ZEN TRAINING

ZEN

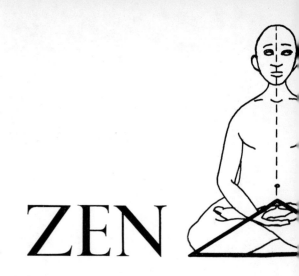

Katsuki Sekida

TRAINING
METHODS AND PHILOSOPHY

edited, with an introduction, by A. V. Grimstone

New York · WEATHERHILL · *Tokyo*

First edition, 1975

Published by John Weatherhill, Inc., 149 Madison Avenue, New York, New York 10016, with editorial offices at 7-6-13 Roppongi, Minato-ku, Tokyo 106, Japan. Copyright © 1975 by Katsuki Sekida and A. V. Grimstone; all rights reserved. Printed in Japan.

Library of Congress Cataloging in Publication Data: Sekida, Katsuki, 1893– / Zen training. / An expanded English version of An introduction to Zen for beginners, originally written in Japanese. / Includes bibliographical references and index. / 1. Meditation (Zen Buddhism) 2. Zen Buddhism—Discipline. / I. Title. / BQ9288.S4313 / 294.3'4'43 / 75-17573 / ISBN 0-8348-0111-6 / ISBN 0-8348-0114-0 pbk.

Contents

Preface

I SHOULD LIKE to express here my thanks to all those who have helped and encouraged me in the writing and publishing of this book. Parts of it originally appeared in *Diamond Sangha,* the publication of the Zen group of Honolulu, and I must first express my feeling of gratitude to Mr. Robert Aitken, who initially edited my articles and prepared them for publication in *Diamond Sangha,* and to Mrs. Anne Aitken, who typed my manuscripts and generally spared no effort in the work of getting them printed. Without their helping hands, encouragement, and the hospitality of the pages of *Diamond Sangha,* those articles would never have appeared. This also is the place to express my gratitude to the readers of *Diamond Sangha* for their steady encouragement; it has meant much to me.

The articles that appeared at that time were independent of each other and were published separately. The work of organizing those articles into book form, of editing the material that I added later, and of writing the introduction was undertaken by Dr. A. V. Grimstone, in Cambridge, England. I wish to thank him most warmly for the care he has devoted to the task, and for his many helpful suggestions. He has worked on the book as if it were his own.

I also wish to thank Miss Debra Graynom, of the Maui Zendo, who helped me by typing some parts of the manuscript, and more generally I want to express my gratitude for the encouragement given me by the members of the Zen groups of Honolulu and Maui, and the mem-

bers of the London Zen Society. Among the latter I particularly want
to thank Mr. Geoffrey Hargett for suggesting Figure 20.

I hope that this book will be of interest and help to those who wish
to study Zen. Good luck in your Zen practice!

KATSUKI SEKIDA

Kochi Prefecture, Japan, 1975

ACKNOWLEDGMENTS

The author and editor wish to express their gratitude to the fol-
lowing for granting permission to reprint published material: Chatto
and Windus, Random House, and the literary estate of C. K. Scott-
Moncrieff for extracts from Scott-Moncrieff's translation of Marcel
Proust's *Swann's Way* and *Within a Budding Grove;* the University of
Illinois Press for a figure from the *American Journal of Psychology;* R. D.
Laing and Penguin Books for an extract from *The Politics of Experience
and The Bird of Paradise,* © 1967 by R. D. Laing; David Magarshack and
Penguin Books for passages from the former's translations of Dostoevski's *The Idiot* and *The Devils,* © 1953, 1955 by David Magarshack; A. C.
Guyton and W. B. Saunders Company for material from *Function of
the Human Body;* Iris Murdoch and Routledge and Kegan Paul for passages from *The Sovereignty of Good;* Manchester University Press and
the University of Chicago Press for an extract from Karl Jaspers' *General Psychopathology,* translated by J. Hoenig and Marian W. Hamilton;
and Macmillan Publishing Company and Allen and Unwin for a passage from Edmund Husserl's *Idea of Phenomenology,* translated by W.
P. Alston and G. Nakhnikian in *Readings in Twentieth-Century Philosophy.*

Editor's Introduction

THE AUTHOR OF THIS BOOK, Katsuki Sekida, was born in Kochi, a town in the southwest of Japan, in 1893. He began the practice and study of Zen in his early twenties, in circumstances that are partly described in chapter 16 of this book, and has continued this uninterrupted ever since. His experience therefore extends over almost sixty years. Although his study and practice of Zen have been intense and profound, and although he lived and studied for some years in a Zen monastery, Ryutaku-ji, he has always remained a layman, earning his living as a schoolteacher until his retirement in 1945. In his later years he has become greatly respected as a teacher of Zen. These few biographical facts are important to the reader, I believe, since they help to establish that this book is the work of a man who can write of Zen with the authority of prolonged experience and deep study.

In 1963, Mr. Sekida accepted an invitation to go to Honolulu to join a Zen group that had been founded there at the initiative of Robert Aitken, and he remained in Hawaii until 1970. It was in Honolulu that Mr. Sekida began working on an expanded English version of a book he had written in Japanese, *An Introduction to Zen for Beginners,* and early drafts of various chapters of this book were circulated with a newsletter, *Diamond Sangha,* published by the Honolulu Zen group. I met Mr. Sekida in 1968, when I was working in Honolulu for a time, and again in 1971, when he came to England for several months at the invitation of the London Zen Society. At that time he asked me if I would assist him in the final preparation of his manuscript for publication. I gladly agreed to do this, since it seems to me that his ideas are interesting and important and his book is a most valuable one. I can claim no profound knowledge or experience of Zen myself, but in the course of my professional activities as a scientist I have acquired a certain experience of writing and editing, and it seemed to me that it was this that Mr. Sekida chiefly needed, rather than a deep knowledge of his subject. Mr. Sekida completed his manuscript in 1972, and the final version is now before the reader.

Mr. Sekida also asked if, in addition to editing the book, I would write an introduction to it. With some diffidence, I agreed to do this. The book is, I believe, well able to stand by itself, and the reader will lose little if he proceeds straight to chapter 1. However, Mr. Sekida's view of Zen is different in many respects from that which has previously been presented to Western readers, and a few words of explanation at the outset may help some readers to orient themselves in unfamiliar territory and to relate what is said here to what is to be found in other books. In particular, I think it may be useful to state explicitly some of the things that Mr. Sekida takes for granted and does not comment on.

For Mr. Sekida the unquestioned basis of any serious practice of Zen is *zazen,* the exercise in which the student sits and learns to control his body and mind. A substantial part of the book is devoted to describing how zazen is performed and what its effects are. Perhaps for some readers this concentration on zazen will need justification, for in Daisetz T. Suzuki's writings, which were chiefly responsible for introducing Zen to the West, no such emphasis is to be found, and this inevitably influenced those introductory books on Zen that were largely based on his work.[1] Suzuki wrote about Zen largely from a theoretical and cultural viewpoint and was not much concerned with the practical aspects of Zen training. Traditionally, the practice of Zen has been taught to students personally, usually in a monastery. Suzuki took this for granted and perhaps assumed that it would always be the case. At any rate, his books contain little mention of zazen, and certainly nothing by way of instructions on how to perform it. It needs, therefore, to be emphasized at the outset that the experiences and insights that Suzuki described are, and always have been, gained by the assiduous practice of zazen.

This point has already been made by Philip Kapleau,[2] whose book went further than any that had hitherto appeared—in the West, at least—in describing how Zen is actually practiced. Kapleau's book is undoubtedly a most valuable and interesting one. Largely consisting of translations of lectures and other material by contemporary Zen teachers, some older Zen texts, and autobiographical accounts by a number of Zen students, it comes nearer than any other book in English to describing how Zen functions as a religion. But still it falls short of being the book that is so badly needed in the West: nowhere does it give the reader the kind of precise instructions for performing zazen that he will need if he is to practice—as most Westerners inevitably will—without the guidance of a Zen teacher. Like Suzuki and the writers of the classical Zen texts, the authors of the material that Kapleau translates did not see the necessity of giving highly detailed practical instructions of this kind. As far as I know, such information has not so far been published in any European language. The first great merit of Mr. Sekida's book, then, is that it tells us exactly how zazen is to be performed.

When we read what Mr. Sekida has to say on this topic, however, we discover that he is not content to confine himself to the essential practical requirements. He goes far beyond this, for he undertakes a remarkable analysis of the whole exercise of zazen, conducted largely in physiological terms. Posture, breathing, the function of the abdominal muscles, muscle tone, the mechanisms of wakefulness and attention—all are discussed in detail in the language of the physiologist. The value of this, it seems to me, is twofold. In the first place, it helps the student to understand what he is trying to do when he sits doing zazen. He is not merely instructed to sit and concentrate on, shall we say, counting his breath or saying "*Mu*," but is told precisely why, if he manipulates his body in certain ways, he will find himself better able to carry out such an exercise. Secondly—and for some people this will be even more important—Mr. Sekida's analysis, logical and scientific as it is, helps to make the whole matter of practicing zazen more reasonable. For many people, and especially those with any sort of scientific or philosophical training, the seeming irrationality of Zen, as it has so often been presented, constitutes a formidable barrier. It is a decided help to find that an experienced Zen teacher is prepared to discuss the basic form of Zen practice in such cool terms.

This analysis of zazen is, however, only the start of what Mr. Sekida has in store for us. For having provided the first clear description of how to do zazen, he goes on to present an account of the aims of zazen, and of Zen training in general, that differs markedly from most of those we have hitherto been offered. To appreciate this we must pause for a moment to consider what other writers on Zen—and here I am again thinking of writers in European languages—have in general considered to be the principal aims of Zen practice.

I think it would be hard to deny that the impression given by much of the literature on Zen is that the overriding aim of the student must be to achieve enlightenment—to experience *kenshō,* or *satori,* in which one "sees into one's own nature" in the deepest sense. For many Western readers, Zen is identified as the Buddhist school characterized by its emphasis on "sudden enlightenment."

The emphasis in Mr. Sekida's account of Zen is significantly different. As will be seen, he by no means ignores or belittles kensho, but he does not place it before the student as something he must strive for in his practice of zazen. It is not merely that, like some other writers on Zen, he regards kensho as something that must be allowed to come naturally, in its own time, rather than be sought or induced by artificial methods. For Mr. Sekida the primary, initial aim of zazen is the attainment of the state of absolute *samādhi:* the condition of total stillness, in which "body and mind are fallen off," no thought stirs, the mind is empty, yet we are in a state of extreme wakefulness. "In this stillness, or emptiness, the source of all kinds of activity is latent. It is this state that we call pure existence."

The discussion of samadhi is in itself one of the most valuable features of Mr. Sekida's book. It is a term that has been used in a confusing variety of ways. Mr. Sekida helps to clarify the situation by making a distinction between two kinds of samadhi. The term has customarily been applied to the condition in which the activity of consciousness is almost totally stopped. If in doing zazen, however, we engage in a practice such as counting the breaths or working on a *kōan,* we may also reach a state in which the normal, logical, sequential activity of consciousness is arrested, yet the mind is still very much active with whatever it is concentrating on. This may also happen in ordinary life when, for example, we become wholly immersed in a physical activity. In all these situations we experience a kind of samadhi, yet they obviously differ in important respects. Mr. Sekida recognizes this difference by designating the first condition "absolute samadhi" and the other "positive samadhi." Both are important, both must be mastered by the Zen student, yet it is the former that, for Mr. Sekida, "constitutes the foundation of all Zen activities."

We may experience kensho when we emerge from samadhi, and Mr. Sekida does not seek to diminish the importance of this. Entry into the state of absolute samadhi is, however, the essential prior condition, and is in itself precious. To experience absolute samadhi may be altogether more important than to have a "poor, commonplace kensho." Like other Zen teachers, Mr. Sekida suggests that the effects of undergoing kensho are not by any means necessarily permanent or even long-lasting. Zen students do not necessarily persist in their practice even after undergoing kensho, and there are, in any case, marked differences in the quality of their experiences. In Mr. Sekida's view, the nature and effects of kensho depend on what foundation of zazen practice and experience of absolute samadhi it rests upon. I have no doubt that Mr. Sekida is skeptical of the value of the more extreme measures—such as shouting and beating—used by some Zen teachers to drive their students to kensho. They may succeed, but the kensho so achieved may be of little lasting value.

This reorientation of our views of Zen is, I think, of much importance. One of its implications, in particular, deserves comment.

It has long been apparent that kensho-like experiences are not restricted to the practitioners of Zen. They have been undergone by adherents of other religions, and also quite outside any religious context, as William James decisively established. More recently it has become apparent that they can be induced by certain drugs.[3] They seem, too (and this has been less frequently commented upon), to be experienced by at least some epileptics.

13

In this connection I think it is worth quoting at some length from the writings of Dostoevski, who was himself an epileptic. In a letter, he wrote: "For a few moments before the fit, I experience a feeling of happiness such as it is quite impossible to imagine in a normal state and which other people have no idea of. I feel entirely in harmony with myself and the whole world, and this feeling is so strong and so delightful that for a few seconds of such bliss one would gladly give up ten years of one's life, if not one's whole life."[4]

What Dostoevski experienced at these times is described in more detail in *The Idiot*, in the words of the prince: "He was thinking, incidentally, that there was a moment or two in his epileptic condition almost before the fit itself (if it occurred during his waking hours) when suddenly amid the sadness, spiritual darkness and depression, his brain seemed to catch fire at brief moments, and with an extraordinary momentum his vital forces were strained to the utmost all at once. His sensation of being alive and his awareness increased tenfold at those moments which flashed by like lightning. His mind and heart were flooded by a dazzling light. All his agitation, all his doubts and worries, seemed composed in a twinkling, culminating in a great calm, full of serene and harmonious joy and hope, full of understanding and the knowledge of the final cause. But those moments, those flashes of intuition, were merely the presentiment of the last second (never more than a second) which preceded the actual fit. This second was, of course, unendurable. Reflecting about that moment afterwards, when he was well again, he often said to himself that all those gleams and flashes of the highest awareness and, hence, also of 'the highest mode of existence', were nothing but a disease, a departure from the normal condition, and, if so, it was not at all the highest mode of existence, but, on the contrary, must be considered to be the lowest. And yet he arrived at last at the paradoxical conclusion: 'What if it is a disease?' he decided at last. 'What does it matter that it is an abnormal tension, if the result, if the moment of sensation, remembered and analysed in a state of health, turns out to be harmony and beauty brought to their highest point of perfection, and gives a feeling, undivined and undreamt of till then, of completeness, proportion, reconciliation, and an ecstatic and prayerful fusion in the highest synthesis of life?' These vague expressions seemed to him very comprehensible, though rather weak. But that it really was 'beauty and prayer', that it really was 'the highest synthesis of life', he could not doubt, nor even admit the possibility of doubt. For it was not abnormal or fantastic visions he saw at that moment, as under the influence of hashish, opium, or spirits, which debased the reason and distorted the mind. He could reason sanely about it when the attack was over and he was well again. Those moments were merely an intense heightening of awareness—if this condition had to be expressed in one word—of awareness and at the same time of the most direct sensation of one's own existence to the most intense degree. If in that second—that is to say, at the last conscious moment before the fit— he had time to say to himself, consciously and clearly, 'Yes, I could give my whole life for this moment', then this moment by itself was, of course, worth the whole of life. . . . 'At that moment,' he once told Rogozhin in Moscow during their meetings there, 'at that moment the extraordinary saying that *there shall be time no longer* becomes, somehow, comprehensible to me. . . .' "[5]

Again, in *The Devils,* Kirilov speaks in similar terms: "There are seconds,—they come five or six at a time—when you suddenly feel the presence of eternal harmony in all its fullness. It is nothing earthly. I don't mean that it is heavenly, but a man in his earthly semblance can't endure it. He has to undergo a physical change or die. This feeling is clear and unmistakable. It is as though you suddenly apprehended all nature and suddenly said: 'Yes, it is true—it is good.' God, when he created the world, said at the end of each day of creation: 'Yes, it is true, it is good.' It is not rapture, but just gladness. You forgive nothing because there is nothing to forgive. Nor do you really love anything—oh, it is much higher than love! What is so terrifying about it is that it is so terribly clear and such gladness."*

The similarities between such passages and the descriptions that

*Translated by David Magarshack (Harmondsworth, England: Penguin, 1953), p. 586. On this passage Shatov, another character in the book, comments: "Take care, Kirilov. I've heard that's just how an epileptic fit begins. An epileptic described to me exactly that preliminary sensation before a fit, exactly as you've done."

15

Zen students give of their kensho experiences cannot, I think, be denied.*

If one were to take kensho to be the ultimate aim of Zen training, one could hardly avoid asking in what way this experience differs from that of the epileptic or the drug taker. Why should anyone submit himself to long years of arduous training in order to reach this condition? Mr. Sekida does not discuss this question explicitly at any length. His remarks on page 179 suggest that he is skeptical about the supposed similarity between drug-induced and other kensho-like experiences on the one hand and true kensho on the other. It may indeed well be the case that we have incorrectly grouped together as "kensho-like" a variety of quite different mental states. However (and this is implicit in Mr. Sekida's book, though not overtly stated), even if this were not the case, this need not lead us to minimize the value of Zen training. For, to repeat, the aim of the Zen student is not, or ought not to be, simply to achieve kensho. The essential requirement, if Zen training is to have any lasting effect on a person's life, is not kensho but the repeated experience of the state of absolute samadhi. This, I believe, is sufficient to dispose of the arguments of those who would advocate the use of drugs as a substitute for zazen, and also of those who would call in question the value of Zen because they believe it has as its aim the attainment of a mental state that would, in other contexts, be regarded as evidence of abnormality.

The significance of kensho is brought further into perspective when we read what Mr. Sekida has to say about the later stages of Zen training. Much of what has previously been written about Zen in the West has been concerned only with the earliest stages of its practice. Kensho has been presented as the ultimate aim, and we have been left somewhat in the dark about what happens next. Mr. Sekida makes it clear that Zen training continues endlessly. To cast off the delusive way of ordinary consciousness while sitting on a cushion in a quiet

*Compare, for example, Philip Kapleau's Three Pillars of Zen, p. 228: "All at once the roshi, the room, every single thing disappeared in a dazzling stream of illumination and I felt myself bathed in a delicious, unspeakable delight. . . . For a fleeting eternity I was alone—I alone was. . . ." There are many similar passages, both in the same book and elsewhere.

room is only the beginning. The student must learn to live in the ordinary world, while yet retaining the quality of his experience of absolute samadhi. In his deeply interesting final chapter, as well as elsewhere in the book, Mr. Sekida discusses these problems in a way that helps us to reach an altogether more balanced picture of the aims of Zen training. For many, perhaps, there has been something unattractive in the notion, not infrequently conveyed, of the Zen student as a person who subjects himself to a prolonged, highly disciplined form of training, usually in the artificial conditions of a monastery, in order to undergo some kind of private, revelatory experience. The picture that emerges from Mr. Sekida's book is quite different. Zen training is a means of enabling us to live our ordinary lives supremely well. I think few readers will be able to resist the appeal of the sketch Mr. Sekida gives in his final chapter of the aged Zen master who has "forgotten Zen and everything like that" and reached a condition of mellow harmony.

It would be possible to single out and discuss many other features of Mr. Sekida's book that are quite new. He tells us, for example—and again I believe it is the first time that such a detailed account has been attempted—how to work on a koan. And throughout the book he introduces and comments on traditional Zen stories and sayings in a way that is original and illuminating and which, instead of inducing the state of baffled (and exasperated) perplexity that so many writers on Zen seem to have as their principal aim, leaves us in a mood to ponder and reflect, and even perhaps to think that we are beginning to understand what these stories and sayings are about. These are matters that the reader can safely be left to discover for himself. There are, however, two features of the book, in addition to those already discussed, which I believe merit some particular comment here.

In chapter 10 and elsewhere, as a framework for his analysis of Zen practice and experience, Mr. Sekida draws a picture of the operation of the mind. His scheme is worked out in terms of *nen,* a Japanese word that has no precise English equivalent, which may be translated as "thought impulse" but which has somewhat wider meanings than that, since it can be used to denote (among other things) a distinctive type of action of the mind. Mr. Sekida distinguishes three kinds of nen-actions, which differ in the immediacy of their contact with the outside world and the degree of self-awareness they involve. A short summary here would not do justice to the whole scheme, and I am in any case not competent to discuss it in any detail. I do not know, in particular, how far it is likely to prove convincing to the professional philosopher or psychologist. I should not be surprised if they demanded somewhat greater rigor in the definition and use of the term "nen" and asked for a more objective demonstration of the reality of the different nen-actions that Mr. Sekida describes.

The reader will observe that the scheme is based wholly on the results of diligent introspection. There are, I think, two points that need to be made here. The first is that, whatever its ultimate merits or defects may prove to be, Mr. Sekida's sketch of the operation of the mind is undoubtedly most helpful for the description and analysis not only of Zen experience but of mental experience in general. At the very least, it gives us a set of concepts and a terminology for the discussion of the aim of zazen and the nature of samadhi; in a broader context it sheds valuable light on the activity of the mind—both normal and pathological—and on the nature of cognition, self-awareness, and consciousness. The second point I should like to make is that, while it may well be the case that what Mr. Sekida has to say will not in all respects satisfy the philosopher or psychologist, it needs to be borne in mind that the price of the demand for scientific exactitude and philosophical rigor is too often the exclusion from discussion of anything interesting at all. Mr. Sekida is writing about a range of phenomena of the greatest complexity and difficulty, some almost wholly unfamiliar to most Western thinkers. Our initial reaction, I suggest, should not be to criticize and dissect, but rather to read what he says with the utmost care and to try to relate it to our own immediate knowledge of mental life.

The final feature of the book that I should like to single out for comment is a more general one. It is the fact that, throughout, Mr. Sekida has done all he can to relate traditional Zen thought and practice to ideas and activities with which the Western reader is likely to be familiar. When, for example, he wishes to bring home to the reader the importance of the *tanden*—that is, the lower region of the abdomen—as a factor in zazen practice, he does so by pointing out its equally great significance in wrestling, in American football, or in sprinting. When he sets out to illustrate the connection between mental processes and bodily activities, and in particular the way in which a mental disturbance or conflict can be discharged by a bodily action, he does so by inviting us to consider the nature of laughter, which forms the subject matter of a splendid chapter. Seeking patiently for parallels between Zen thought and that of Western philosophers, he discusses the ideas of Husserl and Heidegger, and though he finds them wanting, the fact that they have been brought into the discussion at all helps us enormously to get our bearings in this unfamiliar territory. We feel the same when we come across passages from the Bible, or from Proust. No other author, I am sure, has written in this way while at the same time presenting so authoritative an account of Zen theory and practice.

In writing as he does of the physiology of zazen, in seeking to describe the psychology of consciousness, of cognition, of samadhi, of kensho, Mr. Sekida tacitly accepts that these are matters that can be brought within the scope of scientific investigation and analysis. Indeed, he quotes enthusiastically the reports of electroencephalographic studies of Zen masters and Indian yogis that have been carried out in recent years. A scientific approach to meditation and "altered states of consciousness" (to quote the title of a recent book[6]) is not now uncommon, though I believe this is the first time that anyone has written of them from this viewpoint with the personal experience that Mr. Sekida has of them. This is not the place to attempt any detailed assessment of what has been achieved in this field, but I think the results obtained so far support the obvious view that the practice of zazen (or of any other meditational exercise, for that matter) induces a mental state, or series of mental states, with unusual but scientifically definable properties. We are very far from understanding the psychology or physiology of samadhi or kensho, but we are far from understanding the nature of *any* mental state, and I can see no reason why they should not in time be analyzed, at least to the extent that it proves possible to analyze mental events and conditions in general.

This conclusion may well be unwelcome to some. It is one thing to read the following words, on page 194: "For a while she stood in mute amazement, gazing at the sight newly revealed there, and then she felt an emotional welling up—different from anything she had experienced before—as if an indescribably pure spring were overflowing within her. It was an endless stream of ample volume: the outburst of the great delight of which we hear so much." It is quite another thing to discover that the development of samadhi is characterized by the appearance "first of alpha waves, then an increase of alpha amplitude, followed by a decrease of alpha frequency, and finally the development of a theta rhythm" (page 63). We sense a danger that a profound, intensely precious experience cannot but lose in significance if it should prove to be amenable to description in terms of certain patterns of electrical activity of the brain. Furthermore, if the result of practicing zazen is merely the induction of a certain pattern of cortical activity, then it will seem obvious to some that an easier method of inducing that state should be sought; indeed, efforts of this kind are already under way, apart from those involving the use of drugs, to which reference has already been made. I think it is also the case that when we start to talk in this way, in terms of "mental states" or "patterns of cortical activity," it becomes less obvious why one state or pattern should be preferred to another.

This situation was foreseen, with characteristic perceptiveness, by Arthur Waley in an essay, written over fifty years ago, that could justifiably be regarded as the first balanced account of Zen to appear in English. He wrote: "It is not likely that they [Western converts to Zen] will rest content with the traditional Eastern methods of self-hypnosis. If certain states of consciousness are indeed more valuable than those with which we are familiar in ordinary life—then we must seek them by whatever means we can devise. I can imagine a kind of dentist's chair fitted with revolving mirrors, flashing lights, sulphurous haloes expanding and contracting—in short a mechanism that by the pressure of a single knob should whirl a dustman into Nirvana.

"Whether such states of mind are actually more valuable than our ordinary consciousness is difficult to determine. Certainly no one has much right to an opinion who has not experienced them."[7]

There is no simple answer to this line of thought. It helps, perhaps, to point out that to describe a phenomenon in scientific terms is not necessarily to diminish it. The grandeur of the Alps is not reduced by giving an account of their geology; the two are separate, and can co-exist. In the case of mental states this is surely even more strikingly so. However diligently we study the electrical activity of someone's brain, we never discover—never *can* discover—what his mental experience really is, for it is by its nature something utterly private. If you wish to know what a mango tastes like, it is no use subjecting it to chemical analysis: you must peel and eat it. I believe it would be possible, along these lines, to mount a convincing refutation of the argument that the discovery of a physiological correlate of, say, the state of samadhi necessarily diminishes the value of that state. However, having said that, I would add that I do not believe it is really necessary to defend the practice of Zen in that way. I believe we can find all the reasons we may need for practicing Zen by observing the results of doing so. I have in mind here the quality of the people themselves. I count myself fortunate to have met, in addition to the author of this book, a number of Japanese Zen masters. Without exception, they struck me as wholly admirable people. There was about them a serenity, a dignity, and a spontaneity that I have not encountered in other people. It was not the case that a rigid system of training had produced a uniform product, for the individuality of the person was always strikingly apparent. At its best—and it is, of course, obvious that much of what now passes as Zen training is far from being that—the discipline of Zen seems to result in the shaping of enviably complete people. Their quality is manifest not only in their lives and their everyday actions, but in their products—their painting and calligraphy, their buildings and gardens, and so on.

Why should it be the case that man needs to submit himself to anything so arduous and strange as zazen in order to arrive at the fullest development of his potentialities? I have in mind here the fact that the point of Zen training, as will emerge from a reading of this book, is as much the correction, or eradication, of an already existing faulty mode of functioning as the development of latent capacities. It is implicit in Zen teaching that ordinary man is unenlightened, that he is burdened with an ego shell like the confining carapace on the back of a crab, that he has lost contact with reality. Mr. Sekida points to our habit, developed from an early age, of treating the world "in the context of equipment." Not merely things, but people too, are so many tools for our use and exploitation. Thus we become set apart from them. Why should so unenviable a state apparently be our normal lot, escapable only through arduous discipline?

It would be absurd for me to attempt any thoroughgoing analysis of the reasons why this happens, for even if I had the necessary knowledge of psychology, I do not believe that that embryonic discipline can yet offer any satisfactory account of such matters. I would, however, suggest that we must take very seriously the fact that the way out of our condition which Zen provides involves th e experience of a total cessation of the ordinary process of conscious thought—of what Zen calls "topsy-turvy delusive thought." This is what occurs when we enter absolute samadhi.

The medium of our thoughts is language. Words are the means by which we handle reality. This ability to use words has been one of the main reasons for man's prodigious success as an animal. It is also, seemingly, the source of our troubles, for the ability to use words and concepts, while so plainly of enormous value, all too readily becomes hypertrophied. Unconsciously, we come to suppose that to give something a name is to gain some measure of control over it. We come to live in a world of words and thoughts, which takes the place of direct contact with reality. We say, "There is a tree," but do not really see the tree. Indeed, as Iris Murdoch has put it: "Our minds are continually active, fabricating an anxious, usually self-preoccupied *veil* which partially conceals the world."[8] To see the world as it is we have to check this all too pervasive mental activity, to empty our minds, to relinquish what we imagine to be our verbal hold on the world.

The mature Zen student, by dint of long practice, has divested himself of the tissue of thoughts, conceptions, misconceptions, falsifications, and daydreams that our mind normally weaves. He experiences the present moment in all its fullness, as it is, and he is able to see truly what is before him. His perception of the world is clear and undistorted.

I believe it is worth pointing out that, thus described, the aim of Zen training is not markedly different from what has been identified by some Western writers as the correct object of moral effort. I should like to quote again from Iris Murdoch in this connection. She suggests that the prime need, if we are able to reach correct moral decisions, is to develop the capacity for *attention*: "I have used the word 'attention', which I borrow from Simone Weil, to express the idea of a just and loving gaze directed upon individual reality. I believe this to be the characteristic and proper mark of the active moral agent."[9]

"Attention," she writes, "is rewarded by a knowledge of reality"; and again: "The love which brings the right answer [to moral problems] is an exercise of justice and realism and really *looking*. The difficulty is to keep the attention fixed upon the real situation and to prevent it returning surreptitiously to the self with consolations of self-pity, resentment, fantasy and despair. The refusal to attend may even induce a fictitious sense of freedom: I may as well toss a coin. Of course virtue is good habit and dutiful action. But the background condition of such habit and such action, in human beings, is a just mode of vision and a good quality of consciousness. It is a *task* to come to see the world as it is."[10]

Zen has long been, in Mr. Sekida's words, "a mysteriously shrouded wilderness." Traditionally, the student has had to explore this wilderness for himself and try to find his own way through it. His instructions on how to do this, such as they are, have come directly from his teacher. As I understand it, the student has not been encouraged to reflect upon the nature of the territory he is exploring, or on the technique for doing so. And if this is the position in the East, how much more so is it the case for the would-be student of Zen in the West. Here we do not have any established tradition, monastic or otherwise, with which to align ourselves. The need for guidance is acute, yet I think it is correct to say that little of what has so far appeared on Zen in the West is of much use to the person who wishes to study and practice Zen by himself. The wilderness, for us, has more the character of an impenetrable jungle.

Mr. Sekida wishes to change this whole situation. He believes that the time has come for Zen to make use of the knowledge gained in other fields of study and inquiry. He is not in favor of mystification or the deliberate withholding of information. Zen is not mysticism or something esoteric: it is a rational method of helping us to become better people. The territory we have to explore may seem strange at the outset, but Mr. Sekida draws us maps, sets up signposts, gives us instructions. He knows that each of us has to make the journey by himself; he knows that the going is difficult. He has given us more guidance about how to undertake the trip, and what sort of country we shall find ourselves in, than any previous writer. It seems to me that his book will stand as a great pioneering effort.

I think it is right for me, in conclusion, to state briefly what I have done in preparing Mr. Sekida's manuscript for publication. In general, I have seen it as my main task to produce a text that gives the clearest and most straightforward possible expression of Mr. Sekida's ideas. I have in the first place done a good deal by way of rearranging the material into what seems to me the most logical sequence and dividing it into chapters. Secondly, I have as far as possible eliminated unnecessary repetitions. This involved a good deal of anxious thought. Important and difficult ideas are not always grasped by the reader immediately. To have the opportunity to meet them more than once may be valuable, and I have therefore not thought it necessary or desirable to remove all overlaps and reiterations. I have, however, done a good deal by way of pruning the text. Thirdly, I have here and there introduced sentences or short passages where they seemed helpful or necessary to make the meaning or the sequence of ideas plain.

To avoid cluttering the text with italics and diacritical marks, non-English terms are italicized, and provided with macrons where appropriate, on first mention only, while names and other proper nouns are treated like English words throughout. All index entries are rendered in the form in which they first appear in the text.

Finally, I have revised the English extensively. I should make it clear in this connection that Mr. Sekida has an excellent command of English. He can express himself clearly and his meaning is rarely if ever in doubt. To write accurate English, however, is a troublesome and time-consuming matter for him, and he has rightly judged that his time is better spent in other ways.* As explained in the preface, Robert Aitken initially revised a good deal of the material, and I have completed the process. The task has not been without its problems. Mr. Sekida's prose, for all its imperfections, has a charm and originality of its own; he can on occasion produce passages of startling beauty and intensity. It has not been easy to correct the English without losing the individual quality of the original. In general, when a choice had to be made, I have opted for clarity rather than charm, in the belief that the former is more important in a book of this kind, at the present stage of Zen studies in the West.

As a result of all these revisions and rearrangements the book no doubt has a somewhat brisker, more matter-of-fact air than the original. I need hardly say that Mr. Sekida has checked my version with great care, and that the final text has his approval.

*He is at present translating and annotating two important Zen texts, *Mumonkan* and *Hekigan Roku*. It is hoped that these works will appear in the near future.

ZEN TRAINING

CHAPTER ONE

Orientations

IN THIS INTRODUCTORY CHAPTER I want to review briefly some of the main topics that are to be dealt with in this book. A summary at the outset may help the reader to find his way about the rest of the book more easily, and to understand how different ideas and concepts relate to one another.

In studying Zen we start with practice. Now, it is true that Zen is concerned with the problem of the nature of mind, so it necessarily includes an element of philosophical speculation. However, while the philosopher relies mainly on speculation and reasoning, in Zen we are never separated from our personal practice, which we carry out with our body and mind. Edmund Husserl, the founder of phenomenology, may seem to come close to Zen in his ideas when he advocates a technique called "phenomenological reduction." He says that he ignores "the ego as a person arranged on objective time," and arrives at the "pure phenomenon." However, like other philosophers, he does not seem to go beyond a purely mental exercise. In Zen training we also seek to extinguish the self-centered, individual ego, but we do not try to do this merely by thinking about it. It is with our own body and mind that we actually experience what we call "pure existence."

The basic kind of Zen practice is called *zazen* (sitting Zen), and in zazen we attain *samādhi*. In this state the activity of consciousness is stopped and we cease to be aware of time, space, and causation. The mode of existence which thus makes its appearance may at first sight seem to be nothing more than mere being, or existence. However, if you really attain this state you will find it to be a remarkable thing. At the extremity of having denied all and having nothing left to deny, we reach a state in which absolute silence and stillness reign, bathed in a pure, serene light. Buddhists of former times called this state annihilation, or Nirvana. But it is not a vacuum or mere nothingness. It is utterly different, too, from the unconscious state of the patient under anesthesia upon the operating table. There is a definite wakefulness in it. It is a condition of existence that recalls the impressive silence and stillness that we experience in the heart of the mountains.

In ordinary daily life our consciousness works ceaselessly to protect and maintain our interests. It has acquired the habit of utilitarian thinking, looking upon the things in the world as so many tools—in Heidegger's phrase, it treats them "in the context of equipment." It looks at objects in the light of how they can be made use of. We call this attitude the habitual way of consciousness. This way of looking at things is the origin of man's distorted view of the world. And he comes to look upon himself, too, in the context of equipment, and fails to see into his own true nature. This way of treating oneself and the world leads to a mechanical way of thinking, which is the cause of so much of the suffering of modern man, and which can, under some conditions, lead to the development of mental illnesses. Zen aims at overthrowing this distorted view of the world, and zazen is the means of doing it.

On coming out of samadhi it can happen that one becomes fully aware of one's being in its pure form; that is, one experiences pure existence. This experience of the pure existence of one's being, associated with the recovery of pure consciousness in samadhi, leads us to the recognition of pure existence in the external world too. Discussion of these topics inevitably leads us into epistemological tangles, but let us proceed for the moment, granting that such recognition of pure existence is possible. To look at oneself and the objects of the external world in the context of pure existence is *kenshō*, or realization. And this has been achieved, since Buddha himself did so, by men and women of every generation, who bear witness to its feasibility.

30

This experience, as we have stressed, is attained by the training of body and mind. Reason comes later and illuminates the experience, and thus the two wheels of the cart of cognition are completed.

If one goes climbing in the Alps, one is probably led to do so in the first instance by the beauty of the mountains. When one starts to climb, however, one finds it is a matter of working one's way along patiently, step by step, progressing with great care and caution. Some knowledge of climbing technique will be essential. It is the same with Zen. We take it up in search of the meaning of life, or in hope of solving the problem of our existence, but once we actually start, we find we have to look down at our feet, and we are faced with practice followed by more practice, training followed by more training. It must be done patiently and seriously. Much of this book is concerned with the technique of zazen.

Our aim in practicing zazen is to enter the state of samadhi, in which, as we have said, the normal activity of our consciousness is stopped. This is not something that comes easily to us. The beginner in Zen will usually be told to start by practicing counting his breaths —that is, to count each exhalation up to ten, and then start again (see chapter 5). The reader (assuming he is inexperienced in Zen) should try this for himself. Quite probably you will look on this task with some contempt, thinking that you can do it without any difficulty, but when you start you will soon find that wandering thoughts come into your head, perhaps when you have reached about "five" or "six," and the thread of counting is broken. The next moment you come to yourself and cannot recollect where you left off. You have to start again, saying "one" and so on. How can we prevent our thoughts from wandering? How can we learn to focus our attention on one thing? The answer is that we cannot do it with our brain alone; the brain cannot control its thoughts by itself. The power to control the activity of our mind comes from the body, and it depends critically (as we shall show in later chapters, in detail) on posture and breathing.

With regard to posture, we need only say at this stage that stillness of body engenders stillness of mind. Immobility is a first essential. Traditionally, and for good reasons, we sit down to practice, because (among other reasons) it is in this position that we can keep our body still but our minds wakeful. Chapter 2 is devoted entirely to a discussion of the posture we should adopt while sitting.

Immobility results in a diminution of the stimuli reaching the brain, until eventually there are almost none. This will give rise, in due course, to a condition in which you cease to be aware of the position of your body. It is not a state of numbness, for you can move your limbs and body if you want. But if you keep your body still, it is not felt. This condition I call "off-sensation." In this state the activity of the cortex of the brain becomes steadily less and less, and we can regard this condition as a preliminary to entering samadhi.

We continue to breathe, of course, as we sit, and it will be shown later that our ability to concentrate our attention, to remain wakeful, and ultimately to enter samadhi depends on our method of breathing. Even those who have not practiced zazen know that it is possible to control the mind by manipulating the breathing. Quiet breathing brings about a quiet state of mind. If, when you feel like shouting with rage, you keep your breath bated and make yourself quiet, you will find you can control your anger. Particular forms of breathing automatically appear in connection with various forms of activity, as we shall describe later. In zazen, we breathe almost entirely by means of our abdominal muscles and diaphragm. The muscles of the thorax are scarcely used. If the lower abdomen is allowed to fill out, the diaphragm is lowered, the thoracic cavity is enlarged, and air is taken into the lungs. When the abdominal muscles contract, the contents of the abdomen are pushed up, which in turn forces the diaphragm up, reducing the volume of the thoracic cavity and expelling air from the lungs. The slow, sustained exhalation that we adopt in zazen is produced by keeping the diaphragm contracted so that it opposes the action of the abdominal muscles, which are trying to push air out of the lungs. This opposition generates a state of tension in the abdominal muscles, and the maintenance of this state of tension is of the utmost importance in the practice of zazen. All other parts of the body are motionless, and their muscles are either relaxed or in a state of constant, moderate tension. Only the abdominal muscles are active. In ways that we shall explain later (see especially chapters 3 and 7), this activity is a vital part of the mechanism by which concentration and wakefulness of the brain are maintained. Traditionally, in the East, the lower part of the abdomen (called the *tanden*) has been regarded as the seat of human spiritual power. Correct zazen posture ensures that the weight of the body is concentrated there, producing a strong tension, and the method of breathing that is adopted reinforces that tension. In chapter 3 we develop a hypothesis in physiological terms about the way in which stimuli from the tanden help to maintain wakefulness, and in chapter 7 and elsewhere we deal in some detail with the importance of the tanden in both zazen and other activities.

The essential point we want to make at present is that it is the correct manipulation of the lower abdomen, as we sit and breathe, that enables us to control the activity of our mind. Posture and breathing are the key to concentration, to stilling the activity of the mind, and to entering samadhi. Stated so briefly, our conclusion may seem far-fetched. The reader will find our reasons for this conclusion set out in more detail later, and we hope that they will seem convincing. And if they do not seem convincing on the page, the reader should experiment for himself along the lines we shall indicate. Zen is above all a matter of personal experience. The student is asked to accept nothing the truth of which he cannot demonstrate for himself, with his own mind and body.

We have already referred to the state of off-sensation, in which we lose the sense of the whereabouts of our body. Subsequently, by stilling the activity of our mind, a state is reached in which time, space, and causation, which constitute the framework of consciousness, drop away. We call this condition ''body and mind fallen off.'' In ordinary mental activity the cerebral cortex takes the major role, but in this state, apparently, it is hardly active at all. ''Body and mind fallen off'' may seem to be nothing but a condition of mere being, but this mere being is accompanied by a remarkable mental power, which we may characterize as a condition of extreme wakefulness.

To those who have not experienced it, this description may seem strange, yet the condition really does occur in samadhi. At the time, however, we are not aware of it, because, as we shall explain in chapter 10, there is no reflecting activity of consciousness, and it is thus hard to describe. However, if we were to try to describe it, it would be as an extraordinary mental stillness. In this stillness, or emptiness, the source of all kinds of activity is latent. It is this state that we call pure existence. This, perhaps, is the most simplified form of human existence.

If you catch hold of this state of pure existence, and then come back into the actual world of conscious activity, you will find that Being itself appears transformed. Because of the possibility of this transformation, Being is said to be "veiled in darkness" to the eyes of those who have not experienced pure existence. When mature in the practice of zazen, Being is seen with one's own eyes. Or, as it is said in the sutras, "The Tathagata sees Buddha Nature with his naked eyes."

However, just as energy can be used for many different purposes, so can pure existence be experienced in relation to any phase of life—anger, hatred, or jealousy, as well as love and beauty. Now, every human action must be carried on through the ego, which plays a role analogous to that of a pipe or channel through which energy is conducted for different uses. It may be asked what this ego is. We usually think of the ego as a kind of constant, unchanging entity. In fact, however, it is simply a succession of physical and mental events or pressures, which appear momentarily and as quickly pass away. However, so long as our mind operates subjectively, there must be a subject that functions as the ego. As there is normally no cessation of subjective activity, there can normally be no state in which we are devoid of an ego. However, the nature of this ego can change. Every time we succeed in banishing a mean or restricted ego—a petty ego—another ego with a broader outlook appears in its place, and eventually what we may call an "egoless ego" will make its appearance. And when you have acquired an egoless ego, there is no hatred, no jealousy, no fear; you experience a state in which you see everything in its true aspect. It is a state in which you cling to or adhere to nothing. It is not that you are without desires, but that while desiring and adhering to things you are at the same time unattached to them. The Diamond Sutra says, "Abiding nowhere, let the mind work." This means, "Do not let your mind be bound by your desire, and let your desire occur in your mind." True freedom is freedom from your own desires.

When the Zen student has once experienced pure existence, he undergoes a complete about-face in his view of the world. But unfortunately, as long as he is a human being, he cannot escape from the inevitability of living as an individual. He cannot leave the world of differentiation. And he is thus placed in a new dilemma, which he did not encounter before. Inevitably, this entails a certain internal conflict, which may cause much distress. To deal with this, further training of the mind has to be undertaken in order to learn how, while living in the world of differentiation, we can avoid discrimination. We have to learn how to exercise the mind of nonattachment while working in attachment. This is called training after the attainment of realization, or cultivation of Holy Buddhahood, which constitutes an essential part of Zen (see chapter 17). There is a Zen saying, "Equality without differentiation is bad equality; differentiation without equality is bad differentiation." This is a very commonplace saying, but the level of understanding to which it refers is not common, since it can be attained only in a mature state of Zen practice.

Zen training continues endlessly. The mean or petty ego, which was thought to have been disposed of, is found once again to be secretly creeping back into one's mind. The long, chronic habit of consciousness has implanted evil impulses so firmly in man's mind that they haunt us perpetually, and it is impossible for us to inhibit them before they appear. However, the longer we train ourselves, the more we are liberated from the petty ego. When the petty ego appears, do not be concerned with it. Simply ignore it. When an evil thought strikes you, acknowledge it honestly, saying, "Such and such an evil thought has occurred in me," and then drop it. The Zen saying goes, "The occurrence of an evil thought is a malady; not to continue it is the remedy."

Zen talks about "emptiness." What is meant by this? Perhaps a story will help. The guardian deity wanted to have a look at Tozan Osho, but found he could not, and so he devised a trick. He took some rice and wheat from the kitchen of the monastery and scattered it in the yard. In the monastery, things are taken good care of, simply because they exist. (This idea is conspicuously different from that inherent in modern economic thought.) Tozan found the rice and wheat strewn on the ground and said to himself, "Whoever could have been so thoughtless as to do this?" And at that moment the deity was able to have a look at Tozan. Usually Tozan did not abide anywhere. That is why the deity could not have a look at him. Tozan allowed his mind to work when he saw the grain strewn on the ground. A cloud appeared in the empty sky; it soon vanished, but at that moment the deity could have a glimpse of him.

A student of Christianity, hearing that Zen talks of emptiness, offered for comparison a definition of holiness. Holiness, he said, means completeness, with nothing to be added to it. The word holiness is found in Buddhism, too. A Buddha is holy. But in Buddhism, when a man has become a Buddha, he is supposed to forget he is a Buddha. While you are conscious of being a Buddha, you are not truly a Buddha, because you are ensnared by the idea. You are not empty. Every time that you think you are achieving something—becoming a Buddha, attaining holiness, even emptiness—you must cast it away.

Emptiness is a condition in which internal mental pressure is totally dissolved. When a thought appears in your mind, it is necessarily accompanied by internal pressure. Even when you think, "It's fine today," a certain internal pressure is generated in your mind, and you feel you want to speak to someone else and say, "It's fine today, isn't it?" By doing this you discharge the pressure. These matters are discussed in detail in chapter 10. In Zen texts the word *mushin* occurs. Literally, this means "no mind" (*mu*, no; *shin*, mind), which means "no ego." It means the mind is in a state of equilibrium. We think every moment, and an internal pressure is generated, and we lose equilibrium. And in Zen we train ourselves to recover equilibrium every moment. The ego is built up from a succession of internal pressures. When the pressures are dissolved, the ego vanishes, and there is true emptiness.

There is a Zen topic, or *kōan*, that asks, "What is the meaning of Bodhidharma's coming to China?" And the answer given is "No meaning." This means "no purpose." Bodhidharma spent three years traveling to China. The hardships of the journey are scarcely conceivable to us today, yet he is said to have had no purpose. The point is that "no purpose" means emptiness. When Bodhidharma arrived in China, the first distinguished person who met him was Emperor Wu of Liang. Emperor Wu was called "Emperor Wu of Buddha Mind." He was a devout believer in Buddhism. He built many temples, supported monks, and set scholars to translate the sutras into Chinese. He himself was deeply versed in Buddhist scriptures and put on a sacred golden robe to give lectures on the sutras. It is said that on that occasion flowers rained down from heaven and changed the earth to gold. It was thought that this was a reward for great merit. However, if Wu had had true understanding of Buddhist emptiness, and if that emptiness had been realized in himself, the flowers would not have rained down and the earth would not have been changed into gold. Emperor Wu said to Bodhidharma, "I have erected temples and supported monks; what virtue will come out of it?" He expected Bodhidharma to reply, "Great virtue!" Bodhidharma's answer, however, was "No virtue." Emperor Wu perhaps realized his failure and made another attempt. He asked, "What is the first principle of the holy teachings of the Buddha?" Bodhidharma said, "Emptiness, not holiness."

In a famous Zen episode, Joshu asked his teacher Nansen, "What is the way?" "Ordinary mind is the way" was Nansen's answer. But how can we attain this ordinary mind? We might say, empty your mind, and there is ordinary mind. But this is to resort to exhortation, or to a merely verbal explanation of what Zen aims at. The Zen student must realize it for himself, and we must now start to explain in detail how he can come to do this. Only after we have dealt with the practical aspects of Zen training, in the first part of this book, do we go on to consider its theoretical and philosophical aspects.

CHAPTER TWO

Zazen Posture

WHEN DOING ZAZEN one normally sits on the floor, facing the wall, on a cushion or a folded blanket about three feet square. Another cushion or pad, smaller and thicker, is placed under the buttocks (Fig. 5). It is important that this pad be thick enough, since otherwise it will be difficult to take up a correct, stable posture as described below. The pad should be placed under the buttocks alone and should not reach under the thighs.

A number of different postures can be used in zazen, and the student should experiment to discover which suits him best. Some are easier than others, and can be used in the early stages of practice. Provided the student can maintain a stable, motionless position without discomfort for twenty to thirty minutes, it does not matter much what posture is adopted. If it is found impossible to sit comfortably on the floor, one may try sitting on a chair or stool, adopting the essential features of the postures described below as far as possible. One should wear loose clothes that do not constrict any part of the body. Much patient practice and experiment may be necessary in order to learn how to sit well.

Figure 1 shows *kekka fuza,* the so-called "full-lotus" position. It is symmetrical, with the right foot on the left thigh and the left foot on the right thigh. The reverse position can also be adopted. In this, as in all other positions, both knees rest firmly on the cushion. The hands rest in the lap, usually with the right hand under the left and the palms turned upward. The thumbs may touch at their tips, forming a circle, or they may rest parallel to the other fingers. An alternative hand position is to grasp the thumb of one hand in the palm of the other (Fig. 2). Kekka fuza is a rather difficult position for most people when they start their practice. However, it is a completely balanced, self-contained position and one that is most conducive to good practice.

A less difficult posture is *hanka fuza,* the "half-lotus" position (Fig. 2). Here the right foot is under the left thigh and the left foot is on the right thigh. (Again, the reverse position is also possible.) The hands are held as in the full-lotus position. Hanka fuza is an asymmetrical posture and tends to pull the spine out of line, one of the shoulders being raised in compensation. It is possible to correct this with the aid of a mirror or another person, but it should be recognized that this position sometimes results in other defects in posture, notably certain slight distortions of the upper body. We cannot recommend this position very much. You might as well place the edge of one foot on the shin of the other leg. Then the style approaches that shown in Figure 3 and can be recommended.

Figure 3 shows a modified Burmese style, with both feet flat on the cushion. Take care not to fall into the cross-legged posture of a tailor, in which the waist is lowered backward. The waist should always be pushed forward in the way that will be described below. This position is completely symmetrical and conducive to the relaxation of the upper body.

A quite different posture is shown in Figure 4, in which the student straddles his pad, resting his weight on it and on his knees. This style is very effective, especially for beginners wishing to learn how to stress the lower abdomen correctly. If you adopt this position and push the waist forward, the stress will naturally be thrown into the bottom of the abdomen as we shall describe below.

In all these positions the stable base for the body is a triangle formed by the buttocks and the two knees. Hence it is important to find a posture in which the knees rest firmly on the cushion and bear the weight of the body. The pelvis is held firmly fixed, and the trunk is placed squarely on it, not leaning in any direction.

The trunk is held upright by the action of the waist muscles. These

39

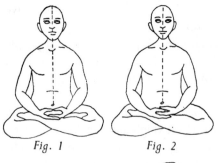

Fig. 1   Fig. 2

Fig. 3   Fig. 4

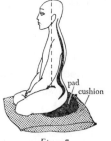

1. The *full-lotus position* (kekka fuza).
2. The *half-lotus position* (hanka fuza).
3. *A modified Burmese posture.*
4. *A posture in which the legs are directed backward and placed on either side of the pad.*

5. *The configuration of the spinal cord in a correct posture. Note that the spine is not held in a straight line.*

6. *This figure illustrates the method of relaxing and lowering the shoulders by placing the hands on the legs and exhaling deeply. In a correct posture a vertical line can be drawn through the center of the forehead, nose, chin, throat, and navel.*

7. *In a correct zazen posture the buttocks and knees form a triangle that acts as a base for the body. The weight of the body is concentrated in the lower abdomen, with the center of stress in the tanden (T). The trunk is perfectly vertical.*

pad
cushion

Fig. 5   Fig. 6   Fig. 7

muscles are of great importance in bodily posture. They spread out widely, some penetrating deeply in the body, and their upper portions reach high into the upper regions of the back. In all postures it is these muscles that hold the trunk up straight, and it is these muscles alone that are particularly contracted. It is important that, as far as possible, the body be kept perfectly upright when viewed from the front. It should be possible to draw a vertical line that takes in the center of the forehead, nose, chin, throat, and navel, and ultimately extends down to the coccyx (Fig. 6). Any deviation of these landmarks from the vertica should be carefully corrected, not only in zazen but in one's ordinary carriage.

Having taken up any of the above postures, the next step is to make sure that the waist and lower abdomen are correctly positioned. The essential movement here is to push the waist forward. This will in turn push the lower abdomen forward and at the same time throw the buttocks backward. This movement will be effectively performed if you try to tilt the top of the pelvis forward. The importance of pushing out the belly in zazen has long been advocated. When you hold your trunk up straight the weight of the body will necessarily be concentrated in the lower abdomen, and the region a few inches below the navel will be the center of the stress. This region is called the tanden (Fig. 7; note that in a more general sense this term is applied to the whole of the lower abdomen). We shall have much to say about the tanden later (see especially chapter 7). Here we may simply observe that when the weight of the body is concentrated in the tanden, the most stable posture and the quietest mental condition are achieved. In zazen the lower abdomen should fill out naturally by the combined action of the forward movement of the waist and the funneling of the weight of the body into this region.

Viewed from the side, the spinal column is not a straight line but is gently curved, as illustrated in Figure 5. The position of the neck and head is of some importance. It is not a bad thing if the face is turned slightly downward, just as some images of the Buddha look down, with the forehead very slightly stuck out and the chin drawn in a little. Keeping the neck slightly slanted forward and quite motionless helps one to get into samadhi; you may, indeed, find yourself doing this

41

involuntarily as your practice develops and you approach samadhi. However, if the student prefers (because of his physical build) he may simply hold his head and neck upright.

The body as a whole must be held quite motionless, since this is a necessary condition for entering samadhi.

Finally, the chest and shoulders should be lowered. By doing this, tension in the shoulders, neck, and the pit of the stomach will be relieved. Place the hands on the knees, with the knuckles forward, and exhale deeply. This is not the formal position of the hands in zazen, but you will quickly discover in this way how to lower the chest and shoulders and thereafter do it routinely. The movement of the buttocks backward also pulls down certain muscles in the shoulders and helps to release stress in the chest and shoulders.

FAULTY POSTURES   We may come to appreciate better the essential features of good posture by considering some of the faults that commonly occur. In Figure 8, for example, the trunk is not placed squarely on the pelvis. Point A must be moved to the right; then the shoulders will be level. If, instead, the shoulders alone are corrected, a still more distorted posture will result (Fig. 12). A fault such as this is not easily detected when the student is wearing clothes; one should sit before a mirror, stripped to the waist, and carefully examine one's posture, moving the body into various positions in order to find out which part of the body must be relaxed, and to what extent, and which part tensed. Minute and delicate manipulation of the muscles and skeleton cannot easily be taught by others and is best learned by patient self-investigation. However, even when using a mirror, a student often fails to recognize his faults for himself. He has not developed an eye to judge his own posture, and may fail to see faults unless they are pointed out to him in detail. I stress this point because I myself for a long time failed to notice my own mistakes. Many of the faults in posture that I describe were once my own. Painful experience makes me rather quick now to notice the faults of others, and makes me feel much concern about them. I used, for example, to experience a dull pain in one of my buttocks after sitting for a long time. I assumed it was inevitable and never thought to ask myself the reason. But the fact

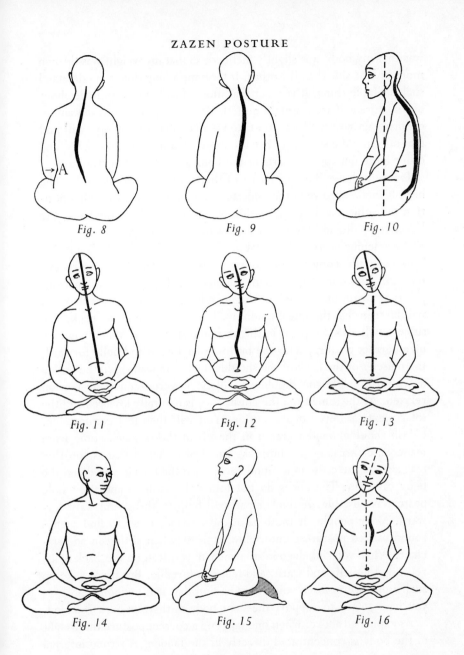

Fig. 8   Fig. 9   Fig. 10

Fig. 11   Fig. 12   Fig. 13

Fig. 14   Fig. 15   Fig. 16

8–16. Faulty zazen postures.

43

was that my body was slightly inclined, so that my weight was thrown more on one side than the other. It took me a long time to understand such a simple thing. It is a fact that most of us know very little about our posture and we maintain quite faulty habits, both in zazen and in ordinary activities. When you take up a correct posture you will find that not only the shoulders but the muscles of the back, the sides, and other quite unexpected parts of the body are relieved of strain.

Figure 9 shows the upper part of the trunk tilted to one side. The head is inclined to the other side to maintain balance. In such a position the subject will feel a tension on the right side of the neck, the lower left side, and the upper right side of the body.

A crouching posture, like that of an old man, is shown in Figure 10. This generally comes from failing to perform the "belly forward, buttocks backward" movement adequately. The subject often complains of a pain in the back of the neck because of the stress there. It will be seen that the spinal column is bent too much at the neck. The subject will also feel pains in the back and shoulders. When you take up a correct posture, with the buttocks backward and belly forward, the muscles of the back of the shoulders (the trapezius) will be pulled downward, while the shoulders will be lowered and their tension relaxed. At the same time the chest, too, is naturally lowered and the solar plexus relieved of its tension. You will then feel comfortable.

Stiff shoulders and a cramp in the pit of the stomach come from inadequate thrust of the buttocks backward. A pad that is too thin may also be the cause of a round back, with the hips lowered and the belly caved in. The knees do not touch the cushion and the whole posture is unstable. A thicker pad will help to thrust the waist forward. Many people, it must be acknowledged, seem to find such a round-backed posture comfortable, at least when sitting in an armchair. When you sink deep in an armchair you lean on the back of it, relaxing the belly and waist, and feel comfortable. But if you take up such a posture in zazen you will soon find that it is uncomfortable, as you have to try to support the bent body with your back rounded.

As explained above, when one takes up a correct posture the weight of the body is concentrated directly in the tanden. A strong internal pressure is produced there and, as we shall see later, this is important for controlling the mind and entering samadhi. A mature Zen student has only to sit down to enter almost immediately into samadhi. It is an outcome of his correct posture. On the other hand, with twisted trunk, rounded back, and other deviations not only will one be uncomfortable, but the weight of the body will not fall correctly into the tanden and it will be correspondingly difficult to reach samadhi.

If one maintains a faulty posture of any kind for a while, one will inevitably begin to feel uncomfortable. In an effort to relieve the discomfort, other parts of the body will be tensed. The shoulders are particularly quick to react in this way, and stiffness of the shoulders is a very common complaint. Furthermore, when we strain our shoulders it creates tension in the upper region of the trunk. This tension disturbs the balance of the internal organs, and this in turn disturbs our mental stability. Thus, tensing the shoulders necessarily results in physical and mental disturbance. We can see this happening, incidentally, not only in zazen but in other situations. The baseball pitcher's sudden loss of control, for example, is often attributable to the unusual straining of his shoulders due to his excitement. We must use the same care in zazen that we would in athletics or gymnastics.

Figures 11–13 illustrate other faulty postures and require little comment. In Figure 14 the face looks sideways. In this case the shoulders and chest are often found to be projecting farther forward on one side than the other. This results in a twisted trunk. The same fault may also arise in some people who sit a little carelessly, without ensuring that their body is facing the wall squarely. That is to say, the line joining their knees is not parallel to the wall. If the face is then directed squarely toward the wall, this will inevitably bring about a twisted trunk.

In the posture shown in Figure 15 the chin projects and the nape of the neck is compressed. As a result, there will be an unnatural pressure on the nerves passing through the neck, and this will disturb one's getting into samadhi.

Figure 16 is a noteworthy example and shows the result of the sternum's deviating from the line running from nose to navel. The trunk is distorted and the shoulders are not level. The neck tilts to one side to balance the posture. If the subject tries to assume a "correct" posture while having this physical fault, tension will develop in the neck, shoulders, and even the face and head. Moreover, a certain pain will be felt in the right side of the chest above the nipple. It may well be almost impossible to correct the curve of the sternum in such a case. For such a person the posture he has been accustomed to may be natural, and should be retained. Such an example is only one of many; careful observation will reveal others. Partial distortion of the spinal column is found in many people. Some are able to right it by sitting correctly, but with others the distortions seem irremediable. Inborn, or acquired while very young, one's settled constitution has to be regarded as semipermanent. It may therefore be mistaken to try always to impose the "correct" posture. A person may well be comfortable with his accustomed posture, and in that case he may as well continue with it. A slight deviation from the standard posture does not necessarily prevent one's getting into samadhi.

What I have been speaking of in this chapter are general principles. I will quote just one example to illustrate how one may need to adapt these to suit one's particular constitution. A certain English correspondent wrote to me recently saying, "After the last five-day *sesshin* I lost the feeling in my feet. This has continued for about a fortnight now. The doctor I have consulted has told me that my fifth lumbar cartilage was destroyed in a car crash some years ago, leaving only 10 percent of the cartilage in place." Now, in the operation of pushing the buttocks backward, the region around the fourth and fifth lumbar vertebrae is sharply bent, and this may have been the cause of the trouble. I advised him to reduce the backward movement of the buttocks. It is a fact that one can get into samadhi even sitting in an easy chair in a casual posture, and there are many examples of sick people, confined to bed, who have attained maturity in Zen. For most of us, however, it will help greatly if we follow as closely as possible the general principles of correct posture that I have described here. Incidentally, this correspondent later wrote to tell me that in the course of time he ceased to lose the feeling in his feet, even if he sat with buttocks pushed backward. A doctor told me that perhaps calcification around the vertebrae had fused them into one solid bone.

CHAPTER THREE

The Physiology of Attention

LET US FIRST TRY an experiment that we call "one-minute zazen." With your eyes wide open, stare at, say, the corner of a building outside the window, or at a point on a hill, a tree or hedgerow, or even at a picture on the wall. Stare at a fixed part of the object and do not allow your eyes to move. At the same time stop, or nearly stop, breathing, and with your attention concentrated on that one point, try to prevent ideas from coming into your mind. You will find that you really are able to inhibit thoughts from starting. You may feel the beginnings of some thoughtlike action stirring in your mind, but that, too, can be kept under control. Repeated practice will give you the power to inhibit the appearance of even the faintest shadow of thought.

This inhibition can be sustained as long as the breath is kept stopped or almost stopped. It is true that your eyes are reflecting the images of outside objects clearly, but "perception" does not occur. No thinking of the hill, no idea of the building or the picture, no mental process concerning things inside or outside your mind will appear. Your eyes will simply reflect the images of outside objects as a mirror reflects them. This simplest mental action may be called "pure sensation." William James, in his classic study of psychology, depicts this pure sensation as follows: "*Sensation distinguished from Perception.—* It is impossible rigorously to *define* a sensation; and in the actual life of consciousness sensations, popularly so called, and perceptions merge into each other by insensible degrees. All we can say is that *what we*

47

mean by sensations are FIRST *things in the way of consciousness.* They are the *immediate* results upon consciousness of nerve-currents as they enter the brain, and before they have awakened any suggestions or associations with past experience. But it is obvious that *such immediate sensations can only be realized in the earliest days of life.* They are all but impossible to adults with memories and stores of associations acquired. Prior to all impressions on sense-organs, the brain is plunged in deep sleep and consciousness is practically non-existent. Even the first weeks after birth are passed in almost unbroken sleep by human infants. It takes a strong message from the sense-organs to break this slumber. In a new-born brain this gives rise to an absolutely pure sensation. But the experience leaves its 'unimaginable touch' on the matter of the convolutions, and the next impression which a sense-organ transmits produces a cerebral reaction in which the awakened vestige of the last impression plays its part. Another sort of feeling and a higher grade of cognition are the consequence. 'Ideas' *about the*

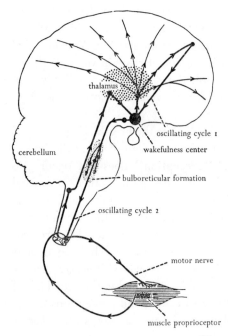

17. Diagram illustrating the pathways of the two oscillating cycles concerned in maintaining wakefulness. (From Guyton, Function of the Human Body*)*

48

object mingle with awareness of its mere sensible presence, we name it, class it, compare it, utter propositions concerning it, and the complication of the possible consciousness which an incoming current may arouse, goes on increasing to the end of life. In general, this higher consciousness about things is called Perception, the mere inarticulate feeling of their presence is Sensation, so far as we have it at all. To some degree we seem able to lapse into this inarticulate feeling at moments when our attention is entirely dispersed."[1]

In our experiment of one-minute zazen, pure sensation resulted from strong inhibition of the process of thinking. While James considered that "to some degree we seem able to lapse into this inarticulate feeling at moments when our attention is entirely dispersed," in our one-minute zazen strong mental power controls our mind and inhibits dispersed attention and wandering thoughts. It is not an inarticulate state of mind but a strong, voluntary, inward concentration. Where does this mental power come from? In our experiment it came from stopping (or almost stopping) breathing. And stopping breathing necessarily involves straining the abdominal respiratory muscles—in other words, developing tension in the tanden. Mental power, or we might say spiritual power, in the sense of this strong inward concentration, comes from tension in the tanden. At first this may sound rather ridiculous. But it proves true, as we shall try to show. Let us first listen to the physiologist, discussing the wakefulness center of the brain: "Two oscillatory pathways have been found in the nervous system that, when excited, can cause wakefulness. Both of these pass through the sympathetic center in the posterior hypothalamus, for which reason this area is often called the *wakefulness center*. In one of the oscillating cycles signals pass from the wakefulness center into the anterior thalamus, and then are relayed in all directions into the cerebral cortex. The cortical areas in turn transmit impulses back to the wakefulness center, reexciting it and initiating still more impulses to stimulate the cortex. This sequence of transmission occurs over and over again, creating an oscillating cycle which is illustrated as 'oscillating cycle 1' in Figure 221 [reproduced here as Figure 17].

"The second oscillatory cycle that can cause wakefulness is the following: Signals are transmitted from the wakefulness center to the bulboreticular formation of the brain stem, and this increases the muscular tone throughout the body. The tension in the muscles in turn stimulates the proprioceptors and other sensory nerve endings over the entire body, resulting in sensory signals that are transmitted back up the cord to the thalamus and finally to the wakefulness center. Thus, a second oscillating cycle is established, the wakefulness center exciting the muscles, and sensations from the body then reexciting the wakefulness center."[2]

Figure 18 shows how, if it is assumed that in zazen sensory signals from the body originate principally in the tanden (and this fact will become clearer as we proceed), then the two oscillating cycles can be related in a simplified scheme.

The two oscillatory streams of impulses affect each other when they pass through the wakefulness center. The decreased tone of one of them will decrease the tone of the other. Especially when the second cycle becomes quiet the first cycle tends to be strongly affected. Judging from the experience of zazen, we would say that it is doubtful whether the first cycle can by itself carry out completely the activity of consciousness. It is at least certain that thought cannot be controlled by the action of the first cycle alone. If you doubt this, try the following very simple experiment. You have only to sit down quietly for a time with the intention of not thinking anything. Presently, however, some idea will come into your head, and you will become absorbed in it and be forgetful of yourself. But before long you will suddenly become aware of yourself and start once again trying not to think anything. However, before perhaps twenty seconds have passed you will once again find a new idea cropping up and will be drawn into thinking about it, forgetful of yourself. You will repeat the same process time and time again, and at last come to realize that you cannot control the thought occurring in your own mind. This is what we mean when we say that the first cycle really is unable to regulate by itself what happens within its own cycle. It necessarily needs support from the second cycle to control itself. William James is thinking along similar lines when he writes, ". . . the one mental state is not immediately induced by the other, . . . the bodily manifestations must first be interposed between.''[3]

The leading party of the first cycle, the cortex of the brain, knows this naturally. When it wants to control its own thought it naturally brings into play the tension of the respiratory muscles. The activity of these recruits the awakening power of the wakefulness center, and by that power it succeeds in controlling itself. In the experiment of one-minute zazen described above, you stopped or almost stopped breathing. The purpose of that was to create tension in the respiratory muscles and so bring about the effect referred to.

The thought-controlling power of the wakefulness center can be regarded as a mental or spiritual power. However, the power is sustained by the stimulation coming from the tension in the respiratory muscles of the abdomen, which do not themselves think, of course, but by their straining permit that power to be generated. So we may regard these muscles—or the tanden in general—as the root of spiritual power.

The physiology textbook tells us, it is true, that the second cycle is formed between the wakefulness center and the peripheral muscles in general. But we suggest that among the muscles the respiratory ones alone can provide a strong enough stimulus to control thought for any length of time. When you strike a hammer blow, or leap out of a window, no thought occurs in your mind. The momentary tension of the skeletal muscles here presumably generates a strong impulse that is transmitted to the wakefulness center, which it occupies, with consequent inhibition of thoughts. But this inhibition is mo-

18. Simplified diagram showing the proposed mode of operation of the two oscillating cycles in zazen. It is postulated that in cycle 2 the tanden is the chief source of stimuli from the body to the wakefulness center.

51

mentary. On the other hand, the tension of the respiratory muscles of the abdomen can be maintained in such a way as to take possession of the wakefulness center for a much longer time.

If now we return once more to the experiment of one-minute zazen and observe carefully how it is done, we find that a tremendous amount of effort is being used. Even in spite of this, certain lapses of concentration appear and thoughts threaten to creep in. Each time, this is inhibited by a renewed effort of concentration. The effort is that of keeping up or renewing the tension in the respiratory muscles. The respiratory muscles, too, it seems, can transmit only a short-lived stimulus, which is strong enough to control thought if constantly repeated. Our conclusion is that we successfully perform one-minute zazen to the extent that we can repeatedly generate new tension in the abdominal respiratory muscles.

Speaking from the experience of zazen practice, we would say that attention, too, can be sustained by the tension of the respiratory muscles. And in just the same way, the fact that attention can be sustained at its peak for only a few seconds is due to the fact that these muscles can be maintained maximally tensed for only a few seconds. Hence, to maintain continuous concentration of attention we have repeatedly to generate new tension in these muscles. This requirement forms the basis of the method of breathing in zazen that is described in subsequent chapters.

The condition of samadhi in zazen is a steady wakefulness, with thoughts controlled and spiritual power maximally exerted. We suggest that it can be described physiologically as a mental force, which appears in the second cycle and which results from the stream of impulses between the tanden and the wakefulness center. In this case, the cortical activity of the first cycle is reduced to all but nothing. One may ask, What benefit is there in producing such a mental and physiological state? The answer will appear later. What we want to emphasize for the present is that breathing has an extremely important role in controlling thoughts in zazen practice.

CHAPTER FOUR

Breathing in Zazen

IN THIS CHAPTER we shall consider some simple facts about the physiology of breathing and their relevance to zazen. First, we need to discuss the volumes of air that can be taken into and expelled from the lungs. These are illustrated in Figure 19.[1]

In this figure, toward the bottom, there is a line at approximately the 1200-milliliter level that corresponds to the so-called *residual lung volume.* This means that even though all of the muscles of expiration are fully contracted, 1200 milliliters of air still remain in the lungs and cannot be expelled. The reason for this is that no amount of muscular contraction can completely collapse all of the alveoli and respiratory passages. This, incidentally, is why it is that in zazen practice we can exhale as much air as possible and then remain without breathing for a considerable period. The rising and falling curve in Figure 19 between the levels of 2300 and 2800 milliliters represents normal respiration. The lung volume increases from 2300 to 2800 milliliters when we breathe in (inspiration) and decreases again to 2300 milliliters during expiration. The inflow and outflow of air with each respiration is known as the *tidal volume,* and it will be seen that this is normally approximately 500 milliliters.

When none of the respiratory muscles is contracting, the lungs contain approximately 2300 milliliters of air. This is the content of the lungs under passive conditions. Normal quiet respiration is performed almost entirely by the inspiratory muscles, and so this passive volume is equal to the volume of the lungs at the end of normal expiration. The horizontal line at the 2300-milliliter level we shall refer to as the *horizon of breathing*.

When, at the end of a normal expiration, one contracts all the expiratory muscles as powerfully as possible, one can force approximately 1100 milliliters of additional air from the lungs. This extra air that can be expired only with effort is known as the *expiratory reserve volume*.

With this as background we may turn to consider breathing in zazen in detail. There is, of course, some variation here in the practice of different students, and at different times in any one person's practice. We merely present here what we regard as some essential features. The line AB shows the maximal volume of breathing in zazen. It will be seen at once that we are concerned chiefly with the expiratory reserve volume. If we make the maximal effort, the whole of the reserve volume is exhaled. However, we do not do this repeatedly. Following such a deep expiration, some three to five cycles of normal breathing will usually follow, as shown in Figure 19, and then another maximal expiration is performed. Some students will not go so far toward the bottom of the reserve volume but will return from around midway or so, as shown by the dotted lines. If you do not go so far below the horizon, you will not need the tidal recovery breathing. However, the farther you go below the horizon, the more quickly you will attain samadhi and the deeper it will be.

The major muscles of inspiration are the diaphragm, the external intercostals, and a number of small muscles in the neck. The inspiratory muscles cause the pleural cavity to enlarge in two ways. First, if the lower abdomen is allowed to fill out or inflate, this facilitates the downward movement of the diaphragm, which in turn pulls the bottom of the pleural cavity downward. This is called abdominal respiration. Secondly, the external intercostal muscles and the muscles of the neck combine to lift the front of the thoracic cage, directing the ribs farther forward than previously and thus increasing the depth of the pleural cavity. This may be called thoracic inspiration. In zazen it is exclusively the former method that is used. This is because the thoracic method elevates the thoracic cage and displaces tension upward, thereby partly depriving the lower abdomen of its internal pressure, while the abdominal method pulls the cavity downward and increases the pressure in the lower abdomen. As we have already emphasized, in zazen, tension and pressure must be kept in the lower part of the abdomen as much as possible, as this brings about both physical and mental stability.

The major muscles of expiration are the abdominals and, to a lesser extent, the internal intercostals. The abdominal muscles cause expiration in two ways. First, they pull downward on the chest cage and reduce its thickness. Secondly, they force the abdominal contents upward against the diaphragm, reducing the length of the thoracic cage. The internal intercostals help in expiration to a small extent by pulling the ribs downward, which also reduces the depth of the thoracic cage.

In zazen, we repeat, the thoracic cage is to be kept as still as possible. Inspiration is performed by inflating the lower abdomen, while expiration is performed by contracting the abdominal muscles. There is, however, an important difference between the method of expiration in normal breathing and in zazen. In normal abdominal respiration the abdominal muscles are simply contracted, which pushes the

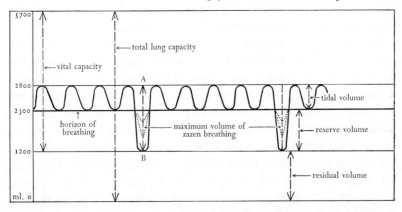

19. Diagram illustrating the volume of air taken into and expelled from the lungs in breathing. The thick, continuous line shows the successive inhalations and exhalations in zazen. Deep exhalation, in which all or most of the expiratory reserve volume is expelled, is followed by a number of cycles of normal breathing. (Adapted from Guy-ton, Function of the Human Body*)*

55

viscera upward, causing them to press on the diaphragm, which in turn expels air from the lungs. However, in zazen, the free contraction of the abdominal muscles and their upward pushing movement are opposed by the diaphragm. This produces bated breath.

The instruction to oppose the contraction of the abdominal muscles by the diaphragm sounds complicated. In fact it is very simple: you have only to hold your breath. If you then expire slowly, little by little, it is necessarily done by holding the diaphragm down and steadily checking the upward pushing movement of the abdominal muscles. The latter are placed in opposition to the diaphragm, and the contraction of each is increased. This is what we mean when we speak of "throwing strength into the tanden." It results in the generation of what ultimately proves to be spiritual power, as we have described above. If you manage to keep the diaphragm and the abdominal muscles contracting in opposition with almost equal strength, your breath will be almost stopped. There may be some quiet and almost imperceptible escape of breath from the lungs because of the natural bodily pressure. You can stop even that, too, if you want to, but to do so will result in an uncomfortable pressure in the chest and is inadvisable. When we speak of stopped, or almost stopped, breath, we generally mean the above state of very quiet respiration.

In the previous chapter we described the experiment of "one-minute zazen" and found we could control thoughts occurring in the brain by dint of holding our breath. That control and inhibition of thought came from this opposed tension in the abdominal muscles and diaphragm. From the experience of zazen we are bound to conclude that by maintaining a state of tension in the abdominal respiratory muscles we can control what is happening in the brain. Even those who know nothing about Zen will throw strength into the abdomen, by stopping their breath, when they try to put up with biting cold, bear pain, or suppress sorrow or anger. They use this method to generate what may be called spiritual power. Furthermore, the abdominal muscles can be regarded as a kind of general manager of the muscular movements of the entire body. When doing heavy manual work, such as weight lifting or wielding a sledgehammer, you cannot

bring the muscles of the rest of the body into play without contracting these muscles. Even in raising a hand or moving a leg you are
straining the abdominal muscles. Scribble with your pen or thread a
needle and you will find tension developing in the diaphragm. Without
cooperation of the respiratory muscles you cannot move any part of
the body, pay close attention to anything, or, indeed, call forth any
sort of mental action. We cannot repeat this fact too often: it is of the
greatest importance but has been rather ignored up to now.

Let us now return to consider once more the horizon of breathing.
This lies at the border between the tidal volume and the expiratory
reserve volume, at about 2300 milliliters. In a passive condition, at
the end of a normal expiration, the lungs contain about this amount of
air and the tension in the respiratory muscles is at zero. Inspiration
starts from this point, and tension starts to develop in the muscles
used in inspiration. In normal respiration, when the lung volume
reaches 2800 milliliters, inspiration automatically turns into expiration; the inspiratory muscles relax, the volume comes down to 2300
milliliters, and all the tension returns to zero. Normally, inspiration
then automatically starts to take place again. In zazen, however, you do
not stop expiration at 2300 milliliters but continue to expire, and
this calls for effort. In general, then, we may say that above the horizon of breathing it is inspiration that requires effort, while below this
it is expiration. Normal respiration is performed above the horizon,
using the tidal volume alone, and expiration comes about by the relaxation of the inspiratory muscles. In zazen, expiration goes down
below the horizon, and it is in this phase that most effort is exerted.
It is this expiration below the horizon that is principally effective in
bringing about samadhi, because it is here that the diaphragm and abdominal muscles are brought most strongly into opposition.

It is important to note that this opposition between the diaphragm
and the abdominal muscles must not be brought into play when there
is still a good deal of air in the lungs, as this will cause a choking and
oppressive feeling in the chest. A certain amount of breath should
first be allowed to escape rather quickly, and then you may start to
expire more slowly. When expiration above the horizon is restricted

57

and the breath is allowed to escape too slowly, the result is rather like applying a brake on a car descending a hill. This is not a positive attitude but a negative one.

A similar negative effect can also appear in inspiration below the horizon, when you control the intake of breath and inhale too slowly. If you do this, you must necessarily put the brake on the relaxation of the abdominal muscles, and such a negative effect, when carried beyond a reasonable degree, again brings about an unnatural, oppressive feeling in the chest. In recovering the expired reserve volume, a rather quick inspiration is natural and desirable. In both expiration and inspiration, therefore, avoid these negative effects, since they will lead to a shallow and uneasy mental condition. If one delays exhalation when there is too much air in the lungs, or delays inhalation in spite of an urgent need to recover the breath, then no composed performance can be achieved, not only in zazen but in other disciplined activities, such as the tea ceremony, flower arrangement, and archery.

With regard to the method of inspiration to be used in zazen, we suggest that this can be divided into two phases. In the first, during inspiration *below* the horizon, breath is taken in naturally and easily by relaxing the diaphragm and abdominal muscles, at the same time allowing the lower abdomen to inflate (that is, performing abdominal inspiration). In the second phase, *above* the horizon, inspiration is performed by contracting the diaphragm. In this second phase it is desirable to begin once more tensing the abdominal muscles so as to inflate the abdomen (that is, perform active abdominal inspiration). This will prevent the occurrence of chest breathing. Otherwise, there may be a tendency to gasp and the abdomen may cave in. The method may sound somewhat complicated, but in practice it is done very naturally and easily if you only take care not to gasp (that is, not to do chest breathing).

With regard to expiration above the horizon, this is done naturally, avoiding negative strain. At around the horizon and below it you may start to contract the diaphragm, to make it work in opposition to the contraction of the abdominal muscles, which pushes the viscera upward.

The material in this chapter constitutes what we regard as the essential general principles of breathing in zazen. In the following chapters we shall describe in more detail how these principles are applied in the various methods of zazen practice. What is described in this chapter is not found elsewhere in Zen literature. It is a new proposal. Of course, if you are experienced in zazen and do not like the method proposed here, you may ignore it. However, as your practice develops you may come to see the value of it.

CHAPTER FIVE

Counting and Following the Breath

COUNTING THE BREATH   It is usual to begin the practice of zazen by counting your breaths. There are three ways of doing this:
(1) Count both inhalations and exhalations. When you inhale, count "one" inwardly; when you exhale, count "two," and so on up to ten. Then return to one again and repeat the process. Perhaps at first it may be helpful to whisper the count inaudibly, or even audibly. Then, except for occasions when you feel the need for audible counting, concentrate on the counting inwardly, stressing your vocal cords but not making any sound.
(2) Count your exhalations only, from one to ten, and repeat. Let the inhalations pass without counting them.
(3) Count your inhalations only, letting the exhalations pass without counting them.
Of these three, the first method is generally used for the initiation of beginners, the second is recognized as a more advanced step, and the third is somewhat difficult for a beginner but gives good training in inspiration.

When, in the first method, you have said "one" with your inhalation, and begin to exhale, if you try to say "two" immediately, you will experience an oppressive feeling in your chest, though it may be very slight. This results from a negative effect of the kind we have described on page 57. This is avoided quite naturally by allowing a little bit of breath to escape from the lungs before you say "two." Why the pain in the chest? When you stress the vocal cords, whether you utter a sound or not, an extra tension, somewhat stronger than in an ordinary exhalation, will develop in the lungs, and if much air still remains in them, a pain will be felt in the chest. The same will prove true when you recite "Mu" or work on a koan (see chapter 6). Of course, in practice, we naturally take steps to avoid this sort of breathing almost before we are aware of it, but it is better to do this knowingly than unknowingly.

In practicing the second method the procedure is to say "won-n-n" with a lengthened expiration, and, after taking a breath, to say with the next expiration "two-oo-oo." With each count the expiration will naturally go down below the horizon of breathing. Thereafter you keep on, saying "three-ee-ee," "four-r-r," and so on, up to ten. But in the middle of the counting, some other idea will suddenly come into your head, and you will find yourself involved with that thought for a while. However, you will soon return to yourself and take up the counting again; but now you discover that you have forgotten where you left off and must go back to the beginning and start from one again. Any beginner who has tried this practice for the first time must have experienced this failure and been surprised by his inability to control his thoughts as he wanted. Some readers may find this hard to believe. Then they should try it themselves, and they will say, "Indeed!" and say to themselves, "This won't do." That, incidentally, is what a Zen teacher wants to hear, for he will then say, "Then you may as well train your mind with this method for a while."

The third method is a training in inspiration. The most important thing in this case is to inflate the lower abdomen and inhale. In the course of saying "one," generally the tidal volume will be filled. As you approach the end of the inhalation it will tend to become chest breathing and you will have to make an effort to keep up the abdominal breathing. Here you will discover the value of the two-phased inhalation that we described on page 58, in which fresh tension is applied in the abdomen in each phase. If you try to inhale in one phase, before you are aware of it tension will move up to the chest and gasping will occur. The two-phased inspiration is very helpful in keeping you doing abdominal breathing, even in tidal respiration, which is done solely above the horizon.

POSITIVE SAMADHI AND ABSOLUTE SAMADHI Although we shall discuss samadhi in detail in chapter 8, we want at this stage to introduce a distinction between two kinds of samadhi, since it is relevant to the discussion of counting the breaths. We shall refer to the two kinds as *absolute samadhi* and *positive samadhi*. People generally associate the term samadhi with Nirvana, in which the activity of consciousness is almost stopped. But the samadhi reached in counting the breaths involves a very definite action of consciousness. This, then, is an active sort of samadhi, and we shall call it positive samadhi, to distinguish it from the other kind, which we shall call absolute samadhi. We do not call it negative samadhi, because absolute samadhi constitutes the foundation of all Zen activities and also because it leads us to experience pure existence.

To date, these two kinds of samadhi have not been clearly distinguished, and confusion has resulted. The *kanna* Zen (working on koans; see chapter 9) of the Rinzai sect involves a large element of positive samadhi (although training in absolute samadhi is also found in this school), while in the practice of *shikantaza* of the Soto sect (see page 80), absolute samadhi is more important (though of course here, too, positive samadhi is developed as well). We suggest that the right course is to develop positive and absolute samadhi equally. To enter the silence of absolute samadhi is to shake off what we call the habitual way of consciousness—in an old phrase, "topsy-turvy delusive thought." By doing so we purify body and mind. Then, going out (or coming back) into the world of actual life and of the ordinary activity of consciousness, we enjoy positive samadhi and freedom of mind in the complicated situations of the world: this is real emancipation.

Returning to the question of counting the breaths, a useful analogy can perhaps be drawn with the state of mind necessary in driving a car. When driving you are obliged to exercise two kinds of attention. The first is sharply focused, directed upon a certain limited zone ahead of you. The second is quite the opposite and is diffused over a broad area; you are on the lookout for emergencies arising in any direction. Similarly, in counting the breaths, both sharply focused and diffused attention are required. We have to concentrate on reciting the numbers, while at the same time being alert not to miss their order. This may sound easy, but in fact, the more you concentrate on the individual breaths and counts, the more difficult it is to keep the attention widely diffused at the same time. To accomplish the two things at once with real success requires the utmost effort. Incidentally, we may remark that after a sesshin in which we may have worked on Mu for a long period, we have to be very careful in driving, since we have been concentrating for so long in a sharply focused manner and have not employed the more diffused type of attention.

It seems likely that the two types of samadhi are correlated with distinctly different patterns of electrical activity in the brain. An electroencephalographic study of seven Kundalini yogis in Calcutta by Das and Gastaut[1] demonstrates the appearance of an intensified beta rhythm during samadhi. The beta rhythm is understood to denote animated cortical activity. On the other hand, studies of Soto Zen masters in Japan by Kasamatsu and Hirai[2] show the appearance, in the course of zazen, first of alpha waves, then an increase of alpha amplitude, followed by a decrease of alpha frequency, and finally the development of a theta rhythm. It is known that alpha waves appear when a person is awake but not thinking hard. The increase in amplitude of these waves seems to denote the progress of mental calming, while the appearance of theta waves may be presumed to denote the advent of absolute samadhi. Comparable studies of Zen masters in positive samadhi have not been reported, so far as I know. However, we may guess that they would show an active pattern of electrical activity, perhaps like that of the yogis.

One final word on the topic of counting the breaths. If, after making good progress in zazen, you return to this practice once more, you will find that it leads to the development of an extraordinarily brilliant condition of consciousness. But this is not to be expected in the zazen of beginners. Therefore, the teacher is usually satisfied if his pupil can master just the elements of counting the breaths and will then pass him to another kind of practice. The pupil may suppose that he has finished with this sort of discipline and that he will not have to practice it again, but this is mistaken. Students practicing alone may also revert to counting the breaths from time to time, even though they have gone on to other kinds of exercises.

FOLLOWING THE BREATH   A certain understanding of Zen (in Japan, at least, probably arising from the general cultural background) makes people vaguely seek after absolute samadhi, even though perhaps not consciously. When you practice counting the breaths, recognizing that it is a training in positive samadhi, you will find it brilliantly illuminating. But this will come only when you have made considerable progress in your study of Zen. And when beginners have worked on breath counting for a while they will find, without knowing why, that the counting is something of an encumbrance to them. They will wish to practice a quiet form of meditation in which the activity of consciousness will be transcended. Then, very naturally, they turn to the practice of following the breath.

Instructions for following the breath are very simple. Follow each inhalation and exhalation with concentrated attention. At the beginning of your exhalation, breathe out naturally, and then when you reach a point near the horizon of breathing, squeeze the respiratory muscles so as nearly to stop breathing. With the epiglottis open, the air remaining in the lungs will almost imperceptibly escape, little by little. At first this escape will be so slight that you may not notice it. But presently it will become noticeable, and as the exhalation goes below the horizon you will find that the air is being pushed out intermittently. If you regulate the escape of air in a methodical manner you will advance more effectively toward samadhi. The longer the exhalation, the sooner you will be there. However, a very long exhalation must necessarily be followed by short, rather quick respirations, to make good the oxygen deficiency that results. This more rapid respiration need not disturb samadhi, as long as you continue with abdominal breathing. However, if you find such an irregular method of breathing uncongenial, try shorter exhalations. These seem to be used by many Zen students.

When using such moderate exhalations, however, even those who have made considerable progress in zazen will often find it difficult to control wandering thoughts. Let us consider these wandering thoughts for a moment. They are of two kinds. The first type is that which appears momentarily and disappears as quickly. The second is of a narrative nature and makes up a story. The first type may be subdivided into two: (1) noticing someone coughing, the window rattling, birds chirping, and similar disturbances that intrude momentarily from outside; and (2) the momentary thought that springs up from within, so that we think, "Now I am getting into samadhi," or "I am not doing well today." This sort of thinking does not disturb one's getting into samadhi very much, and as samadhi progresses, such thoughts gradually disappear of themselves.

The second type of wandering thought is the sort of narration that occurs in daydreaming, in which one thinks, for example, that one had a conversation with certain people and one is once again absorbed in the situation. While the body is apparently sitting in meditation, the mind is getting angry or bursting into laughter. This type is quite a nuisance. Now, it is to this type of thought that one very often falls a victim when practicing moderate exhalations. Every so often one comes back to oneself, notices the wandering thoughts, and plucks up concentration to control the fantasy. But eventually one finds that one's power is too weak. How can one get out of this condition? There is no way other than by generating tension in the respiratory muscles by stopping or almost stopping the breath. If now you were to use the vocal cords and inwardly say "Mu," you would find that a greater strength is thrown into the abdomen and mental energy is increased. That strength and energy give you the power to control wandering thoughts. However, you are now working on Mu, rather than following the breath, and that forms the subject of the next chapter.

Finally, we may note that when you are mature, following the breath will naturally lead you to shikantaza.

CHAPTER SIX

Working on Mu

WE CAN DIVIDE our practice of working on Mu* into three stages.

THE FIRST STAGE When you sit down to practice you will almost certainly find that your mind is in a condition like boiling water: restless impulses push up inside you, and wandering thoughts jostle at the door of consciousness, trying to effect an entrance onto the stage of the mind. Strong measures are required to hold all this in check. The important thing is to stop the first thought. If you once casually allow its intrusion, an endless succession of thoughts will follow in its train and you will be helplessly carried away. Thus you must completely shut out wandering thoughts from the very beginning. The earlier you check them, the faster you can enter samadhi and with the least waste of time and energy. This first stage of practice, then, is solely dedicated to checking wandering thoughts.

Breathing at this stage is done with the mouth slightly open; the breath is forced out through the narrow gap between the lips. This practice will give a tension to the respiratory muscles much stronger than in respiration through the nostrils, and it effectively controls wandering thoughts. As we do this we say inwardly, "Mu. . . Mu . . . Mu . . ." You will find that at the start of each new phase of saying "Mu" fresh tension is produced in the tanden. The abdomen

---

*Mu is traditionally the first koan assigned to the Zen student. For an account of the background, see The Three Pillars of Zen by Philip Kapleau.—ED.

will cave in by degrees, but do not allow the lowest part of the abdomen to cave in completely. Exhale until the reserve volume is almost expired. Then inflate the bottom of the abdomen and begin inhalation. Inhale using the lower part of the abdomen.

After a deep exhalation of this kind you will have to recover your breath, and a few short respirations within the tidal volume will naturally follow, as previously described (page 54 and Fig. 19). In this recovery breathing, both inhalation and exhalation are performed in two (or three) phases (Fig. 20). When the tidal volume is regained, another long exhalation is possible. After you have gone through this procedure two or three times, you will find your lower abdomen inflated and equipped with a strength such as you have never experienced in your ordinary respiration. In other words, a strong pressure is generated in the tanden. It gives you the feeling, we might say, that you are sitting on the throne of existence. When you are mature, two or three repetitions of this practice will be sufficient, but if you choose you can repeat it a number of times.

At this stage the eyes can be either open or closed. Those who find it hard to control their thoughts may find it helpful to stare fixedly at a point on the floor or the wall in front of them, as if glaring at an enemy. As we shall discuss later, concentrated visual attention (sustained by the tension of the muscles of the eyes) exercises a strong controlling power over wandering thoughts, just as does that of the contracted respiratory muscles.

At this first stage you can, if you wish, work on counting the breaths instead of saying "Mu." Counting the breaths is recommended by many Zen teachers as a most effective way of checking wandering thoughts at the start of practice. I believe the reason for this is that when we say, for example, "won-n-n" very slowly, we tend to divide the word up into separate sounds, and when passing from one sound to the next we give a fresh contraction to the respiratory muscles.* The process is very natural, and we do not have to worry about when to renew the stress, as might be the case when we are

---

*This is more true if one is counting in Japanese, in which the words concerned are polysyllabic: hitotsu, futatsu, mittsu, and so on.—ED.

simply saying "Mu." If you decide to count your breaths at this stage, there is no need to count up to ten. You may simply say "won-n-n" or count up to three and begin again.

All this may sound rather complicated, but in fact it is very simple. Whatever you decide to say to yourself at this stage, the essential thing is to perform firm exhalations, continued for as long as possible. If you take care not to relax the tension in the lower abdomen, all the

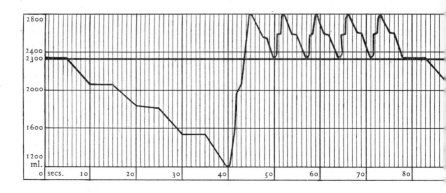

20. *Diagrammatic representation of the bamboo method of breathing. An initial deep exhalation (left) is shown as taking place in four stages, with a brief interval between each, and is followed by five cycles of breathing of normal depth, in which exhalation takes place in two stages. Inhalation is two-phased in all cases. Then the entire sequence*

other manipulations should follow naturally of themselves. Even I, who am advocating the method, could not remember all the details and had to practice it myself just now and write down the sequence of events. With some people a slightly modified method may develop, depending on their constitution and degree of maturity. And that is all right. I do not myself always follow exactly in every detail the procedure just described or those described elsewhere in this book. Zazen training, after all, must be contrived by everyone for himself.

However, to know something of the experience of those who have gone before one will save unnecessary trials and errors.

Dogen Zenji, in his *Rules of Zazen,* says, "When posturing is completed, perform *kanki* exhalation once." This kanki is interpreted as an exhalation through the mouth. Exactly what sort of practice this was is not known. Zen teachers of old taught their disciples individually, according to their degree of maturity, and their instruction was given

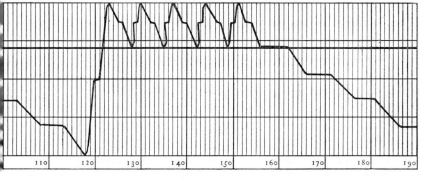

is repeated. The diagram is intended merely to illustrate the principle of the bamboo method; the exact time taken for each stage, the number of pauses during exhalation, and the number of cycles of normal breathing after each deep exhalation are matters of personal choice and will in any case change during the course of zazen.

largely verbally, to the student himself. Hence, much of their teaching is inevitably lost now. However, it is clear that at the start of zazen sitting, Dogen exhaled once through his mouth. One such exhalation may have been enough for a mature master, but more than one may be desirable for people at an earlier stage of training.

THE SECOND STAGE   The first stage is designed mainly to check wandering thoughts, and the method of breathing is strong, even

69

rough. The sound of your breathing may even be audible. When you have carried out the first-stage breathing a few times you will find in your lower abdomen a condition analogous to what is called "the boundless stretch of the earth." It is as if your lower abdomen stretched out, as firm and stable as the earth itself. Now, taking over this condition intact, you begin breathing by the second-stage method.

At this stage the mouth is closed and the tongue pressed firmly against the palate and upper jaw. You breathe through the nostrils. It is not advisable to do zazen habitually with an open mouth, and the reason why you do in the first stage is that when you exhale forcibly between almost closed lips you generate the strongest pressure in the lower abdomen. In the first stage, with the mouth open, you were in fact probably saying inwardly something more like "hu" than "Mu." In the second stage, with the mouth closed, the word "Mu" will naturally, though soundlessly, accompany your exhalation.

Now, "Mu" means "nothing" and is the first koan in Zen. You might suppose that, as you sit saying "Mu," you are investigating the meaning of nothingness. But that is quite incorrect. It is true that your teacher, who has instructed you to work on Mu, may repeatedly say to you, "What is Mu?" "Show me Mu," and so on, but he is not asking you to indulge in conceptual speculation. He wants you to experience Mu. And in order to do this, technically speaking, you have to take Mu simply as the sound of your own breath and entertain no other idea. Only intensely keep on saying "Mu," and when you are successful in this practice, quite without any philosophical speculation, you will one day come to realize that the answer is already given, and you will clap your hands and burst out into a great shout of laughter. If, on the other hand, you start trying to think of the meaning of Mu you will lose touch with immediacy and be left all at sea, drifting about bewildered among conceptual ideas.

At the start, then, simply keep on saying "Mu." Say it inwardly, with the vocal cords in the attitude of saying "Mu." Using the vocal cords in this way is a most effective way of throwing strength into your tanden. As you go on, you may find that the "Mu" changes slightly into "u . . ." or even "n . . . " These are natural developments

70

and are perfectly all right, since these sounds can be more easily voiced with the tongue pressed firmly against the palate.

THE BAMBOO METHOD OF EXHALATION   I want to discuss here in detail a method of breathing that we have already touched upon, which to my mind is of great value in zazen and which, to my knowledge, is not described elsewhere in Zen literature. In practice, however, I believe many Zen students must have used this method without being aware of it. It has not been explicitly described before simply because nobody has previously taken the trouble to analyze in detail what he was doing.

The method is to say, in one breath, "Mu . . . Mu . . . Mu . . ." or "Mu-u-u," with intermittent or wavelike exhalation. We hit upon the name "bamboo method" for this type of exhalation, for just as a bamboo trunk has successive joints or nodes, so exhalation is stopped now and then for a little while, giving short pauses. The length of the intervals and exhalations may be decided according to the length of your breath. The possible variations are too diverse to be described here. I once foolishly tried to give much too detailed a procedure, going so far as to specify for how many seconds the breathing was to be stopped at each pause and how long the exhalations should be. This was a mistake. The method had developed as a result of long practice and thus came quite naturally to me, but to others who tried it such a rigid specification proved altogether too stiff and inflexible, and they found the method too troublesome to adopt.

If you think of trying this method, do it as if you were pushing repeatedly at a closed door that will not open, saying, "Mu-u-u-u-u-u." Then in the course of time your own way of doing this will become more or less established. That method will itself no doubt undergo some modification as your training progresses, and eventually you will find that you have developed your own style.

When we say "wavelike" this refers to a continuous but repeatedly stressed way of exhaling. "Intermittent," on the other hand, implies rather long intervals between exhalations. When one's samadhi becomes deeper, exhalation may seem almost stopped for a long while,

71

with only an occasional faint escape of breath and almost imperceptible inhalation. Such variations of breathing appear spontaneously, according to the degree of development of one's samadhi. With any of these patterns of breathing, however, we generally go down deep into the reserve volume.

Why do we practice this kind of breathing? Once more, the answer is: (1) in order to make the tanden replete with power; and (2) to send repeated stimulation from the tanden to the wakefulness center of the brain, by which means, as we have already discussed (pages 50–51), we inhibit the occurrence of thoughts and so bring about absolute samadhi. Consciousness is by nature constituted so as to be always thinking something, and if left to itself it starts daydreaming. These wandering thoughts are quite a natural thing, but one cannot get into samadhi if one's mind is occupied with them. The bamboo method of exhaling is nothing more than a device for controlling wandering thoughts. Anyone who has practiced zazen will know how difficult it is to control wandering thoughts. We suggest that if you use the method just described you will find it somewhat easier to bring them under control.

We have already drawn an analogy between intermittent exhalation and the repeated hard shoves we give to a sticking door, rather than a steady, continuous pressure. Another analogy might be with a tug-of-war, in which it is far more effective to tug intermittently than to pull on the rope without interruption. Yet another analogy may be taken from painting. When a Japanese artist draws a bamboo trunk, he places his brush at the bottom of the paper and pushes it upward for a few inches. Then he stops, lifts the brush slightly from the paper, and begins again a bit higher, pushing the brush upward again for a few inches. The tiny space between the strokes represents the bamboo joint. This process of pushing, stopping, and again pushing the brush upward is repeated until the full length of the bamboo is drawn. The artist carries out this operation in one exhalation. With each pause his breath also stops; with each new stroke his breath is allowed to escape slightly. Thus the painting illustrates not only the bamboo trunk but every phase of his exhalation. Such a picture allows no retouching;

it represents the spiritual power of the artist at the moment of his painting. This pattern of exhaling while painting bamboo is an excellent analogy to the intermittent or wavelike exhalation that we have advocated for zazen.

Figure 20 illustrates the bamboo method of breathing diagrammatically.* We must stress again that there is no need to try to follow this too exactly.

A NEW STAGE OF MIND   On one occasion of my own practice, nearing deep samadhi, I happened to notice that the stage of my mind was quietly turning and a new scene was appearing. In this new scene no wandering thought popped up its head; there were absolute stillness and silence, as if one had landed on the moon. Clearly, since at times I was noticing this condition, some activity of consciousness was going on within my brain. But it was no more than an instantaneous activity of what I wish to call the reflecting action of consciousness (on this, see chapter 10), and it disturbed my approaching samadhi hardly at all. The condition that had been established was not to be disturbed by that sort of interference. But it would be premature to call this state of mind absolute samadhi. It is only the start of samadhi. You must step further into genuine samadhi. Nevertheless, the experience was a great thing for me. I made a springboard of it and was able to take a further step ahead.

There really comes a stage as your samadhi develops when you may even call out to the stray thoughts to come—and they do not. After repeatedly going through such an experience I tried to discover what I was doing to reach such a stage. And at last I realized that, directly before the appearance of that stage, I was attuning myself to my intermittent exhalation, to push ahead, as it were, inch by inch, just as a wounded soldier crawls along, scratching at the earth, and I cried out, "Oh, this scratching along inch by inch!" From that time I made a point of using this way of breathing, and found to my wonderment that the effect was immediate and profound. It saved me from the old

*I am indebted to Geoffrey Hargett for the idea of this figure.

struggle with wandering thoughts, and I found I could rather easily approach absolute samadhi. Of course, there were many ups and downs, but the way was secured. Now I can see clearly the route I took on the climb, just as if I were looking at an aerial photograph of the Alps. How can I help telling you of it?

OFF-SENSATION   Sitting in zazen posture, with our exhalations going down below the horizon of breathing, a new sensation—we call it off-sensation—quite naturally starts to set in, because you are now mentally going down into the soundless depths of the sea, so to speak. Apart from the tanden, all parts of the body are relaxed and motionless. Off-sensation naturally follows.

Off-sensation is not numbness. If you want to move your hands or arms you can do so, and normal sensation returns. But if you let them remain immobile, the position of your hands, arms, and body is not felt. Awareness of the body's existence comes from stimuli arising in the skin, joints, viscera, and the proprioceptors in the muscles. If the skin is not touched, no stimuli arise from it; if the joints are not moved, no signals come from them. And in zazen posture these sensations easily drop away. But certain proprioceptive signals keep on working and continue to give a certain vague, generalized feeling of existence, even when the tension of the muscles is kept neither too strong nor too weak and when the muscle tone throughout the entire body is kept constant. This sensation is different from any ordinary, everyday one. It is felt as a generalized internal and external, somewhat painful pressure, pervading the whole body. One feels as if one were clad in heavy armor. The pressure becomes stronger as samadhi deepens. In actuality, it is probably a very weak sensation, but just as the sound of a nut falling at midnight in the heart of the mountains resounds throughout the hills, so the pressure is felt to be strong, since all other sensations are minimal.

There are Zen phrases to describe this state as it develops: "millions of miles stretch of steel banks" and "silver mountains and iron cliffs." It is a kind of spiritual power, which becomes the spiritual power of *jishu-zammai*—self-mastery.

However, as samadhi deepens still further, all such awareness of wakefulness, of strong spiritual power, of the feeling of the entire body's rather painful pressure, will die away, and genuine off-sensation appears. That, in reality, is the falling off of body and mind. There is something existing there, it is true, but one cannot say what it is.

Someone may say, "I followed your instructions exactly but did not experience any such result as you describe." "Practice!" is my answer. One may practice zazen for twenty, thirty, even fifty years, and go through failures and frustrations, but every defeat and time of despair is in reality a gain rather than a loss. Any experience is to be regarded as a part of one's assets.

THE EYES AND VISUAL ATTENTION   The eyes have a very important role in practicing zazen and realizing samadhi, and I now wish to make some observations on them. I do this with some reluctance, since what I propose differs from the traditional precepts about the use of the eyes. Zen teachers almost always advocate keeping the eyes open or half-open in zazen. We are indeed usually advised strongly against zazen with the eyes closed. The reason usually given for this is that practice with closed eyes leads to sleepiness and wandering thoughts. This is admittedly good advice for beginners. Personally, however, I always close my eyes when practicing zazen. In my experience, when the eyes are open the mind naturally looks outward. If I want to direct my attention inward, I have to make a deliberate effort to exclude the visual sensations received through the eyes. Closed eyes spare me the difficulty and facilitate inward attention.

Outwardly directed attention is connected with positive samadhi, inward attention with absolute samadhi. It is true that thought can be inhibited even with the eyes open, but one cannot prevent the eyes from reflecting external objects, and sensation inevitably occurs. This fact makes it somewhat difficult for us to enter completely into absolute samadhi. Perhaps those who keep their eyes open are practicing positive samadhi. Unfortunately, most Zen students do not know the difference between positive and absolute samadhi. It is true that even the practice of positive samadhi can bring about kensho, and students who experience this may be well satisfied with their practice. However, my belief is that such a practice will lead to only a partial grasp of Zen. There are numerous cases of people who attain so-called kensho but who by and by disappear from the Zen circle, to be heard of no more. Perhaps they did not penetrate deeply enough into Zen.

We can distinguish two kinds of attention, abstract and sensory, the former operating independently of the sense organs, the latter employing them. Sensory attention is, of course, of various kinds: visual, auditory, bodily, and so on. In zazen practice, sensory attention is more effective than abstract attention. The latter tends to become exhausted rather quickly. If you simply work abstractly on Mu, you will rather quickly be overcome by wandering thoughts, but if you use your visual attention to look into yourself—and more precisely, to look into the tanden—you will reach a state of awareness of your existence itself. And you will also find that you are steadily getting into absolute samadhi. Profound silence envelops you. It is as if you were going down into the depths of the sea, ultimately to settle on the bottom of it.

When I close my eyes and direct my visual attention inward, at first I can see only darkness, but presently the inner scene becomes clearly lit, and the mind's eye is steadily looking into the innermost part of myself. This inward direction of the visual attention always tends to be accompanied by bated breath, and also by bodily attention. These three elements, visual attention, bated breath, and bodily attention, eventually fuse into a single act of concentration that constitutes a powerful driving force toward absolute samadhi. We can call this driving force "will power" or "spiritual power."

Auditory attention naturally tends to be outwardly directed. When you listen to the ticking of a clock, your mind is directed toward the sound, and this leads to positive samadhi. Visual attention, too, is normally directed outward. Only when you close the eyes can you direct attention completely inward.

If, as an experiment, you concentrate attention on the palms of your hands as they lie in your lap, you will feel a delicate tremor there (possibly caused by the bloodstream), and you will be directly connected with the existence of the palms. You are exercising bodily attention. Whenever visual attention is directed upon any part of the body, bodily attention necessarily makes its appearance there. It is as if a spotlight were thrown there in search of some important object. The clear feeling of the palms now occupies your whole attention. In other words, you are concentrating your mind on the palms. In practice, visual attention, bodily attention, and the mind are here one and the same thing.

Or again, direct your visual attention to your arms and try to watch them in imagination. You will find that your breathing slows down, your body becomes quieter than it was before, and a condition of gentle, constant tension develops in the skin. Almost at once, you will probably feel a delicate, thrill-like sensation occurring first around the back of the upper arms and hands, then spreading quietly in all directions. At the same time another thrill-like, delicate vibration will start to appear first around the ears, then will spread to the cheeks, forehead, throat, and shoulders. The sensation of thrilling is accompanied by a clear feeling of delight that calms the body and mind. The condition of the internal organs, the blood circulation, and other psychophysical matters are all reflected in the skin. The thrill will presently subside, and then there comes a peace and silence, dominating the body and mind. Off-sensation sets in before you are aware of it. There is a definite affinity between the thrill-like sensation and off-sensation, and the latter follows the former.

As a beginner you may not immediately experience all this, but the fact of knowing that such a phenomenon occurs will help you to acquire the ability to bring it about rather readily. The thrill-like sensation will be less frequently experienced by more practiced students and will generally be skipped altogether when you are mature. There are also some people who do not experience the thrilling at all, perhaps for constitutional reasons. They have no need to worry about this, as the thrill is not a necessary condition of entering samadhi. Many musicians, poets, and painters, however, seem to be familiar with the sensation of thrilling.

Hakuin Zenji describes another method of inducing off-sensation, which is somewhat analogous to that which we have just described in that it involves concentrated visual and bodily attention. He instructs you to imagine that a soft cake of incense is placed on the top of your head. The cake melts and gradually soaks down into the forehead, cheeks, and throat, and then on into the chest, stomach, belly, and legs. Off-sensation will soon follow.

When you have attained proficiency in the practice of these tricks, a trace will be left in your body and mind, so that even when you do not resort to them off-sensation will rather easily occur in your zazen practice.

If you direct visual attention not to the palms or the arms but to your interior—to be precise, to the tanden—you will find yourself looking steadily into your own existence. When you are mature in this practice, you can enter absolute samadhi in the space of one breath.

Experienced Zen students who are successful in their practice must be using this inwardly directed visual attention, but they seem never to have reflected upon the fact, much less analyzed it clearly enough to be able to tell others about it. There is a great difference between doing a thing knowingly and unknowingly. Lacking a clear understanding of what they are doing, it is likely that they will sometimes find there is something not quite right with their practice, without being able to identify the fault. Some Zen students probably resort simply to abstract attention to Mu and then find that they are subject to stray thoughts, since this sort of attention readily becomes fatigued.

Once again, direct your visual attention to the tanden. The sensation of the tanden will suddenly become apparent and fill your mind. You will find you are steadily and strongly holding and watching yourself. Now let the tension of the respiratory muscles relax, and withdraw the visual attention; you will be merely abstractly thinking of the tanden and you will find that your concentration is drastically weakened.

THE THIRD STAGE   In this third stage, the periods of breath being almost stopped get longer and longer, breathing becomes softer and gentler, and presently the moment will come when it seems that no breath is stirring. You are not strongly stopping the breath and the epiglottis is not closed (that is to say, you are not stopping the breath by using the chest). You are doing all the manipulation with your abdomen, and exhalation comes about mainly by occasional yielding of the diaphragm. Even in this condition, the reserve volume is being gradually used up. But a considerable time elapses before the reserve volume is exhausted: forty, fifty, or sixty seconds or even more. And then inhalation will spontaneously occur in its turn.

In this third stage, samadhi has already begun. You are doing only one thing, which is to look into the tanden with undivided attention. Although no thought occurs, a bright illumination seemingly lights up the mind. Or rather, the mind itself emits the illumination. Rather than speak in terms of light, however, it may be truer to say that everything is dark. Perhaps an analogy will be helpful. Suppose you enter a cave and arrive at the deepest part of it, where a small electric bulb is burning. You can see nothing. But as your eyes become adapted, the light of the bulb becomes brighter. Even though you are in a cave, you feel that the whole universe is stretching boundlessly around you. All is stillness and silence. Strange to say, not a thought stirs in your mind. This is a metaphor, but it may help you to imagine to some extent the condition in which, with no thought occurring, a bright light illuminates the mind. It is as if you were asleep and at the same time wide awake. It is not that a light is illuminating the mind but that the mind is illuminating itself. There is nothing to be found: no world, no others, no self, no time. There is only a subtle existence, of which there can be no description.

Some may ask, "How could you come to know that? The condition you speak of seems to be pure subjectivity, which is not reflected upon and not noticed, which is not known and is beyond description. How do you explain that?" The answer in brief is that the mind retains its action of a moment before, so that I subsequently come to notice the condition as a kind of retreating figure. This point is discussed in more detail in chapter 10.

However, we are not at an end yet. When samadhi becomes yet

deeper, all reflecting actions of the mind are blocked and even the immediate past is not retained. After all your effort, you cannot peep into your own samadhi, much less describe it. What I described above is hardly more than the beginning of samadhi. But perhaps this will be enough to let you imagine what samadhi is.

Let us now return once more to breathing. You may ask, "Isn't the bamboo method used in this third stage?" It is, though without any clearly defined pattern. The breath, as I have said, is now almost stopped, and is allowed to escape only occasionally, bit by bit. And at each escape a change—albeit a very slight one—occurs in the tension of the respiratory muscles and the impulse is transmitted to the brain, and so on. Everything has become quiet. At this stage, if one stops saying "Mu" and enters the state in which one is only holding and watching the tanden, one's practice can be called shikantaza. This is not a state of absent-mindedly sitting; it is a wakeful condition.

I said above that when you begin saying "Mu" you are not supposed to try to think of the meaning of Mu but to take it as the sound of your breath. And if only you will work on, intensely saying "Mu," you will eventually find that the meaning was given long ago. On the other hand, if you engage in conceptual thought about how Mu is to be understood, you will merely pile up concept upon concept, and there will be no end to the job. I repeat, when you once come to have a certain experience of samadhi you will find that the meaning of Mu has long been awaiting you.

CAUTIONS This advice not to think about Mu with your head is of great importance. Reciting Mu with your head is quite different from pushing Mu into the bottom of your abdomen. One student I encountered had worked on Mu long and earnestly, keeping his mind's eye on Mu in the abstract, and thought he was practicing correctly. But for some time he felt that something was not quite right, and in the end he came to realize that he had been doing two things at once. One was working on Mu with his head; the other was watching the movements of the respiratory muscles and the contraction of the lower abdomen. The discovery of this fault was of great importance to him. Now, if you want to practice positive samadhi you do indeed have to work on Mu using your head, and ask, "What is Mu?" But if you want to practice absolute samadhi you must watch—rather, *become*—the movements and contractions of the respiratory muscles.

By practicing positive samadhi (by working on Mu) students often attain so-called kensho earlier than by practicing absolute samadhi, which is the fundamental part of training in Zen. Both of them, in the end, must be mastered. But here we are primarily concerned with the latter. I would go so far as to say that you should not seek after so-called kensho. If you really realize absolute samadhi, there is already genuine kensho in that experience. We shall have more to say on this topic below.

Some people complain that when they work on Mu, a certain painful sensation appears in the middle of the forehead between the eyes, to their great discomfort. This is one of the consequences of the attention not being concentrated on the tanden. They admit that spiritual power is located in the tanden, but habitually they feel that the mind lies between the eyes or in the throat, and they unconsciously focus attention on the forehead or the throat. Such concentrated attention often causes pain, just as a sunbeam concentrated to a point by a lens does. If this becomes a habit, the mere idea of the forehead causes pain there. Even if one thinks one will not think of it, the idea of nonthinking of it proves that one is doing so. One must break such an unconscious habit by focusing attention directly on the tanden.

Finally, we may end this chapter with a few further remarks on inhalation. Most of the important points in connection with inhalation have been described already in connection with the first and second stages of working on Mu. We will merely note one or two points not touched upon. First, the shorter breaths that follow a deep and long exhalation are also very useful in promoting samadhi. They should be inhaled in two phases and exhaled in two or more phases. You may feel impelled to recover the breath quickly and start to gasp (chest breathing). Have patience for a moment if this happens and inhale in two phases, using the lowest part of the abdomen first. Keep the tension as low as possible and gasping will be avoided. Secondly, in addition to

81

this short breathing, you will occasionally find that, almost involuntarily, you perform a very natural and deep inhalation, which is done with the chest. This has come from physical necessity and does not interfere with your samadhi. There is no need to worry about it.

CHAPTER SEVEN

The Tanden

WE INTRODUCED in chapter 3 the notion that the tension of the muscles of the body has a close relationship to one's spiritual condition, and that the tanden, which we regard as the leader of the muscles of the whole body, is of the utmost importance to the Zen student in the development of concentration and what may be called spiritual energy. We shall here take up this topic once more and consider some further examples.

Suppose, first, that we try to look inside ourselves—to reflect on ourselves and catch hold of the mind. The reader should make this experiment for himself. When you try to do it, you are puzzled as to where you can find the mind. Perhaps you turn your attention to the interior of your head, but you find no response there. Or perhaps you look inside your chest, or at the heart: again, nothing comes of it, even if you hear your heart beating. It seems that you cannot locate your mind anywhere. However, if you are determined and continue this introspection intensely, you will eventually find yourself stopping your breath, and then for the first time you will feel something spiritual arising within you. When you began to stop your breath, tension inevitably developed in your tanden and drew your attention, and it was in looking into your tanden that the tension of your mind became apparent.

In according such importance to the tanden we do not question that it is the brain that thinks, plans, and gives orders; but what carries out the directions of the brain is, in the first place, the abdominal muscle structure, together with the diaphragm. If they do not go to work, no scheme is translated into action. You cannot produce a piece of music by simply staring at the score. When the respiratory muscles set to work, mental—or spiritual—power is put into action. The effect of the activity is reported to the brain, which will then think of further orders, and cyclical chains of processes will occur, as we have earlier indicated. Mental action is exercised through this oscillation from the brain to the muscles and from the muscles to the brain. The process is the same with emotional expression: laughter, anger, and sorrow cannot manifest themselves unless the abdominal muscles are convulsed. You may bury a friend up to his chest in the sand at the seaside and tell him a funny story, and try as you may, you cannot make him laugh. He fully understands in his head the effect of the two contradictory ideas in the story, but he does not feel amused. For a feeling of amusement to appear, it is absolutely necessary that a certain physical impulse suddenly thrust up from the bottom of the abdomen. This impulse comes from the convulsive contraction of the respiratory muscles.

Three-quarters of a century ago, the James-Lange theory of emotion was advanced, according to which "the one mental state is not immediately induced by the other, . . . the bodily manifestations must first be interposed between them, . . . we feel sorry because we cry, angry because we strike, afraid because we tremble. . . ." We do not laugh because we are amused but are amused because we laugh. This theory seems not to have been accepted by psychologists, at least in its simple form. However, we must agree that, without the cooperation of the body, no mental action can be brought to fruition. Obviously, man laughs with his body, gets angry, cries, and exercises will with his physical energy. The relation between the head and the body is like that between the general staff and the soldiers in the field: however hard a competent staff may rack their brains, no battle can be fought without troops.

In practice, we stop wandering thoughts through breath control, and by this method we succeed in entering samadhi. The brain first orders the body to take up a certain posture and to breathe in a certain way. However, the role played by the head ends there, and thereafter

84

the action of the respiratory muscles controls the amount of thought going on in the brain. The head knows, or comes to learn, that it cannot govern by itself, so it circumvents the problem and resorts to contracting the respiratory muscles, and thus contrives to control itself. I do not know what the psychology and physiology of our day have to say about this topic, but my own experience in zazen tells me that it is absolutely impossible for an ordinary person to control his thoughts without taking up a good posture and giving an appropriate tension to the respiratory muscles of the abdomen. The art of breathing in zazen is to maintain this tension. Further, when the respiratory muscles are contracted, the muscles of the entire body are put under tension, so that the tanden is the leader of the muscles of the whole body.

In crucial moments, breathing involuntarily comes to a stop. The circus performer knows this, the athlete knows it, the potter throwing a bowl on the wheel knows it, and so does the cartographer, who unconsciously holds his breath when he wants to draw a fine and accurate line. In the tea ceremony, in Noh acting, in judo, and in kendo, the tanden takes the lead in the movements of the body. We have already described how the artist or the calligrapher almost stops breathing when he draws a series of lines and gives new tension to the respiratory muscles every time he comes to an important point. He actually practices what we have called intermittent, or bamboo, exhalation. An elevated type of spiritual activity is manifested in his breathing.

Our contention, then, is that controlled respiration generates spiritual power, and that attention, which is actually spiritual power, can never be exercised without tension in the tanden. Some detailed examples may serve to explain this idea further.

When I first watched an American football game I found it rather uninteresting. Members of two opposing teams are lined up in two rows, and at a signal dash against the opponent's line and in a moment fall down one upon the other. They repeat this same abrupt and jerky movement continually and do not seem to get tired of it. "Monotonous! What fun is there in such abrupt movements?" I thought. Occasionally the ball was thrown over the heads of the opponents, but the moment it was caught they again fell upon each other. To the eye accustomed to watching rugby or soccer, American football lacks any display of serial movements. But soon I began to appreciate the charm of the momentary crash, and I thought I understood something of the American spirit.

Now let us stop and think of the players' posture just before their dash, and consider how they are breathing, and what part of the body is particularly tensed at the moment of darting forward. The breath, of course, will be stopped, arms and legs tensed. But how about the abdomen? In reality, you cannot dart forward if strength is not thrown into the abdomen. Even if you throw your entire body against your opponent, if the center of gravity is not fixed in the lower abdomen, and the hips and buttocks are not supporting the center of gravity from below, you will undoubtedly suffer a severe fall. All Americans must know that the momentary collision is not merely the percussion of two bodies: it is a combat between spiritual powers. That is why people are fascinated by the game. Then where does the spiritual power come from? Do you say it is from the head?

Just as I was at first not interested in American football, so Westerners are likely to feel disappointed when they watch Japanese sumo wrestling for the first time. They see two wrestlers confronting each other in the ring, crouching on all fours, but in a few seconds they stand up, and each goes to a corner to take up some white stuff, which he throws in the ring. Once again they are on all fours in the middle of the ring. They seem to be engaged in a staring match, but before you know it, they are up again. They go through this seemingly meaningless process repeatedly. You soon get bored. "Quick! Hit each other!" you want to shout. At length they grapple, but in a moment one of them is out of the ring, or lying flat on his back or stomach, and you are told the bout is over. Occasionally they grapple with each other longer, but they never perform such spectacular movements as are seen in Western wrestling, in which the participants fall down headlong or hang the opponent upside down and pound his head on the ground. Sumo wrestlers are gentlemen. "Sumo is not particularly interesting," you think. But eventually you may develop an eye for its movements.

As a matter of fact, sumo is a game of measuring one's strength against the other player, but the most important thing is not to lose one's balance in the quick and violent movements—in dashing, pushing, colliding, dodging and being dodged. Infinite training is required to keep the center of gravity in the lower abdomen all the time. The hips must be kept low, the buttocks pushed back. Why do they get down on all fours before starting? The simplest way to find out is to try it yourself. Squat down on your hands and feet, as though you were a lion about to spring on its prey, and stare at your imaginary opponent with a lion's spirit. You will find that a strong force develops in your hips and lower abdomen. Repeat this three or four times—then you will learn something.

The reason the sumo wrestler squats down on all fours and stares at his opponent, and does this repeatedly, is that each time he takes up the posture he develops a greater degree of strength in his body. After five or six times he feels his entire body full of vigorous force. You can see it with your own eyes. His face and, indeed, his whole body become flushed with the increased flow of blood. His skin shines brighter and brighter, and at last he is ready to dash forward with all his might. He is filled not only with physical strength but with spiritual power. We call this being full of *kiai*. *Ki* literally means "breath," which includes both inhalation (*kyuki*) and exhalation (*koki*). *Ai* literally means "to adjust." When "ki" and "ai" are combined in the one word "kiai" the meaning is strong mental and physical power that can be discharged with a brief explosive exhalation. The intensity of kiai is determined by the degree of tension in the respiratory muscles. In short, everything depends on the tension in the tanden.

The maximum tension in the respiratory muscles is developed only momentarily, and the timing of its development is of the utmost importance. This timing is decided by the timing of developing tension in the abdomen. The smallest error makes all the difference, for one cannot then summon up one's utmost power at the right moment. Therefore you must be at the peak of attention in order to fling your explosive power, at its peak, against your adversary. At the moment when sumo wrestlers rush forward, the greatest spiritual energy and concentration are demonstrated, like a flash of lightning, and it is in this that the charm of sumo resides. If any part of the body other than the

87

soles of the feet touches the ground, it means one's defeat, hence one must always keep oneself in good balance. The most important technique in sumo is to keep the center of gravity in the tanden. In zazen this is done by taking up a correct posture, which is then maintained while sitting motionless, but in sumo (and in circus performances, too) this has to be done in the midst of vigorous and strenuous movements. Zazen is child's play compared to the feats of these athletes!

At the start of the hundred-meter race, the initial spring of the runner's legs means a great deal. In fact, the starting dash is generated by the explosive release of energy from the contracted respiratory muscles. If these are tensed a fraction of a second too early or too late, the start will likewise be too early or too late. When you are experienced in the practice of zazen you will naturally become aware of the moment at which the tension of the respiratory muscles begins to decline, and you will spontaneously give an appropriate contraction to them once more—automatically bringing about the bamboo method of respiration.

Now seat yourself in zazen posture and imagine that you are a football player making vigorous dashing movements. You will find yourself tensing your entire body, and especially the abdominal muscles. But the tension is of only momentary duration, and if you want to continue the practice you will have to give the abdomen repeated contractions. In imagination, then, you are repeating the dashing movement on the cushion. After four or five repetitions of this you will find you have to stop to inhale. If you inhale in one movement, the tension developed will be largely relaxed, but if you first make a short inhalation by inflating the lower part of the abdomen and then continue to inhale by expanding the upper region of the abdomen (inhaling in two phases, as we have previously described), you will be able to maintain much of the tension. It is quite an ascetic practice to continue such a strenuous effort for twenty or thirty minutes. But when you have gone through such self-imposed torture to the end, you will emerge to find in your abdomen a kind of strength, both physical and spiritual, such as you may never have experienced before. You will find yourself sitting on the cushion with the spirit of a sovereign. It is simply because your tanden has been filled with vitality.

When I was training myself at a certain monastery I occasionally gave myself the rigorous exercise of dashing, in imagination, against the door of the room with the rush of a sumo wrestler. It was a painful and crazy stunt. I had given a certain American some encouraging words, and I felt I should undergo a pain equal to his. The solemn atmosphere of sesshin in a monastery drives the student into a frame of mind like that experienced on the battlefield and makes him do things that seem ridiculous and even insane to the ordinary man. Now, what was the outcome of my self-imposed torment? Wonderful! It was a new exploration. Many Zen students must have done such things, and have achieved great things from them, but they do not talk much about their methods. They are primarily concerned with reaching a goal, and when the goal is reached the route is forgotten. The stories of their experiments are not recorded to help and inspire us. Anyway, the result of my experiment was remarkable. I attained great physical and mental stability. The lower half of my body was rooted in bedrock, like the rock beneath Manhattan Island, while my body was secured like the skyscrapers upon it. Whatever might happen, there would be no movement.

There is a Zen phrase—we have already quoted it—"silver mountains and iron cliffs." They are a solemn wall, like the snow-clad Himalayas. The Zen student pushes against this wall, pressing it back a millimeter, a tenth of a millimeter, a hundredth of a millimeter at a time. The spiritual power to do this comes from the tension in the tanden. The head is helpless: it can only give orders to gaze into the tanden. The action of gazing is itself maintained by the effort of the tanden, and it is the effort of the tanden that has brought the silver mountains and iron cliffs into being. When we find ourselves confronting them, we feel as if they stood before us as something external. In fact, they are nothing but ourselves, and when the time comes we find ourselves standing as the silver mountains and iron cliffs themselves. While I was dashing myself in imagination against the wall, the wall was the silver mountains and iron cliffs. In the end, I become them myself. I am the sovereign being between the heavens and the earth. I am on the throne of existence. This solemn feeling has come from the power of the tanden.

89

The tanden has come to have such spiritual importance because it forms part of an oscillatory circuit of which the brain is the other main component. As we have already pointed out, the brain is equipped with only sufficient energy to operate its switchboard of impulses. This explains why the brain cannot sustain voluntary attention for more than a few seconds. It has to get new energy—that is, new stimuli— from the body, and particularly from the tension of the respiratory muscles, in order to control its thought. William James was perfectly correct when he wrote that "the one mental state is not immediately induced by the other, . . . the bodily manifestations must first be interposed between." The brain knows this through long experience. In fact, it does not know how to manage wandering thoughts unless the respiratory muscles intervene to help it. It is extraordinary that this obvious point has hitherto been overlooked. The tanden has no conscious functions, but when it functions as one end of the spiritual circuit of the brain, it acquires spiritual importance. The words "abdominal muscles" and "diaphragm" may seem lacking in spirituality; "tanden" is appropriately endowed with spiritual meaning. From our own immediate experience we can confirm the reality of this spiritual power of the tanden.

CHAPTER EIGHT
Samadhi

RINZAI ZENJI'S FOUR CATEGORIES are as follows:
(1) Man is deprived; circumstances are not deprived.
(2) Circumstances are deprived; man is not deprived.
(3) Both man and circumstances are deprived.
(4) Neither man nor circumstances are deprived.
What do these statements mean?

THE FIRST CATEGORY "Man is deprived; circumstances are not deprived" denotes a situation in which one's mind is absorbed in outward circumstances. A famous surgeon was once performing an operation that required great concentration. While he was working there was a sudden earthquake. The shocks were so severe that most of the attendants involuntarily ran out of the room for safety. But the surgeon was so absorbed in the operation that he did not feel the shocks at all. After the operation was over he was told of the earthquake, and this was the first he knew of it. He had been completely absorbed in his work, in a kind of samadhi.

We experience this kind of samadhi when we are watching a football game, reading, writing, thinking, fishing, looking at pictures, talking about the weather, or even stretching out a hand to open the door—in the moment of sitting down or stepping forward. In fact, we are at every moment absorbed in that moment's action or thought. There are various degrees of absorption, various periods of duration, and differences between voluntary and involuntary attention: the dif-

91

ferences, for example, between our watching a football game (involuntary attention) and the surgeon performing his operation (voluntary attention). But we are almost always experiencing a minor or major condition of momentary samadhi, so to speak. When we are in this sort of samadhi we are quite forgetful of ourselves. We are not self-conscious about our behavior, emotions, or thought. The inner man is forgotten and outer circumstances occupy our whole attention. To put it another way: inward concern is absent; outward concern dominates.

It should be remembered that consciousness works in two different ways, one directed outward, the other inward. When consciousness is concerned with outward matters, inward attention is forgotten, and vice versa. There are two kinds and several phases of samadhi. We have already drawn a distinction between absolute and positive samadhi; Rinzai Zenji's four categories provide the basis for a further characterization of the different phases.

Now, it is important to recognize the difference between true samadhi with self-mastery (see pages 94–95) and the false kind of samadhi without it. In the first, even when the inner man is forgotten, he is not forsaken. The firmly established man is getting along well within, ready to make his appearance at any time. False samadhi lacks this self-mastery from the outset. There can be fighting samadhi, stealing samadhi, hating samadhi, jealousy samadhi, worrying, dreading, upsetting samadhi, but all without the guidance of self-mastery. These are not true samadhi as it is understood in Zen.

An animal or bird enjoys samadhi every moment. When it grazes in a meadow it is in a grazing samadhi. When it flies up at the sound of a gun, it is in a flying samadhi. Mellowed by the evening sun, standing quietly for a long time motionless in the meadow, it is in what we might call a "mellowing samadhi"—a beautiful picture and a condition to be envied even by a human being. But the animal has no self-consciousness; though much to be admired, the animal's samadhi is after all an animal samadhi, a lower state than that which man is capable of. The mellow condition attained by some under the influence of drugs like LSD, though greatly attractive to weaker characters, can be compared to that of animal samadhi. It is a retrogression to the primitive life. Not losing self-mastery but at the same time being involved in external conditions is the real meaning of "Man is deprived; circumstances are not deprived." In this state the inner man is simply inactive.

THE SECOND CATEGORY   The second category, "Circumstances are deprived; man is not deprived," denotes inward attention. When we work on Mu or practice shikantaza, we concentrate inwardly and there develops a samadhi in which a certain self-ruling spiritual power dominates the mind. This spiritual power is the ultimate thing that we can reach in the innermost part of our existence. We do not introspect it, because subjectivity does not reflect itself, just as the eye does not see itself, but we are this ultimate thing itself. It contains in itself all sources of emotion and reasoning power, and it is a fact we directly realize in ourselves.

Rinzai Zenji calls this ultimate thing "man." When this "man" rules within us in profound samadhi, circumstances are forgotten. No outward concern appears. This state of mind is "Circumstances are deprived; man is not deprived." It is an inward samadhi and it is what I have called absolute samadhi, because it forms the foundation of all zazen practice. It contrasts with the outwardly directed samadhi described in the first category, which I call positive samadhi. Positive samadhi is a samadhi in the world of conscious activity. Absolute samadhi is a samadhi that transcends consciousness. When we simply use the term samadhi by itself we generally refer to this absolute samadhi.

THE THIRD CATEGORY   The third category is "Both man and circumstances are deprived." A discussion of this category must be preceded by an explanation of self-consciousness. I have said that consciousness functions in two ways, outwardly and inwardly. There is another important action exercised by consciousness: one that reflects upon its own thought. This kind of reflection must be distinguished from general introspection, which deals with character or behavior. When we think, "It is fine today," we are noting the weather, but we are not noting that we are thinking about the weather. The thought about the weather may last only a fraction of a second, and unless our next action of consciousness reflects upon it and recognizes it, our thought about the weather is allowed to pass away unnoticed. Self-consciousness appears when you notice your thought, which immediately precedes your noticing it, and you then recognize the thought as your own.

If we do not perform this noticing action we do not become aware of our thinking, and we will never know that we have been conscious at all. We may call this action of noticing our own thoughts "the reflecting action of consciousness," to distinguish it from general introspection. I take some trouble to identify this reflecting action of consciousness because, as will be seen, it plays an important role in dealing with topics in zazen.

Now, when one is in absolute samadhi in its most profound phase, no reflecting action of consciousness appears. This is Rinzai's third category, "Both man and circumstances are deprived." In a more shallow phase of samadhi, a reflecting action of consciousness occasionally breaks in and makes us aware of our samadhi. Such reflection comes and goes momentarily, and each time momentarily interrupts the samadhi to a slight degree. The deeper samadhi becomes, the less frequent becomes the appearance of the reflecting action of consciousness. Ultimately the time comes when no reflection appears at all. One comes to notice nothing, feel nothing, hear nothing, see nothing. This state of mind is called "nothing." But it is not vacant emptiness. Rather is it the purest condition of our existence. It is not reflected, and nothing is directly known of it. This nothingness is "Both man and circumstances are deprived," the condition Hakuin Zenji called "the Great Death." The experience of this Great Death is no doubt not common in the ordinary practice of zazen among most Zen students. Nevertheless, if you want to attain genuine enlightenment and emancipation, you must go completely through this condition, because enlightenment can be achieved only after once shaking off our old habitual way of consciousness.

JISHU-ZAMMAI   What is the difference between sleep and samadhi? Samadhi never loses its wakefulness. "Jishu-zammai" is the expression that describes the quality of samadhi. *Ji* means "self," *shu* means "mastery," and *zammai* is "samadhi," so the term denotes the samadhi of self-mastery. Jishu-zammai never loses its independence and freedom. It is spiritual power, and it contains within itself all sources of emotion and intellect. When you come out of absolute samadhi, you find yourself full of peace and serenity, equipped with strong mental power and dignity. You are intellectually alert and clear, emotionally pure and sensitive. You have the exalted condition of a great artist. You can appreciate music, art, and the beauties of nature with greatly increased understanding and delight. Therefore, it may be, the sound of a stone striking a bamboo trunk, or the sight of blossoms, makes a vivid impression on your mind, as is related in so many descriptions of kensho (see chapter 9). This impression is so overwhelming that "the whole universe comes tumbling down."

Kensho is nothing more nor less than your recognition of your own purified mind as it is emancipated from the delusive way of consciousness. It is rather seldom that one notices the inner man, because the reflecting action of consciousness is not at work in the most exalted moments of existence. But when your mind is projected to the outside world in the form of, say, the sound of a stone striking bamboo, or the sight of blossoms, and the sound or the sight strikes the door of your mind, you are then greatly moved by this impression, and the experience of kensho occurs. You seem to see and hear beautiful things, but the truth is that you yourself have become beautiful and exalted. Kensho is the recognition of your own purified mind in a roundabout way. We shall deal further with kensho in later chapters.

THE FOURTH CATEGORY This category, "Neither man nor circumstances are deprived," is the condition attained in the Zen student's maturity. He goes out into the actual world of routine and lets his mind work with no hindrance, never losing the "man" he has established in his absolute samadhi. If we accept that there is an object in Zen practice, then it is this freedom of mind in actual living.

To put it another way: when you are mature in practicing absolute samadhi, returning to ordinary daily life you spontaneously combine in yourself the first and third categories. You are active in positive

samadhi and at the same time you are firmly rooted in jishu-zammai—
the self-mastery of absolute samadhi. This is "Neither man nor circumstances are deprived," the highest condition of Zen maturity. True
positive samadhi achieved through Zen practice ultimately resolves
itself into this fourth category.

A man may practice zazen and make certain progress in absolute
samadhi and be successful in establishing the "man" within himself.
Then a new problem will arise, that of how he can exercise this man
in his actual life in the busy world. When sitting on the cushion doing
zazen he can attain samadhi and experience the man, and can realize
that the man is really his absolute self. But when he comes out into his
daily routine and eats, talks, and is active in his business, he often finds
he has lost the inner man. He wonders how he can manage to maintain the man in himself in his daily life.

To take another example, the Zen student may be told first to work
on Mu. At first he does not know what to do with this Mu. But in the
course of practice he comes to know Mu in the pure condition of his
existence that appears in his samadhi, and he realizes that Mu is his
own true self. But when returning to actual life he finds that even in
walking his Mu is disturbed, and he is unable to maintain the condition he enjoyed in his samadhi. When he moves his spoon to his mouth,
or stretches his hand to something on the table, his mind is not in the
same condition as in the samadhi that he experienced at sesshin time,
at the monastery or elsewhere. He would sweep, broom in hand,
earnestly trying to maintain the Mu, but alas! things around him intrude into his mind or attract his eyes, and he finds he is distracted.
Circumstances are rampant; man has no place to settle down in his
mind. Where has the man gone who was described as "not deprived"
in the second category?

The student may now change his attitude and, returning to the state
of the first category, try to be absorbed in outward circumstances.
But he finds this, too, very difficult. While sweeping, he cannot become sweeping itself. In other words, he is unable to forget all other
things besides sweeping, as the surgeon was absorbed in his operation.
Of course, when he sees a football game he becomes absorbed in it.
But this is a case of passive, involuntary attention, in which anyone

can be excited and shout, forgetting all other things, including the inner man. There can be absorption in fighting, absorption in dissipation, absorption in amorous passion, all with the inner man forsaken. The victim is at the mercy of outer circumstances. This is false or superficial samadhi. The samadhi of the first category is not this sort of thing. The missing ingredient is inner control, jishu-zammai. Although the man is not on the stage, in genuine samadhi he is wakeful inside.

In short, the student who is puzzled how to retain the inner man in his daily life—who wonders how he can embody Mu in himself in his actual life—is striving for the condition in which both the inner man and the outward concerns—man and circumstances—are not deprived but are freely in action. In the first category man was inactive; in the fourth category man has returned to the front line. One who has attained maturity in Zen can behave freely and does not violate the sacred law: both man and circumstances are in vigorous activity and there is no hindrance. Only maturity in Zen will secure this condition—the ultimate aim of Zen practice. We shall return to this topic in the final chapter.

CHAPTER NINE
Koans

WHEN THE STUDENT has caught hold of Mu in absolute samadhi, he is told to recapture it in the light of reason. What has been intuitively known gives rise to subjective conviction, but it should be illuminated by reason so that an objectively confirmed understanding is achieved. An objectively confirmed understanding of Zen must be embodied in certain concepts and ideas. There are two ways of manipulating concepts: (1) it can be done as a purely mental exercise, in which we pile concept upon concept, or (2) it can be done by connecting every concept to our own actual experience. The former method means building up construction upon construction, like a tower of Babel, ending in total confusion; the latter is analogous to cultivating an orchard or a rice field, in which every plant is firmly rooted in the ground. It is this method that we adopt in Zen. Whatever type of koan we may be working on, we do not treat it as a matter for abstract intellectual study. It has to become part of us. How is this done?

We may take as a first example the following: "Thinking neither of good nor of evil, at this very moment, what is your Original Nature?" To tackle this topic by resorting to ideas or concepts you have learned from books and philosophies is of no avail. What you have learned is borrowed from others and does not originate in your own experience. Your true understanding must be based on your own experience. Then how are we to work on this koan? Recite it, exerting all your mind, in one exhalation, using the bamboo method of breath-

98

ing. "Think-ing nei-ther of good nor of e-vil at this ver-y mo-ment what is my O-rig-i-nal Na-ture?" Take it syllable by syllable, word by word, and say it with all your attention, dwelling at length upon each word. At each change of sound, give a new stress to the respiratory muscles of the abdomen.

When a word or phrase is kept in the mind for a certain length of time, without being mixed with other ingredients, it seems to infiltrate every part of the brain. Quick as the transmission of nerve impulses in the brain may be, they will take a certain period of time to spread through and infiltrate the brain, with repeated feedbacks. In Zen the term *nen,* which may be translated as "thought impulse," is very important (see chapter 10). The infiltration of a nen-thought throughout the brain produces a wonderful effect. At our ordinary reading speed no such infiltration normally occurs. But it does sometimes happen when you read the work of a poet you particularly admire, or read the Bible, dwelling on every word and taking ample time over it. On such an occasion you may be reading word by word, carefully and with deep appreciation, and suddenly the passage will seem charged with infinite meaning, seeming almost to come as a revelation from heaven. Anyone who has ever read the Bible with devoted piety must have had such an experience. We call this sort of reading "language samadhi," and it is this that we must achieve when reciting a Zen koan.

The nen-thought does not stop working when it has infiltrated throughout the brain. Even though it may leave the focus of consciousness for a while, its underground activity persists and produces a certain effect. When the time comes, this effect will burst onto the plane of consciousness and occupy the focus of attention. So-called inspiration is an example of this happening. It does not really come from outside but is the product of the fermented nen-thought. When you recite, as described above, "What is my O-rig-i-nal Na-ture?" suddenly, sometime, the Original Self will spring up and stand before you, displaying itself in all its magnificence. Original Nature is pure existence, which was already realized within you as your samadhi deepened, and now it has sprung into the focus of consciousness. But it presents itself as if it came from outside. The form it takes varies from one individual to another, and we may consider some other examples.

THE SOUND OF FIREWOOD TUMBLING DOWN A certain monk suddenly realized his Original Self when he heard the sound of a heap of firewood tumbling down. In the sound he heard all things collapse—delusive thoughts, the habitual way of consciousness—leaving pure existence exposed. But in fact, the collapse had occurred long ago in his absolute samadhi. The realization was only a matter of noticing this for the first time, as if the falling away had taken place just at the moment that he heard the sound of the wood crashing down. The pure existence that made its appearance following the collapse wore a universal aspect; at the same time, it was an event inside himself. On such an occasion one hears in the sound of the falling wood the noise of the universe collapsing. The monk heard the hills, valleys, woods, and everything go down into the infernal region with a tremendous roar. Many such experiences have been related by Zen students, and there are many examples in Zen literature. These are the stories of kensho. Kensho is an event in positive samadhi, in which consciousness is in touch with the outer world.

PURE CONSCIOUSNESS Such a state of looking simultaneously both into one's own nature and into universal nature can be attained only when consciousness is deprived of its habitual way of thinking. Working on a koan is one way of doing this. The necessary condition of consciousness that we must achieve is called pure consciousness. Pure consciousness and pure existence are fundamental concepts for the discussion of Zen from a modern point of view.

The phenomenologist Husserl says that when every involvement of the ego as a person is suspended through the method of phenomenological reduction, the pure phenomenon is attained. He carries out this reduction in his head, by changing the attitude of his mind, and seems to suggest that it can be done without much difficulty. The idea of suspending every involvement of the personal ego agrees closely with our view of the need to eliminate the habitual way of consciousness. However, the methods advocated for doing this are utterly different. In zazen we effect it not by a simple change of mental attitude but by hard discipline of body and mind, going through absolute samadhi, in which time, space, and delusive thoughts fall away. We root out the emotionally and intellectually habituated mode of consciousness, and then find that a pure state of consciousness appears. There must, therefore, be a rather considerable difference between what we call pure consciousness and the pure phenomenon of the phenomenologists. Nevertheless, there must also be some resemblance between the two, and we shall have more to say later about the nature of phenomenological reduction (chapter 14).

KENSHO THROUGH SEEING PEACH BLOSSOMS   A monk discovered his Original Nature when he saw peach blossoms in full bloom. No doubt many people are deeply impressed by the sight of peach flowers in bloom. But generally this occurs in the course of the routine activity of consciousness, which is under the influence of its longstanding habit of looking at things in the context of equipment and closes its eye to the purity of the object in itself. In absolute samadhi, on the contrary, this habit of consciousness falls away, and one looks at the external world with unblinkered eyes. Then everything is found to be emitting a brilliant light.

This experience did not happen casually to the monk in question. He had long experienced absolute samadhi, and had made the habit of consciousness fall away, with the consequent exposure of pure existence. But one seldom becomes aware of one's own subjective experience of this state. However, because the experience is universal in nature, it is projected onto the objects of the external world, and it was inevitable that someday the monk would become aware of it. This monk saw pure existence projected onto the peach blossoms.

THE SOUND OF A PEBBLE STRIKING BAMBOO   A monk, sweeping the grounds of a Patriarch's tomb, realized his own nature on hearing the sound made by a pebble that flew from his broom and struck a bamboo trunk. The experience of kensho is very commonly associated with seeing, hearing, touching, and other sensory activity.

In their pure condition the senses directly cognize one's own and others' existence; this is pure cognition. But its pure state is generally contaminated in our ordinary life, and tainted with self-centered desires and views, and then pure cognition is not achieved. The point is very simple: if only the habitual way of consciousness falls away, everything will be all right.

This monk was a man of superb intellect. He had mastered all the learning of his day, from Buddhist teachings to non-Buddhist philosophies. But he was driven into a corner by his teacher of Zen, who requested him to say something original on the subject of his true nature. He had to acknowledge that nothing he knew could set his mind at rest about the problem of life and death. He was greatly troubled. He worked hard with his teacher but could not solve the problem. He fell into despair and thought himself worthless. He decided to live as keeper of the grave of the Patriarch; one must have something to live for. He found the only way to live was by doing this humble job.

In such a state of mind, no thought of making use of others to satisfy his own desires appeared. And now even such an insignificant object as a broom came to be an intimate friend to him. The fallen leaves he gathered each day seemed to convey to him a friendly feeling. A blade of grass, a tiny, insignificant flower put forth by a weed, which had passed unnoticed before, was the object of wonder and respect. In the monastery, even today, brooms and other such tools are made by the monks themselves. The tools are parts of the maker, and when one uses them they are one's hands and arms.

> Familiarized in my daily life,
> How delightful sweeping the ground is!

This monk thought himself a good-for-nothing creature, but he had developed, before he was aware of it, a great embracing ego. Moreover, he practiced zazen each day, and knew intimately the state of absolute samadhi. Living in this way, he was occupied one day in sweeping, when suddenly a pebble struck a bamboo trunk and made a clear, ringing sound. The pebble was alive; the bamboo trunk was alive. And the sound was living, too. Shapes, colors—everything right and left, everywhere, was full of existence. And he heard the voice of existence itself.

The external world is really there around us. That existence is normally veiled is due not to existence but to our eyes. The habitual way of consciousness makes us look at things mechanically and think them dead. If only this mechanical view is abandoned, then existence is exposed in its nakedness. This monk came into direct touch with it. The sound emitted from the bamboo trunk was the voice inside the monk himself, and at the same time, the voice pervading the whole world.

UNBORN   A monk was struck by the word "unborn," and that solved for him his long years of doubt. He realized his own true nature. When still a child he had been set to study a Chinese classic in which he encountered a phrase that runs "to clarify the illustrious virtue," and he became filled with doubt as to what this illustrious virtue was. A precocious child comes to be aware of the problem of life at an early age. Words had to be found to represent this doubt, and the monk found them in this phrase.

To give an adequate answer to a child about his problem of life is not an easy matter. He visited many teachers, but none could satisfy him. One suggested that Zen could help him and he started doing zazen. He must have had a natural inclination toward Zen. He continued his practice for many years without a teacher. Sometimes he went into the mountains where no one was living and spent many days on the verge of starvation. Prompted by the idea that one should ignore the body for the sake of discipline, he sat on top of a crag and never moved until he rolled down from it. Prolonged sitting caused the skin of his buttocks to break and bleed. Eventually, it seems, he became ill with tuberculosis, coughing up blood. He became weak, and was on the verge of death. He thought he would not mind dying but regretted doing so without clarifying the meaning of "illustrious virtue." Members of his family prepared a cottage for him, with a servant to look after his daily needs. But his appetite was almost gone. At this stage the underground activity of the nen-thoughts must have put forth something that came up into the sphere of consciousness; suddenly the word "unborn" struck him, and everything was all right. He began to eat with an appetite and recovered his strength. Later he became a great Zen master.

"Unborn" is an abstract word, but it embodied so exactly all the past training and attainment of this monk that it was as clear and concrete as a key in his hand. There are many abstract Zen terms, but they all represent the concrete experiences of Zen students, and monks find in them vivid expression of their attainment. This monk subsequently talked only of this word, "unborn," throughout his life, and never spoke of any other topic.

The monks whom I have mentioned all became great Zen masters in their later days. Their names are to be found in Zen literature. Much more could be related of them, but for the moment I have said enough. I want, however, to consider one more case.

This monk also suffered for a long time from the problem of life and death. An animal may fear, but it does not suffer. It is simply in moment after moment's samadhi because it does not have the reflecting action of consciousness with which to reflect upon itself. Man suffers because he has this reflecting action, and reflects upon the thought that appeared a moment ago. Thus arises self-consciousness, which produces the problems of self, and of life and death, too. Man divides his mind into two, the one reflecting upon the other. In fact, the mind is not divided, but moment after moment's nen-thought reflects upon the thought that has gone before, worries over it, and becomes agitated.

What has happened has happened; what has gone is gone. If only one understands this, there is nothing to suffer from. But to be able to understand in this way calls for a long period of Zen training, in which one attains absolute samadhi, the activity of consciousness is stopped, and pure existence is exposed. With pure existence there is no problem of life and death. This monk saw pure existence clearly and in a most concrete form at the very moment when he emerged from his samadhi. He sang:

> "You, before me standing,
> Oh, my eternal self!

Since my first glimpse
You have been my secret love."

KANNA   To work on a koan in zazen is called *kanna*. *Kan* means
"viewing"; *na* means "topic." The meaning of the term is therefore
"seeing into the topic." In actual practice we recite each word with
our utmost attention, holding onto it as tenaciously as possible.
This constitutes language samadhi. "The eastern hill keeps running on
the water." This may be recited as follows: "The east-ern hill keeps
run-ning on the wa-ter." Let each word infiltrate your head, taking
time in reciting it. Then this enigmatic saying will become wonderful
and lead you to a certain understanding of reality, which is in a constant state of flux.

BEATING THE DRUM   A monk asked Kasan, an old Chinese Zen
teacher, "What is the condition of a truly enlightened man?" Kasan
said, "Beating the drum." The monk asked again, "What is the true
teaching of the Buddha?" Kasan answered, "Beating the drum." The
monk said once again, "I would not ask you about 'The mind itself is
Buddha,' but I ask what is 'No mind, no Buddha.'" Kasan said, "Beating
the drum." The monk still continued to ask: "When a transcendental
one comes, how do you treat him?" Kasan said, "Beating the drum."
   If a man can existentially realize his own actions, he will be able to
understand Kasan's answer. What do we mean by "existentially"?
This simply means you do not lose your sense. In other words, you are
not bedeviled by conceptual thinking. When you beat a drum, or
strike a match and light a candle—if you do it in genuine positive
samadhi, in that moment you are realizing your existence. You may
bow before the images of Buddha, and you are not worshiping idols.
   Setcho, the author of the *Hekigan Roku* (Blue Cliff Records), puts
his *gāthā*, or poem, in praise of this story in the following words:

> "Dragging a stone, carrying soil,
> You should use the spiritual power
>   of a thousand-ton bow.
> Zokotsu Roshi rolled three wooden balls;

How could they surpass Kasan?
I will tell you, what is sweet is sweet,
What is bitter is bitter!"

"Dragging a stone, carrying soil" comes from certain Zen stories, but here it is enough for us to imagine that we are dragging a stone with a rope and carrying soil in straw baskets over our shoulders. Zen stories are all our own stories. Zokotsu Roshi is a famous Zen teacher called Seppo. (Zokotsu is a place name; it was quite a common practice to use the name of the place where a teacher lived as his surname.) There are many anecdotes about Seppo. One day he rolled three wooden balls before his disciple. What is the meaning of it? Movement! To drag a stone, to carry soil are also movements. Kasan's beating a drum is a movement, too. Setcho was a great master; he did not fail to see Kasan's meaning, and presented these examples of Zen movement in his gatha. This penetrating eye of his makes the *Hekigan Roku* one of the greatest Zen classics. A thousand-ton bow is a formidable weapon. "How could they surpass Kasan?" None surpasses the others. Kasan, Zokotsu Roshi, and the others are on the same level. "What is sweet is sweet, what is bitter is bitter" was Setcho's conclusion. Sweet is absolutely sweet; bitter is absolutely bitter. You can know existence only by directly feeling it, not by indirectly speculating about it. This is the fundamental truth of Zen. Therefore, Setcho said, "I will tell you."

WHY HAS BODHIDHARMA NO BEARD? There is a koan that asks, "Why has Bodhidharma no beard?" Bodhidharma is taken to represent the pure Dharma. He is generally pictured with a beard. But this koan says Bodhidharma has no beard. Its real intention is to say the true Dharma has not only no beard but also no eyes, no nose, no mouth, no face, no hands, no legs, no body. It is written in the *Hekigan Roku,* Case 88: "Blind, deaf, and dumb, it is absolutely insulated from conscious activity." Absolute insulation is nothing but absolute samadhi. But this koan is speaking not only of absolute samadhi but also of the positive affairs of life. How can you be blind, deaf, and dumb in the activity of actual life? In the turmoil of fame and profit, can you be a fool—climb a cliff without using your hands, step off the top of a hundred-foot pole?

If you let go your hold on a cliff, you will fall down and lose your life, but in spiritual affairs you should really do this. You must once cast away what consciousness has accumulated since childhood, that is, your illusory ego. In absolute samadhi it is rather easy to let go your hold, but in the world of active life, to let go the hold on one's ego is difficult. You tell yourself not to hate others, to quench the heat of anger, to be free from temptation, to kill the desire for fame, power, vainglory, and so forth, but you cannot follow your own precepts. You cannot even take off the beard, much less eyes, nose, mouth, and face itself. But a truly enlightened man has no face when he speaks, negotiates, and discusses the serious problems of life. He has nothing to hold to, in the midst of the busiest activity of consciousness. In the midst of the burning flames of life he keeps his mind as serene and shining as the lotus flower in the fire.

CHAPTER TEN

Three Nen-Actions and One-Eon Nen

MAN THINKS UNCONSCIOUSLY   Man thinks and acts without noticing. When he thinks, "It is fine today," he is aware of the weather but not of his own thought. It is the reflecting action of consciousness that comes immediately after the thought that makes him aware of his own thinking. The act of thinking of the weather is an outward-looking one and is absorbed in the object of its thought. On the other hand, the reflecting action of consciousness looks inward and notes the preceding action that has just gone by, wrapped up in thinking of the weather—still leaving its trace behind as the direct past. By this reflecting action of consciousness, man comes to know what is going on in his mind, and that he has a mind; and he recognizes his own being.

These two kinds of actions of consciousness are both called nen, a term which we introduced in the previous chapter and which we may approximately translate as "thought impulse." The nen alternate with each other, from moment to moment, and we may feel as if they were arising almost simultaneously. But nen-actions that occupy the stage of consciousness come forth one at a time. There may be many impulses thronging about behind the scenes, eager to make their appearance on the stage. Every nen-action has its fringe, and these subconscious impulses may make us feel that several actions of consciousness are proceeding parallel to one another. However, the mind's mode of operation is such that there is only one actor on the stage at a time, and the focus of consciousness is upon that one alone.

Suppose a man thinks, "What a detestable fellow he is!" or burns with jealousy. He becomes the incarnation of rage or jealousy itself. He does not realize that he is possessed. A moment later he may blame himself for the meanness his mind has revealed. But however much he may blame himself, he cannot reverse his earlier impulse. His knowledge of it comes after its appearance.

A rigorously trained mind may occasionally be able to detect a subconscious impulse and dispose of it before it springs up into the level of consciousness, but even in that case the impulse comes first, and perceiving it comes after. When you experimented with one-minute zazen, you probably occasionally found something like a premonitory wriggle of nen arising in your otherwise blank mind, and also an inhibiting action following it like a shadow. In this case, too, the order of occurrence was first a subconscious mental action, then a subconscious reflection on it.

The impulse to theft, greed, anger, complaint—all make their appearance before one is aware of them. If the reflecting action of consciousness fails to appear and does not recognize them, they will pass unnoticed and sink into the depths of subconsciousness. However, a nen is an internal pressure of some kind, and if it is not consciously recognized it will remain in the subconscious, unresolved. In this way, some nen will undergo a kind of fermentation and perhaps cause harm to the mind, as we shall explain later.

THE FIRST AND SECOND NEN Let us call the outward-looking action the first nen, and the reflecting action of consciousness the second nen. The first and the second nen come and go momentarily (Fig. 21), and when a serial process of thought is occurring the second nen will frequently arise to illuminate the preceding nen, and the two will intermix as if they were entangled with each other. This makes a person feel that, while thinking, he hears a voice within him that knows his thinking and gives advice to him. For instance, while roaring with anger, one may find another voice whispering in one's ear, "Don't get angry! You mustn't lose yourself in a fit of rage!" This persuading voice is comparatively composed, but the first nen is bawling forth, and this is accompanied by an excitement of the entire body. All the nervous system, internal glands, even the circulation of the blood are thrown into a commotion. They are surging waves, like a mob demonstrating outside a public building, crying out, "Our patience is exhausted! It has gone beyond a question of gaining or losing." Then the other voice will be quietly saying, "No, you should bear it to the best of your ability."

Of course, this is but one example. The first nen will often be quiet humor, the silence of the Himalayas, the mercy of Kannon, or the spiritual power of "silver mountains and iron cliffs."

THE THIRD NEN   The second nen, which illuminates and reflects upon the immediately preceding nen, also does not know anything about itself. What will become aware of it is another reflecting action of consciousness that immediately follows in turn. This action is a further step in self-consciousness. It consolidates the earlier levels. We shall call it the third nen. This third nen will think, for example, "I know I noticed I had been thinking, 'It's fine today.' " Or it may say, "I know I was aware of my knowing that I noticed I had been thinking, 'It's fine today.' "

For the sake of simplicity we may depict these nen as occurring in the first place in a linear progression, with groups of first, second, and third nen following sequentially (Fig. 22). In our example relating to the weather, we have first the observation, second the awareness of that observation, and third the acknowledgment of ourselves becoming aware of the observation. Subsequent acknowledgments may follow and are all in this context third nen, and thus the sequence becomes: first nen, second nen, third nen, third nen, third nen, and so on, as in Figure 23.

However, our minds are complex and dynamic in their operation, and it is not possible to represent the true sequence of our thoughts by such neat diagrams. In order to try to indicate the real complexity of things we have devised more elaborate diagrams (Figs. 24 and 25), which indicate that in the course of the sequence 1, 2, 3, 3, 3 . . . something more subtle is actually happening. This is that during this progression of self-awareness, another first nen and second nen appear as a continuation of the original observation. A change in the wind, or a new shape of clouds, for example, is noticed, and then the next

110

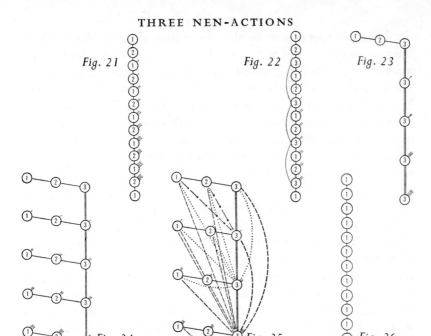

Fig. 21 Fig. 22 Fig. 23 Fig. 24 Fig. 25 Fig. 26

21. *A simple alternating sequence of first and second nen.*

22. *A simple sequence of groups of first, second, and third nen. Such a linear succession (1, 2, 3, 1, 2, 3) is termed the A connection.*

23. *This diagram shows that following a first nen-action (for example, observation of the weather) and a second nen-action (in which we become aware of the observation), there may be a succession of third nen-actions (recognition of ourselves becoming aware of the observation, and subsequent acknowledgments of this, corresponding to a progression in self-awareness). This succession of third nen, shown joined by a double vertical line, is termed the B connection.*

24. *This diagram shows that new first and second nen constantly appear, as time brings new phenomena, so that each successive third nen is fed not only by its predecessor but also by new first and second nen. Each third nen therefore represents in itself all the previous nen.*

25. *This figure portrays in greater detail the actual interaction of each third nen with preceding nen-actions.*

26. *The steady succession of first nen-actions that develops in zazen is shown in this figure. Here there is no interruption by the self-observing second nen or the self-conscious third nen.*

third nen emerges to sum up this observation along the line both of the new nen series and of the previous third nen, each with its own branch line. Thus, in Figure 24, the first series of observations about the weather runs from the top point diagonally down to the right (1, 2, 3), and then vertically downward through the series of third nen. Each subsequent third nen is also fed with a new series of nen (new impressions) as time brings new phenomena. Thus each subsequent third nen dynamically consolidates all of the previous third nen and at the same time brings to itself a new series of first and second nen, which inevitably intervene in the flow of mental action. Thus any given third nen presents in itself all the previous nen.

We have, then, sequences of first, second, and third nen (1, 2, 3), which for convenience we may refer to as the A connection, and another kind of sequence, shown in Figures 23, 24, and 25, which is the series of third nen, shown connected in the diagrams by a double vertical line. This we term the B connection. A and B connections blend with each other and form the stream of consciousness, somewhat in the manner shown in Figure 25. This figure also shows the direct and indirect connections of each third nen with its preceding nen-actions. It shows that the third nen in each series receives directly the preceding third nen and all its possessions, and also the preceding second nen on its own branch line, and that indirectly all the preceding nen are integrated into each current third nen. We say indirectly, but this is so only on paper. Actually this integration results in a unified experience of self-awareness. Everything preceding is integrated into the stream of consciousness and passed along, with new impressions, to the next third nen.

The B connection constitutes the stem that sustains the stream of consciousness, but the stream is composed of a continuous succession of different nen. Each third nen has an internal connection with its preceding ones. But the first nen is constantly receiving new stimuli from the external world, and there is a constant leaping from one nen-action to the next, the whole being integrated by the third nen into the continuing line of thought. The second nen always follows and notices its immediately preceding nen-thought. And thus, just as the abrupt changes on the cinema screen do not startle us, so the continuous changes of the nen projected on the mind's screen are not disturbing.

All this explanation is intended to portray the working of the mind when left to itself. The discipline of zazen encourages absorption in one nen, for example, in Mu. This is illustrated in Figure 26. By consciously repeating "Mu" with each successive exhalation, the student induces the steady succession of first nen-actions, with no reflecting upon them in the form of second nen, and no self-consciousness in the form of third nen. The mind just produces "Mu-mu-mu-mu . . ." Gradually this develops into the condition, which we shall discuss later in this chapter, called "one-eon nen." This, in fact, is nothing more than another term for absolute samadhi, which we have already discussed in a preliminary way, and to which we shall return in chapter 13.

GRASPING A SOUND   If, all of a sudden, just now, a factory whistle started to blow, you would probably be preoccupied by the sound for a moment and then come to recognize it as the whistle of a factory. If it were the noon signal you might have the impression that, from the moment you noticed it, you knew it was the whistle for lunch. But a little careful introspection will show that in reality, when the whistle started, for a fraction of a moment your attention (the first nen) was preoccupied by the sound; it was, so to speak, in a state of slight shock. That state of the mind's reception of the stimulus may be called the pure sensation, which, in turn, will immediately develop into so-called ordinary sensation. Then the second nen will emerge and recognize these, and finally the third nen will appear to integrate the impression of the first and second nen into a perception. Before this perception is achieved, however, reference will be made to some knowledge that you already have stored up as conceptions. Then the sound is recognized as that of the noon whistle. This is the process of perception, and it is the progression of first, second, and third nen, similar to the process of thought.

When you think, "It is fine today," the first nen is a thought, not a single sensation. The second and third nen, too, operate in thought. But before you say, "It is fine today," you must have received the sen-

113

sation and perceptual recognition (a series of the first, second, and third nen) of the appearance of the sun, sky, trees, flowers, and so forth, and that was followed by the intuitive thought, "It is fine today" (again the first nen).

If you say that you do not find in yourself anything like a reflecting action of consciousness when you hear a sound, try listening to the tick of a clock and see whether you can be so wholly absorbed in the listening that you are forgetful of yourself. If you cannot, then you must acknowledge that you could not throw yourself into the action of listening and become listening itself. The reflecting action of consciousness was active, tenaciously whispering in the ear of your mind. It is next to impossible for a person who is not trained in zazen to throw himself voluntarily into the condition of listening itself.

SUBJECTIVITY It must be understood that the action of the mind is always subjective; that is to say, our doing and thinking are all the action of subjectivity. Whatever we may think or do, our subjectivity is thinking or doing, and it is always doing so without being conscious of itself. Whether looking outward or reflecting, in that very moment we are unconsciously engaged in the business. A moment later we may become aware of our doing or thinking, but the action of becoming aware is itself unconsciously done. Unconsciousness necessarily accompanies our behavior in the moment of the act, because this is the intrinsic character of subjectivity.

There is a confusing usage of the word "subjective" that denotes thinking from a self-centered point of view. But we use the term "subjectivity" here simply with reference to the subject thinking or doing. Whether one thinks in a subjective or an objective way (that is, independently of one's own self), one is thinking in one's subjectivity. Subjectivity takes notice of other things but never of itself. As the eye cannot see itself, so subjectivity cannot observe itself. When it is observed, it is converted into an object, and another subject must be viewing it. That which thinks, "It is fine today," is thinking in subjectivity and is not aware of itself. Only when it is illuminated and reflected upon by the subsequent reflecting action of consciousness is it recognized and identified as the subject that thought, a moment ago,

"It is fine today." But it has already been turned into an object by virtue of the fact that it has been reflected upon and objectified by the reflecting action, which is itself now acting in subjectivity.

THE THIRD NEN : RECOLLECTION AND MEMORY   If you listen carefully to a continuous sound and try to notice the quality of your hearing, you will find that the sound fluctuates slightly, sometimes appearing thin, sometimes solid. This may be because your attention is directed outward one moment, inward the next. When looking outward the impression is directly in contact with the sound, while when looking inward the contact is indirect, thus creating the different densities of the impression. This phenomenon is also no doubt affected by the fatigue of attention, which occurs every few seconds.

Every moment of a continuous sound is caught by the successively appearing third nen through the medium of the first and second nen. The final third nen grasps in its present instant all of its preceding perceptions and illuminations and the continuous sound itself, and integrates them into one stream of sound.

When we listen to music, the developmental changes are recorded in the successive series of first, second, and third nen. Each third nen integrates the preceding impressions of the composition up to that moment and hands them on to the next third nen, together with new impressions of the succeeding sounds. Thus the piece of music will be held throughout the whole course of its continuation, development, and changes. The final third nen grasps, in its present instant, the character of the music in its whole extent, losing none of the sections, even though they have already rolled by into the past. This is the retention of the direct past. The sound itself has passed away, but it is held in this present instant in its living phase.

The clarity with which the third nen can go back to grasp direct impressions of the past in their living phase depends on the innate quality of one's consciousness, and also on its particular condition at the moment. When the consciousness is tired, the sphere of its illumination becomes narrow and dark. You can readily notice this in your reading. When tired, your hold is uncertain, and repeated reading does not bring you a clear grasp of the meaning. Next morning you are surprisingly dynamic in your grasp of line after line, which you read through with refreshing clarity.

Recollection, self-criticism, imagination, intention, and speculation that do not belong to the reflecting action of consciousness are all first nen. We said elsewhere that the first nen looks outward. But it also looks back at one's past thought or objectified self, which has ceased to be pure ego. When we recollect past things, we think in imagination. However, the reflecting action of consciousness is neither imagination nor the reproduction of the past, but a vivid grasp of the preceding nen.

Psychological tests show that immediately after a traffic accident, the victim often retains a good memory of the occurrence. But a little later, when asked about it, he is found to be forgetful of the details. This may be explained in the following way. Immediately after the event the third nen, which grasped the accident on the spot through the cooperation of the first and second nen, is still actively at work, and the scene is retained clearly in the mind's eye. In other words, the victim is still seeing the accident mentally. This we describe as the retention of the direct past, and it will generally last for the few moments that constitute the first phase of memory formation. But we cannot hold the immediate past in its living phase for long. We soon transfer it to the second phase of memory formation. In this process of transfer, a new first nen will look at the scene of the accident that is projected by the third nen, and the process will form a circuit from the first series of three nen to the second series and then to a third series, and so on. The circuit will consist of repeating the description of the observation. Some new data may be added or dropped with each repetition, generally quite spontaneously. This constitutes the second stage, the so-called intermediate phase of memory formation.

In this phase, while the circuit is kept active, the memory will survive, generally for an hour or more. If one of the links of the circuit gets tired and drops out, the memory will fail. In the exhaustion that follows the shock of an emergency, the circuit may not get started, or it may have too weak an impetus, so that the transfer fails. This will explain the vanishing of memory a few moments after the accident. However, a nen leaves its trace behind, and when someday the trace comes in contact with the appropriate stimulus, it may once again be fired and recovered on the level of consciousness.

The third phase, in which memory is thought to be permanently consolidated, seems to begin rather independently. We have very little information about how this process is carried out. The physical basis of long-term memory is as yet unknown.

Perhaps at this point we may venture a vague speculation. So long as a memory is recoverable on one's present level of consciousness, there must be something identical or with an affinity to the present condition of consciousness. Now, let us suppose that a so-called memory trace is a consolidated internal pressure of some sort, that every internal pressure has its own mood, and that every mood has been handed down by the successive third nen up to this present moment. Since infancy, every mood has been integrated into the present mood—a process that we can regard as the foundation of personality. Then, when we remember a past thought or action, we identify it as ours. This is done through the identification of the past mood. The mood that we thus recall may be very different from our present one, but it has been handed down by the successive third nen and in the course of time it has successively amalgamated with moods of various kinds—repentance, self-reproach, delight, pride, vanity, depression, and so on—before melting into the present mood. In trying to call up a vague memory, we find first a hazy sort of atmosphere appearing before the mind's eye. It has a certain flavor—warm or cool, pleasant or horrible. It may have the feeling of a misty spring dawn, a summer morning, an autumn evening, or winter severity. From within this vague atmosphere, the figure of the wanted object, at first in a symbolic and then gradually in an embodied form, makes its appearance. Memories must be stored wrapped in a shroud of mood, with symbolical labels.

The feeling of the continuity of our ego is also brought about by the identification of mood, which continues to be felt at every moment and has been handed down to this moment.

INTUITION So-called intuitive judgment may be a more complicated mental process than is generally imagined. When we think, "It's fine today," we may feel as though the thought suddenly comes to us. But before the thought appears we must have been unconsciously appreciating the shining sun, the blue sky, the appearance of the clouds, and the sights of the earth, and, of course, been moved by their beauty. However, before the series of such unconscious perceptions (or sensations) was illuminated, the conclusion from them had been given in the thought, "It's fine today." And this final thought attracted attention so strongly that it was preferentially illuminated, and settled in our mind. At the same time, the preparatory appreciation, which had operated unconsciously, was eclipsed by the final idea, had no chance to be illuminated, and dropped from memory. In other words, the idea "It's fine today" was so refreshing and attractive that, the moment it appeared, it alone occupied the stage of consciousness. Strong attention always works exclusively, and all other thoughts or perceptions are temporarily banished. In short, the reflecting action of consciousness did not appear to grasp the preliminary perceptions or thoughts, in this case about the weather.

In much the same way it is often said that an inventor's original idea, or a mathematician's solution to a difficult problem, is suddenly and intuitively given. However, in those cases, too, much previous thinking of a trial-and-error kind must have been done before the reward was obtained. The thinking may be hours, days, months, or years old, but it has been continuing its work as a subconscious internal pressure.

Commonly we hear someone say, "I intuitively realized the situation the moment I saw his face." But in truth, you received an impression when you met your friend, and the impression was instantaneously referred to a series of past circumstances, and a conclusion was reached. These references were made before you were aware of them, and by the time your conclusion was arrived at they had already gone beyond your reach. You were left with the impression that the conclusion was reached intuitively.

Bankei Zenji was enlightened when he was struck by the word "unborn." It seemed to come to him from a heaven-sent voice. But his life-and-death struggle in zazen had already brought him to the mental condition that was "unborn" itself. However, he needed just once to come across a word by means of which he could catch hold of the voice. Saint Paul heard the voice of God on the road to Damascus. Bankei Zenji heard it in Buddhist scriptures. Monks encounter the same "unborn" when they recite their sutras every day, but to few does it sound as it did to Bankei Zenji. Before the "sudden realization," great men toil in immense labor.

ONE NEN, ONE EON   So far we have considered various actions of nen. In the depths of absolute samadhi, however, these actions disappear. In place of them there appears "one nen, one eon." This phrase means that this moment's occurrence of this very nen is identical to one eon; it also means that one eon is present in this moment's nen-action.

Let us use the term "one-eon nen" as a noun. This one-eon nen is the fundamental form of all other nen-actions. From a certain point of view we called it jishu-zammai, the samadhi of self-mastery; from another point of view, pure existence. Pure existence, jishu-zammai, one-eon nen—whatever term we use for it, this phenomenon makes its appearance in its pure form in absolute samadhi, clearly separated from other nen-actions. We put special emphasis on this, since this state forms the starting point for the reconstruction of the habitual way of consciousness.

In our ordinary life, however, this one-eon nen is manifested, if deluded, as a deluded ego; if angry, as an angry ego; and so on. It is, in fact, no less than the first or the second or the third nen. What is required is the purification of these nen-thoughts, first through absolute samadhi, in which the habitual way of consciousness falls away, and then through positive samadhi—that is, through the so-called cultivation of Holy Buddhahood (see chapter 17)—in which a reconstruction of consciousness is carried out.

The aim of practicing zazen is to lead us to scrutinize our nen-actions, to restore them to their purest form, to give existence its eye to see itself, to reconstruct the way of consciousness, emancipated from its delusive habit, and to let existential life start its proper development.

Existence has no specific phase. It has blindly molded itself in innumerable forms, some successful, some not. Now in Zen we are trying to give it an eye of its own, so that it can see itself clearly and lead the way by itself.

An ambitious project—
Zen intends to control intentional creation.
It wants to control existence.

PSYCHOLOGICAL TIME AND ABSOLUTE SAMADHI In absolute samadhi there is no time. "No time" means there is only the present time. This is true not only in the samadhi reached in zazen, but also when you are engaged in some serious matter. For example, in taking an important examination, you may find time remarkably reduced. An hour seems like five minutes. When you are told that the time is up, you glance at the clock in the hall and suspect that someone must have moved the hands. Actually, you were absorbed in your work in a kind of samadhi, and your psychological time was shortened. Your attention was wholly upon your work and there was no room for the reflecting action of consciousness. Completely absorbed, you were not aware of yourself, your thoughts, or your behavior. You have no time. Or, in other words, there is only the present time, and in that present time many things come and go, events happen and end.

In the same way, in the thick of battle you are forgetful of yourself, forgetful of time. In an emergency—an earthquake or a fire—rescuing people or things from a building, you have no time. There is only a continuation of the present. Present, present, present. This present time is interrupted if a reflecting action of consciousness occurs. You reflect upon your thought and recognize the difference between the moment ago and this moment. You notice the order of events, recollect the past, conjecture about the future. After a catastrophe, you go through the area once again and are astonished by the deeds that were accomplished, deeds that now seem remarkable and almost beyond human powers. During the event itself you knew what to do at every moment, but your thoughts and actions were not reflected upon; they did not remain in your mind but were instantaneously forgotten. Occasionally, in slacker moments, you may perhaps have reflected briefly on your thoughts, or on the situation, but such reflection was rare, and psychological time was drastically shortened.

From these examples we may deduce that psychological time is created by the frequency of operation of the reflecting action of consciousness. In our ordinary life there is an average frequency of this action, and we can roughly estimate by long experience that a certain feeling of frequency corresponds to an hour of physical time. However, in extreme circumstances, when the reflecting action of consciousness fails to operate, our estimates fall short, and an hour seems like five minutes.

Time completely disappears in absolute samadhi, and so does space. Causation also disappears. There is only a row of events. This state of no time, no space, and no causation is simply realized, without discussion, as an immediate experience in absolute samadhi.

Our ordinary consciousness has been brought up and domesticated to live and behave in a world that is fenced in by the limits of time, space, and causation. These distinctions have given rise in turn to the world of opposition and discrimination in which we ordinarily find ourselves. The ordinary consciousness never dreams of the possibility of a world of other dimensions, but this ordinary attitude of mind is in fact projecting a topsy-turvy world of delusion. In absolute samadhi, time, space, and causation have fallen off, and thus our habitual way of consciousness collapses. What follows? There is a sudden realization of the world of nonopposition, when we experience the oneness of all things. It is said in the sutras that the Tathagata sees Buddha Nature with his naked eyes. Face after face, like corn in the field, is looking at us, and they are all the faces of the Buddha.

Moment after moment, only the present comes and goes during the period of samadhi, a continuous stream of the present. Only in the present can we be said to exist. From the nature of samadhi, we do not have cognizance of this fact, but we re-cognize it in the moment we come out of that condition. By this experience we know that life in the present moment is absolutely independent and is our true existence.

On the other hand, when we introspect, we find that every thought that occurs affects all the thoughts that follow. Even the briefest thought, lasting only the smallest fraction of a second, whether it is recognized or ignored, cannot pass away without having its effect upon the thoughts that follow. We have already, we hope, established the truth of this assertion above. Now we can perhaps give it a different aspect by saying that this is a manifestation of karma. Every action leaves its influence upon ensuing actions. This present moment has inherited from all the past events that, without a single omission, have been handed down to us from countless cycles of existence. In this sense, this moment depends upon the entire past. It looks forward to the future, and this looking forward causes a dependence upon the future, as well.

THERE IS NO SELF BUT CAUSATION "No man, but causation" is a Zen saying, meaning that all phenomena result from the succession of cause and effect, and that there is no entity that can be called a self. All is the outcome of cause; everything is itself a cause. We are all of us subject to constant mutation under this law. There is no constant self. It may make you dizzy to reflect that nothing remains of your childhood of twenty or fifty years ago. Quite a different person has slipped into your shoes, and not your innocent baby shoes, either, which would be split by your feet today. Nothing is left of the child except for one thing, your existence itself. The line that runs from your childhood to the present can be replaced by no other line. Link after link of cause and effect have been handed down to the present, and there is nothing to be called a person. There is nothing to hold onto, nothing to cling to. You feel assured and at ease with your present existence, and do not deplore the person who was clad in your clothes and who moved about in them yesterday, and in the days before yesterday, when you understand that the fact that exists can be found only in this moment. Moment after moment this existence succeeds itself and constantly changes.

In the *Mumonkan,* Case 32, Mumon writes, "He treads the sharp edge of a sword. He runs over the steep ridge of an iceberg." Every moment is the sharp edge of a sword. A slight misstep proves fatal. Every moment you are creating yourself; your thought is of your own making and it affects all your succeeding thoughts; it decides the trend of your mind toward integrity or weakness. Every moment and every thought give a new start to the next moment and thought. Every moment we are changing the aspect of our existence. In a word, moment after moment is given us for our free disposal on our own responsibility, the thought after thought of each moment bringing us something new for good or ill. We are responsible for our future, and for the future of humanity. There can be no evasion, no excuse for inattention to the duty of this moment. We have only to think for a moment about this to see that this is a fact almost too obvious to need pointing out, yet hardly anyone has called attention to this simple truth and grave reality.

The theory of karma is a formulation of Buddhist ethics. Karma has been interpreted as the accumulation of one's past actions, but perhaps "behavior" is a better term. Thoughts are a kind of behavior and are the cause of all actions. The theory of karma asserts that you are responsible for your present existence and for what you will become in the future. This moment is like a switch point on a railway track, of which you have free use. You can switch from an evil course to a good one, and vice versa. Everything depends on your behavior now. You are precisely in the position of the leaders of the two camps of East and West, who face world conflagration as they make their decisions.

PURE EGO   Let us now try to relate what we have said of nen to the concept of the ego. Nen is an action of subjectivity, the behavior of the ego. When one becomes aware of one's own nen and recognizes it as one's own, self-consciousness appears. To recapitulate, in the action of consciousness we have found three phases: (1) the first nen, which looks outward, working unconsciously; (2) the second nen, which illuminates and recognizes its immediately preceding first nen; and (3) the third nen, which illuminates all its preceding nen, integrating them into the stream of consciousness. Correspondingly, we can trace three phases of pure ego: (1) the phase that unconsciously thinks or desires—the ego that looks outward and does not recognize itself; (2) the phase that recognizes the unconscious phase that immediately preceded it—the ego that recognizes its preceding ego; and (3) the phase that operates self-consciously—the ego that recognizes the first and second phases of ego as oneself. It is meaningless to ask which of these phases is the real ego. Each nen is the action of subjectivity, and when it appears it constitutes one's real ego of that moment. No ego recognizes itself directly, as we have seen; it is recognized by the following reflecting action of the ego.

It may happen that a person will refuse to acknowledge a certain desire that he has because he pretends to himself that he has another "nobler" one. The desire is banished from the surface of his consciousness. However, such an ignored or unacknowledged idea will remain in the subconscious and in time may break forth. Perhaps one had a secret or open wish—to obtain a situation, an object, or a lover, shall we say—but for some reason one denied oneself or gave up the idea.

Thus, some desires are not given the respect they demand. They are the egos that, consciously or subconsciously, think and wish but are not illuminated by the second and third nen, or, if illuminated, are not duly evaluated; or if evaluated, are greeted with alarm, hurriedly hushed up, and sent down into darkness, remaining as an unresolved internal pressure in the depths of the subconscious. Such a pressure, like a bomb exploding in a strongly fortified building, sometimes displays a devastating and totally unexpected force. Faced by this phenomenon, we may ask whether this explosion is not the real ego. The answer is that it was a real ego when it first appeared, but it was ignored or defeated in the competition with other egos. When it appears once more, it is again the ego of the present.

The vital thing that we must clearly understand is that the ego has no consistent phase. Existence is a continuous mutation. When it has appeared, it has appeared; when it has gone, it is gone. If laboring under a delusion, it is a deluded ego; if angry, an angry ego; if in rebellion, a rebelling ego. If mentally ill or neurotic, it is a deranged or troubled ego.

In short, all things move and flow. The ego also mutates. Therefore it is empty. When it has appeared, it is there; when it is gone, it is gone. As it mutates, it has no definite phase. As it is empty, you can say there is no such thing as ego. But as it is vividly here in this moment, you must say, "There it is." For the moment we must leave this topic, but we shall return to it later on.

ABNORMAL MENTAL EXPERIENCES AND ZEN   Zen students
sometimes come to me and complain in some such terms as these:
"While I am doing zazen, voices come ringing in my ears, some singing, some shouting, some even calling me names." Or again, "They
never stop pestering me, watching everything I do and broadcasting
the news of it to the world: 'Now he is walking down the street, now
he is entering a restaurant, now he is sitting down . . .'"

I am not a psychologist or a psychiatrist, but I cannot help thinking
about what they say. Perhaps their experiences can be understood
along the following lines. Every nen-thought is accompanied by a
certain internal pressure, which never fails to leave its effect behind.
It remains in the depths of the mind, and the accumulation of such
pressures constitutes a tremendous force in an adult's life. Besides
these effects, man has inherited passions (which are also a form of internal pressure) from his parents and ancestors, as well as from his pre-
human forebears. The aggregate of all these effects constitutes karma.
If I had an uneasy feeling yesterday, the consequences are still at work
now. Even if the feeling itself was dispersed, my mind, which was once
affected by the feeling, must have developed a certain mood in response. Anger, sorrow, hatred all leave their effects behind, and they
build up layer upon layer of mood.

Man's mind can be compared to a long-neglected ditch, into which
rubbish and litter have been thrown carelessly for generation after
generation, forming thick layers of decaying matter. This is constantly
decomposing and fermenting, producing poisonous gases as it does so.
The sound of the fermentation and the escaping bubbles of gas are
ignored during the daytime, but when night comes and everything is
quiet, you hear its low grumbling: "Bzzzz . . . bzzzz . . ." In
just the same way, when your mind begins to quieten, in bed or doing
zazen, the internal pressures of yesterday, of the day before, or of a
long time ago rise to the surface of consciousness and have to be dispersed. Internal pressures that thus force their way onto the stage of
consciousness may be translated and expressed in symbolic form—a
feeling of unease or of being threatened, for example, manifesting itself as a witch's cursing or the shrieks of a ghost, or, of course, as
some more ordinary voice. A normal mind, though it may hear such

voices, does not believe in them, but when the structure of nen-thoughts collapses, mainly through the breakdown of the third-nen activity, then the voices are perceived by the first nen, which normally looks outward, as coming from the external world.

Zazen is the practice of dredging the layers of internal pressure. "Empty the mind" is the Zen phrase for this dredging. Afflicted minds have practiced zazen from the earliest times to rid themselves of their sufferings. Sakyamuni Buddha himself started the practice to liberate himself from agonies that he did not know how to escape. Zazen is a self-operated psychiatric method. But it must be acknowledged that there are some minds that are too devastated to be able to sit quietly and regain a peaceful condition.

Recently, just as I was setting out on a trip, a young man came rushing in to ask my help. As I had only a few minutes to spare for him, I said point-blank, "Do you hear the voices?" "Yes, the voices," he said. "Oh, they are unbearable." In his distress, he gestured as if he were being pierced through with a sword. "Men, women, witches—their voices go through me!" "Get to work," I said. "To start with, take this luggage to the car." He took up the bag and set off. I stood at the door of the zendo and watched him. He was carrying the heavy bag very earnestly, walking quickly, throwing his whole body and mind into the job and doing it as if his salvation depended on it. He was not hearing any voices at that moment. He was in positive samadhi. But how was he to keep that up? That is a great problem. I advised this young man to become absorbed in farm labor. But guidance by an experienced therapist would certainly be necessary.

SUBCONSCIOUS NEN ATTRACTION   A monk from a remote mountain district once told me of a bizarre experience. His native village was sparsely populated, and a path along the side of a steep cliff was the sole route to the neighboring village, which was miles away. A deep abyss, with a lake at the bottom, lay at the foot of the cliff, and it was said that a spirit lived in it and enticed into the abyss men who happened to pass by on a dark night. In fact, sometimes a dead man was found floating in the lake. People were afraid to pass there by night. A new postman heard of the story and laughed at it, boasting that he would pass there one dark night to prove no such monster existed in these civilized days. A few days later he was found dead, floating in the lake. People made a fence along the path to protect those who passed there.

One dark night, in an emergency, the monk, who was still very young, had to go on an errand to the neighboring village, passing along the path. He groped his way along, keeping carefully to the cliff face all the time. Suddenly demonic arms came stretching up from the abyss and caught hold of him. He desperately elbowed them away and heard a dull metallic sound. He found that what he had thought were demonic arms was the fence itself. He had tried strenuously to keep to the cliff, but before he was aware of it, he was unconsciously drawn to the abyss side. But for the fence, he would have fallen into the abyss and died. This can be called subconscious nen attraction.

The more a frog strives to keep away from the snake, the more it is attracted, and eventually it is swallowed up. A psychotic person is obsessed by the idea that he tries to evade.

When Christ said, "Rise up and walk," the paralyzed man straightway rose up, took up that whereon he lay, and departed to his own house. Christ was a great therapist. I would be interested to know what happened to the man in later life.

CHAPTER ELEVEN

Existence and Mood

IN EARLIER CHAPTERS we have frequently talked of existence. In chapter 7, for example, I referred to a state in which one could say, "I am on the throne of existence." It was the outcome of a condition in which the tanden was full of strength. But what does it really mean to say that I am on the throne of existence? What is existence? Perhaps we can approach an answer by saying tentatively that mood is the keynote of existence. Mental activity may be the primary function of the brain, but this does not embrace the whole of existence. Living vitality is a characteristic of the body, and mood is a psychosomatic production. The most exalted existential life is the refined mood stemming from a purified wisdom—a wisdom that in Zen tradition is likened to the lotus flower blazing like a diamond in the heart of a fire. We shall consider later where this purified wisdom originates. With regard to the living vitality, I repeat my conviction that it comes mainly from the body itself, and in particular from the tanden. When the tanden is filled with strength, we are filled with spiritual power, and we may find ourselves saying, "I am on the throne of existence."

EVERYONE HAS NARROWED HIS WORLD   Everyone, without exception, has narrowed his world by his own doing. From the most magnanimous sovereign to the most wretched schizophrenic, each lives in his own limited sphere. A schizophrenic may be a person of excellent intellect; he may be able to describe and analyze his condition with great accuracy. But his world narrows day by day. At the outset he was one with humanity, a person with a justifiable pride in himself, but as his condition deteriorates he is driven into a state hardly better than that of a worm, and in the end he cannot survive. A normal person's world does not dwindle progressively in this way. At a certain point there is a barrier to any further diminution. But the barrier does not seem absolutely secure. Almost all people suffer from the narrow world they inhabit, brought about by their delusive thought. For the most part, unfortunately, they are not aware of this.

Some people try to resolve their problems of life by a sort of guesswork. They think that if their problems are solved, they will be saved. But so long as they are still imprisoned in their narrow world they are just like an insect that gets indoors by mistake and dashes itself against the window or the ceiling, tiring itself out, suffering helplessly. Some people ask themselves, "What am I?" and struggle endlessly with that question. But their presupposed idea about this "I" is the very factor that creates their narrow world and drives them into a mood of estrangement from others. There is subjectivity in one's thinking as long as one thinks at all. However, this "I" is the product of illusory thinking. There is no such "I."

MOOD   Man lives in his mood as long as he lives. Even the experience that we have in the depths of absolute samadhi—which we call the experience of pure existence—is permeated by a mood that forms, as it were, its identifying color: a mood of annihilation. We recognize it when we come out of absolute samadhi as an immediate memory of its retreating form. It is not something philosophically abstracted. If it were an abstraction, we could not directly feel it. An abstract production may tally with real existence, just as a statistical computation may tally with the contents of a warehouse, but abstract is abstract: it is not existence itself. In Zen we want to catch hold of existence directly.

A child's life, which is not yet greatly influenced by the delusive activity of consciousness, and the life of an adult, which is under the almost complete control of a deluded consciousness, constitute two different worlds of mood, one warm, the other cold; one soft, the other hard. Everyone will remember that when he was a child he inhabited a world quite different from an adult's. Some of you still keep the evidence to testify to this in the form of drawings or poems you produced as children.

I remember when I was a first-year pupil at primary school, we were set to work on Japanese calligraphy. We had two or three lessons a week and an expert came to help in instructing us. Calligraphy was accorded much importance as a form of art education. It has much in common with Japanese ink painting. In both, retouching is impossible. The artist's spirit at the moment of execution is projected intact onto his production. His breathing, which directly controls his spiritual power, proves to be very important. The calligrapher and artist spontaneously master the way of breathing, without being specially taught it, and their way of breathing is very much like that employed in zazen, as I have described. When one goes heart and soul into the practice of an art, a certain pattern of breathing necessarily appears. Child as I was, I was almost stopping my breath as I handled the brush at my work. I remember this specifically because my grandmother, who acted as my adviser on calligraphy, made a comment once that made me notice that I stopped my breath while writing. When earnestly at work, children are soon in samadhi. I took up the brush and was lost in my work. The classroom, the desk, the boy next to me, the teachers faded away. All of a sudden I came back to myself and found the two teachers standing beside me. The old master calligrapher was pointing to my writing. He looked at the class teacher and excitedly said a few words. The class teacher was nodding in reply. On such an occasion the child is innocent. I did not understand what the teachers were marveling at. I must have felt they were praising something around me, and not knowing what it was, I remained utterly indifferent. Children do not appreciate the beauty of their productions. Something existential makes them produce fine works. It is in later years, when their consciousness is equipped with the eye of the artist, that they begin to appreciate their own work.

The work I produced on that occasion was kept for a long time afterward, and whenever I looked at it I was struck with admiration. It was two characters of the Japanese syllabary called *katakana*, one with only one stroke, the other with two (Fig. 27). The first was done with a rather thick and rich line starting at the right and drawn easily down toward the left, across the upper half of the sheet, which was about ten inches wide. There was a strong, heavy touch at the start, richness in the trace of the brush on the way, and again the beautiful and powerful stroke when the brush left the paper. "Did I do this?" I thought later. "Now I could never do it. There was certainly good reason for the wide-eyed wonder of the teacher." Fifteen or twenty years later I would look at it with renewed admiration. The other character I wrote at that time occupied the lower half of the sheet and was also beautifully done. At the next lesson the two teachers frequently came and watched me, and when I finished writing they exclaimed admiringly.

After this the teachers and my family began to show special interest in my work at calligraphy and gave me much encouragement. They placed me at a desk and made me do special practice. And what was the outcome? The more they admired me, the worse I wrote. My calligraphy grew shy, timid, and stunted, and eventually the characters were reduced to miserable dwarfs.

There are so-called prodigies. They can constantly produce wonderful works that command the admiration of the adult. They show no decline in their ability for a long time. They must be genuine ones. I, it seems, was an imitation. However, even a genuine prodigy does not know why his productions are admired. One said that if he worked in a certain way adults were pleased, so he continued that way. It is remarkable that, though aware of this, his creativity showed no decline in quality. In my case the effect of the intrusion of the activity of consciousness was to cause a hopeless deterioration in my work. My innocent mood was spoiled. The idea that I had to follow adults' advice and try to produce the kind of works they admired ruined me.

There is obviously a dimensional difference between adult life and the mood of a child. Let us imagine that an infant is born. As it grows and develops awareness, it is colored by the action of its conscious-

27. *The Japanese katakana syllables* no *(above) and* me *written with a brush.*

ness. In the course of its growing up, through the years from two, three, four, through five, six, seven, through eight, nine, ten, and to eleven, twelve, thirteen, and fourteen, consciousness more or less completes its development. Consciousness from the start finds itself as "Being-in-the-world," for others are an essential background against which its existence is defined. From its first appearance, consciousness identifies itself as a being coexistent with others. And it happens that the necessity of living makes consciousness look on things in the world as being in the nature of equipment. This encourages the development of the egocentric "I," and this development in turn reinforces the tendency to view the world as so much equipment. This placing of things in the category of equipment is not limited to relationships with things but applies also to relations between man and man. Your employees are your equipment. Your father and mother and brothers and sisters are many times treated as equipment, if not constantly. Even your dearest wife—if you carefully introspect yourself you will find that she is no exception and that at least in a thoughtless moment, or at times when you are more than usually egocentric, she is treated, in Heidegger's phrase, in the context of equipment.

> The man who said for the first time,
> "Brothers are the beginning of strangers!"
> Must have begun to say it
> With a breaking heart.

You cannot help being engulfed by this abyss of heartlessness, exclaiming, "It should not be so! It should not be so!" Others, of course, also treat you as equipment. The situation has now reached the point where man has completely isolated himself from the world. While a "Being-in-the-world," he is the most forlorn, desolate, and miserable creature. He has no one to help him except himself. This relationship with the world leads him into a terrible condition. Opposition after opposition: wherever he may go he is faced by opposition. He is surrounded by hostility. Ultimately the world begins to descend upon him as soon as he awakens in the morning, when his unprepared mind is not yet ready for combat.

Fighting against the world, fighting against his loneliness, fighting

132

against himself, man has lost the sense of richness of his childhood. Everything is looked upon in the context of equipment, assessed in terms of its utility and serviceability. The cup on the table is simply for carrying tea to the lips (while the tea master, acting in the spirit of Zen, passes his hands lovingly over his bowl, gazing at it untiringly with aesthetic affection). The bee that flies across the sun does not catch the adult's eye, because it has nothing to do with him (while to the eyes of a child the flight, like a meteor shooting across the Milky Way, is infinitely beautiful). He shows no interest in the falling leaves (while a child is immediately caught up in the falling itself). His vividness of sense and mood has died out, replaced by a conceptual way of thinking. He is an intellectual being and has killed the precious sense and mood of childhood.

Need our existence develop only in this way? Can no other way be found? Could our existence continue to develop in the mood of a child? In fact, this type of existential development is preserved in man. An infant does not discriminate himself from his mother. As the infant becomes a child and plays with his friends, he is often forgetful of the difference between himself and his playmates. They play as a united group. Sometimes the awakening activity of consciousness interferes and makes the child discriminate himself from others, and the world of opposition appears. However, the next moment it is all forgotten. Children quarrel but are soon friends again. Thus, sometimes the world of unity, sometimes the world of opposition appears in the lives of children. This experience is repeated daily and the two discrepant worlds gradually settle down, side by side, in their minds. Children are very adaptable, and in ordinary daily life the two worlds do not conflict. Their flexible minds accept things as they are.

When a baby comes out from behind the curtain and says, "Boo!" what a beautiful world he finds! He is looking at the world with an artist's eye. Zen students also find things truly existing when they come out of absolute samadhi, and in that moment the phenomenon of kensho occurs. With ordinary adults, however, there is only a conceptual understanding of men and things. They do not see things as they truly are.

When you walk along a street, perhaps you merely look at things as

133

you usually do. But once equip yourself with a pencil and drawing block and face the street, and what a different aspect you find there, if only you have the eye of an artist. Everything is alive. What symmetry! What beautiful unity of colors! The curve of the street, roofs, windows, signs, trees, people stepping to and fro, and in the far background, the hills and the beautiful sky! The stage of your mind has undergone a complete change. You are existentially looking at the world, existentially absorbed. This is the artist's world, and the child's, too. Absorbed in this way, we are in a state of true positive samadhi.

A monk asked Ummon, a great Zen master, "What is the samadhi in particle after particle?" Ummon answered, "Rice in the bowl, water in the pail!" A great question, and a great answer. But no one can understand them at the first, second, or even hundredth hearing if one is trying to understand them intellectually. I will tell you how we can come to understand this question and answer. Recite the question with the keenest concentration, spending five or ten seconds on each word. Do it in one exhalation. Look into each word as you say it. It may take you a minute or more to recite the question. Do not worry, however, about the timing, or about the passing minutes. Only look into each word with the keenest attention until your mind penetrates it. Then turn to Ummon's answer and recite it, and meditate on it, in the same manner. Repeat this many times. Do not think it silly to do such a thing. At first, four or five repetitions may produce no effect. Do not be disappointed even if that happens, or question the value of the exercise. Continue it patiently.

Presently you will be entering into this dialogue; a kind of samadhi is being established. You should be sitting in good zazen posture while you do this. In time, you will find that a certain solution to the problem arises spontaneously in your mind. It is not a solution arrived at by your intellectual thinking but is a natural product of your samadhi. The solution is not of a kind that proves either true or false, but nevertheless, you have reached an answer. The answer is the counterpart of yourself. You cannot show or do any more than you have or are. The solution may not be true, but you have advanced toward the real realization of the problem. If you repeat the practice day after day, month after month, you will one day come across the true meaning of this dialogue.

"Particle after particle," in the question, means moment after moment, that is, present after present. In this present moment you can truly realize your own existence, and in no other time. Existence is only revealed to you *now*. There is no existence except in this moment. The monk's question, therefore, can be translated, "What is the samadhi in the present moment after moment's existence?" or "What is the samadhi in looking into individual after individual's being?" From the outset, the question contains its own answer in itself. There is a Zen saying, "The answer is in the question." But what does Ummon's answer really mean? If you look existentially into the boiled rice in the bowl, or the water in the pail, or the flower on the the table, or the bustling street scene, the fall of leaves or the flight of butterflies, you find there the rice is, there the water is.

You must once have this experience and you will discover what a splendid thing the boiled rice in the bowl is. It shines like diamonds in the incandescent heat of a fire. It is perhaps rather easy to realize existentially that the butterfly flies. The rice lying there quietly is more difficult. However, if you are truly in positive samadhi, either is the easiest thing to realize. Ummon used the more difficult example, and that is always his way. Ummon is kind. Butterflies might deceive through intellectual understanding, but this rice defies all conceptual fraud. If you really look into this difficult rice lying here, what a revelation you have. It is the ultimate in spiritual revelation; you have looked into existence.

Some Zen students who value tradition may scold me, saying I have revealed the secret of this koan prematurely and thereby harmed budding Zen students. But have you really realized this koan by reading this commentary? If you suppose you have, you are mistaken. To repeat, all intellectual, conceptual understanding is simply dead understanding. In order to reach true realization of this koan you must go all the way through the practice I suggested above. You must do it with your body, with your respiratory muscles, with your tanden.

"And Jesus departed from thence, and came nigh unto the sea of Galilee." You have perhaps read this passage in the Bible many times. Possibly you did not find it particularly interesting. No doubt some will casually pass it by. But some pious Christian must be reading it just now, spending time on every word of it, with eyes penetrating it, in deep meditation, his body motionless. He is in the same frame of mind as when he is offering a prayer. He has a vivid image of Christ walking along the beach of Galilee. He is with Christ.

AN IDYLLIC WORLD   I remember when I was four or five years old, I went to a kind uncle's shop, where books and stationery were sold. A large signboard in the shape of a writing brush hung from the eaves above the entrance. It was a country town and there were few passers-by. My uncle said he wanted to go to a back room to wash his hands and asked me to tell him if any customer came. I felt a great sense of responsibility and was all attention, watching the front of the shop. For a long while—to a child's perception—no one came; there were no passers-by. I was, if I remember rightly, rather wishing that no one would come.

The morning sun shone on the signboard. The air was clear. Suddenly a wasp came humming by, her wings glittering in the sun. She approached the signboard and hovered, perhaps with the intention of alighting on it, then moved away. I watched with keenest attention as she continued to fly around and earnestly hoped she would not alight on the board. However, at last she landed on it. "Oh! My duty! Is she going to make away with the board?" She moved around vigorously as if to take possession of it. "Must I tell my uncle?" She continued her vigorous movements. "Stop! Stop!" But she did not stop. Tormented with indecision, almost desperately, I said to myself, "I must." I went to the back of the house and, finding my uncle, told him all about the wasp. At first he seemed somewhat alarmed by my serious attitude, but suddenly he burst into laughter and said it was of no importance. His words dissolved my anxiety and I felt pleasantly at ease. He led me into the shop once more. How happy I was at the sight of the shop and the street! Beautiful sunshine, clear air, and the vigorous movements of the wasp gleaming in the sun!

136

EACH SEPARATELY PASSES AWAY   The child takes it for granted that he and his father, mother, brothers, and sisters will live everlastingly in unity. He never dreams of any other possibility. He lives in an idyllic world. However, one day he encounters a situation that makes him realize that his father is an individual man, that his mother is an individual person, and that he, too, is an individual being, separate from father, mother, brothers, and sisters. The discovery may come as a shock. However, the shock can be minimized if the discovery comes little by little, in the course of the child's ordinary life. A child is extremely adaptable to circumstances and naturally learns from the petty events of each day the necessity of accommodating himself to the world of an adult. The repetition of the once-shocking experience of his individuality habituates him to it, and gradually he is drawn into the world of discrimination and opposition.

In short, the development of consciousness necessarily encourages the growth of the individual ego. Eventually the world of discrimination and opposition occupies the larger part of the consciousness of the growing child. However, it also happens that when the child encounters such a serious matter as death and is made to realize that father, mother, brothers, sisters, his much-loved aunt and uncle, and even he himself are all destined to pass away, one by one, separately and alone, he may once again be thrown into a state of grief and despair. Grief brings him face to face with the serious problems of life. Socially, too, he is obliged to confront many kinds of dilemmas. He finds that the world attacks him. I want now to relate a life story that will bring out my conception of these matters.

THE STORY OF A NISEI GIRL   As a child, this nisei girl lived in California with her parents and brothers. At the outbreak of World War II the family were quite suddenly visited by the government authorities, who took them all away to a concentration camp. She was eight years old and could not understand why they should be taken into custody like this. Up to that moment she had thought of herself as an American, and rather an ordinary little girl. She had taken things as they were. Now she was told that things were different, and that she and her family were Japanese. Why this discrimination?

How could it be? She had believed in the world, accepted life, relied upon it, enjoyed it. She had never dreamed of any other kind of life. Now the heavens came tumbling down. Her child's world was completely upset, and she felt nothing but disgrace, contempt, restriction, and misery. "How am I different from them—from my friends, my teachers? Why have I been deserted? Why has this happened?" At first she experienced all this as a strong, generalized emotion rather than as a set of specific questions. This emotion never left her. The situation in which she found herself was unbearable. She could not help thinking in her child's mind, "Why?" and a great doubt about life took hold of her.

This kind of betrayal teaches children, for better or for worse, the way to adapt to the world. However, if the situation is too acute, and the child by nature too sensitive, he may suffer irreparable damage. Doubt and distrust are implanted in his mind and come to constitute his characteristic mood. He may suffer from this throughout his adolescence. Perhaps he will unconsciously take revenge upon his unknown enemies by resigning himself to the life of a troublemaker. Love and achievement may divert his mind for a while, but distrust remains the keynote of his life and at every point may come forward to preoccupy his mind. Some will suffer inwardly, some outwardly. On waking in the morning, chronic uneasiness appears. The weird idea of death rumbles like distant thunder. With the end of one's life, all is reduced to nothing: love, home, money are all meaningless. Oh, the idea of nothing! Under the steady gaze of death there is no place to take refuge. This state is already neurotic. The world has greatly narrowed.

The girl in our story grew to womanhood and married. But she could find no remedy for the trauma that had been inflicted upon her mind when she was eight years old. She moved to Japan with her husband, and when she heard of Zen she thought it might solve her problems. She read books on the subject and, following their instructions, tried to practice zazen. She had no opportunity of meeting a teacher, but her strong internal pressure (*gidan*) never stopped knocking from within at the door of her mind, demanding to be resolved. This constant gidan is strongly encouraged by Zen teachers. Knock at the door and it will be opened. One day, when she was about to take a bath, a certain change occurred in her. Although this was later confirmed as kensho by a teacher, she had no idea what it was. However, once the change occurred she found she was in quite a different mood. She felt freed from all worry. The world that had confronted her, presenting an appearance of menacing persecution, underwent a complete change and now appeared entirely friendly. She found herself looking at the world with a different eye. She was filled with delight. Whatever she did, whatever she saw, she felt happy, grateful, and blessed. She did not know why it was, but she felt liberated from her burdens. The inner person who had been confined in a shell was now freed. The gloomy, depressing mood that had enshrouded her was gone. She wondered what had happened and decided to try to consult a Zen master about her experience. A friend was able to arrange this, and the roshi who tested her confirmed that the experience was kensho.

The world in which each one of us finds himself is of his own making. Some may find themselves in a narrow, menacing world, others in a more amicable one, depending on each person's ego. If the mood of the ego toward others is an aggressive one it creates around it a world that, reciprocally, seems to be descending upon it. The ego develops its shell to defend itself against the world. At first there is unity between the ego and the world; they are originally one. However, as consciousness develops it begins to discriminate between its own ego, the egos of others, and the world.

If the ego shell is broken, then all is broken—truly all is broken. The world of persecution is also eliminated. The ego shell is, of course, the product of individual consciousness, but it is often forced upon us from outside. In the case of the girl in our story, the outside agency (the government authorities) forced her to develop an ego that started to entertain doubt and resentment against the outer world. This doubt and distrust of the world and life (even though she herself earnestly wanted to trust them and be reconciled with them) imposed upon her a lifelong problem. While this was unsolved her mind could never be at ease. However, quite suddenly she experienced what we call a "turning of the mind." All her problems were solved, and she stepped forth into the world of unity.

Man has to put food into his mouth in order to stay alive. If it is put into another man's mouth, his own stomach is not filled. He has to put clothes on his own back to keep warm; it is no use putting them on another man. In the world of opposition one must serve oneself first, otherwise one will not survive. Thus, a discriminating ego is inevitably born. The habit of regarding others as equipment develops naturally, as we have explained earlier in this chapter. Although any "Being-in-the-world" recognizes others from the beginning, the recognition is incomplete. A man knows that others exist, but he does not fully appreciate that the emotions and will that operate in himself are also at work in others. In other words, he cannot completely feel the action of the minds of others, which will, so to speak, bleed if cut, though he feels the action of his own mind well enough, and knows how it bleeds.

The fact that men do not really recognize each other, that they therefore treat each other as equipment, makes them confront each other as enemies. The actual condition of our world at present tells us that this is so. "Being-in-the-world" takes the world as an enemy that wants to persecute him and, if possible, eliminate him. To cope with this, his ego develops the habit of returning blow for blow. This is essentially the mood of an adult who has become a slave to the habitual way of consciousness.

Can we not cast off this mood? We can. There is another world of mood, different from that of the adult's world. It is the world that we have tried to depict in this chapter, the world of children. When I described this as an idyllic world, perhaps some readers identified it with the romantic vision of pastoral poets and dismissed it as being no more than a subjective dream that could never become a reality. That is not so. The experience of zazen tells us that there is a certain stream of mood running continuously in our minds from babyhood through to our adult life. If a Zen student reaches pure existence at the bottom of absolute samadhi, he emerges and finds this stream. If you doubt this, you should do zazen yourself, just as a scientist makes an experiment to confirm the findings of other scientists. The practice of zazen was started 2,500 years ago and has been handed down through the earnest efforts of outstanding men of every generation. The results are reported in the massive literature of Zen, which is there for everyone to read.

So there are two worlds of mood, one represented by the child's world, the other by the adult's world. Even in adult life, however, the mood of the child's life is not completely extinguished. It occasionally reveals itself through some chink or crevice of consciousness. The more accustomed to it you become through zazen, the more often you will return to the mood of your childhood, and the more frequently you will be visited by the mood in your daily life. When you first become aware of it you may well be struck chiefly by its strangeness. Some will ignore it. You will catch hold of it firmly only if you are determined to find a way out of your spiritual deadlock.

THE REVERSIBLE ACTION OF CONSCIOUSNESS   The mind oscillates like a swing, in a manner similar to that in which we perceive the reversible figures studied by psychologists. Figure 28, for example, shows the outline of a goblet at first glance, but if you continue to look at it you will suddenly find that the goblet is gone and two human profiles have made their appearance. If you continue to gaze, the faces will disappear and the goblet will return. The change repeats itself endlessly and, picking up tempo, finally ends in a dizzy visual confusion. Figures 29 and 30 show other reversible figures.

The reversible figure is generally used to illustrate the figure-ground phenomenon. But we want to ask why this change occurs. Consciousness always seeks change as it flows along. It is subject to fatigue. Sustained attention does not last more than a few seconds. In the reversible figures the two designs alternately alleviate the fatigue of perception. But in our ordinary daily life things are not so favorably arranged,

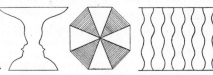

28–30. Examples of reversible figures.

141

and many instances of perceptual confusion may be experienced. For example, if you fix your eyes upon a corner of a building and continue gazing at it you will presently find that the whole building begins to move. If you stare at a certain fixed point on a hill, the hill will start to rotate endlessly along the horizon. If you watch a stone in the garden, the garden, with all its plants, flowers, and hedges, will start creeping sideways. The most startling experience is one you may encounter at a railway station. Stare at the straight edge of the platform, and in a short time this straight line will begin to wind and bend toward the railway track. If you continue staring, the winding movement will become more and more violent, and the whole platform will rise and break like the dashing of heavy waves. Although nothing is actually moving, you may almost fall in the effort to keep your balance. "Danger!" you cry, and stop looking. Then, instantly, the weird phenomenon is gone, and there is the platform, with people moving peacefully to and fro, silently and impressively, as in a newsreel of a strange, distant country. Midnight apparitions in a haunted house must similarly be a result of such unnaturally continued strained attention.

Reversible figures relate to perceptual phenomena, but similar patterns of oscillating activity also occur in relation to other mental functions. At any rate, the mood of childhood and the mood of the adult interchange with each other before one is aware of it. The change occurs very naturally in a child's mind, but as one's ego shell becomes stronger the change is often blocked.

Adults all carry ego shells on their backs. Their lives are narrowly confined, as if they were living in a fortress under threat of attack. To secure himself against the enemy's onslaught, man takes on heavy burdens. He experiences great suffering—all the troubles, difficulties, strife, worry, and solitude that come from confining himself in his ego shell. He is unconsciously asking for help of some sort; he craves deliverance from his burdens. He is, in fact, surfeited with his own ego. Then there appears the reversible phenomenon: the child's world pops up in the world of the adult. This often happens, but usually it is ignored.

The reversible figure contains in itself two patterns, and each of

142

them appears alternately to alleviate perceptual fatigue. But the shifting of mood is hindered because of the strength of the firmly rooted ego. The effect of this obstruction is disastrous. Man must give vent to his pent-up worries and problems, and it often happens that he runs from the torture of actual life to become steeped in alcohol, or takes up some other would-be diversion that is in fact no more than a trap. Some go to the golf course or some other pleasant place to try to divert themselves and give some comfort to their egos. Others, however, will be forced by their situations, or by their own natures, to continue to gaze without relief or comfort at a world that is progressively narrowing down on them. Then a phenomenon occurs that is comparable to what happens when we stare at the edge of the railway platform: mental turbulence takes possession. The sufferer goes to a psychiatrist for consultation about his case. However, what he complains of to the doctor is only the symptom. The real cause of it is his narrowed-down mood.

31. A drawing that contains two faces. (From E. G. Boring, American Journal of Psychology 42 [1930]: 444)

Look at Figure 31. It conceals two faces. You can find one right away, but what about the other? Perhaps the face you see first will prevent your finding the second one. If you were not told that there is a second face concealed there, you would never dream of searching for it. But if you know it is there, and if you only try to find it, it will in time be revealed to you. In the same way, man clings to the old world to which he is habituated, even if it tortures him, and never dreams of seeking another. But if only he is mindful of recovering the old, idyllic world, someday he will be rewarded by discovering it again. For the nisei girl whose story we told earlier in this chapter, the reward was given suddenly, like a cork popping out of a bottle. The reversible figure of the mind turned automatically, as it were. With a young woman or a child, kensho often comes in this way, like an apple falling from a tree. A more mature adult, whose consciousness has perhaps developed more complicated, tenacious habits of thought, may have to fight for it.

SAUL ON THE ROAD TO DAMASCUS   "Then they cried out with a loud voice, and stopped their ears, and ran upon him [Stephen] with one accord, and cast him out of the city, and stoned him; and the witnesses laid down their clothes at a young man's feet, whose name was Saul.

"And they stoned Stephen, calling upon God, and saying, Lord Jesus, receive my spirit. And he kneeled down, and cried with a loud voice, Lord, lay not this sin to their charge. And when he had said this, he fell asleep.

"And Saul was consenting unto his death. . . . He made havoc of the church, entering into every house, and haling men and women committed them to prison . . . yet breathing out threatenings and slaughter against the disciples of the Lord. . . . As he journeyed, he came near to Damascus: and suddenly there shined round about him a light from heaven:

"And he fell to the earth, and heard a voice saying unto him, Saul, Saul, why persecutest thou me? . . . And Saul arose from the earth; and when his eyes were opened, he saw no man: but they led him by the hand, and brought him into Damascus. And he was three days without sight, and neither did eat nor drink."

Beautiful! Not a word can be altered. The reader will excuse me for having omitted some passages, not because I do not value them but for the sake of brevity. I quote the case of Saul here because it seems to me that it can be taken as an example of the reversible phenomena of the human mind. You can imagine the internal strife that Saul experienced. "And he was three days without sight, and neither did eat nor drink." Zen has many similar examples. Kensho often comes when it seems that hundreds of bombs are raining down from the heavens.

Let us take another case. Late one evening, near the end of the year, a certain couple were considering double suicide, as they were faced with many financial and social difficulties. Suddenly there came a knock at the door. An old friend from the country had come to see them. They talked together until late at night. The next day the friend left. Alone once more, the wife said to her husband, "I thought a great deal last night, and it occurred to me that perhaps we can survive if we live with our minds ready to die." The husband said, "I was going to say the very same thing." The period of one night had given them time for their minds (or more accurately, their mood) to reverse. Very often we find that at a time of deadlock in life a new idea strikes us and a new perspective begins to open up. If only we wait, after the rain comes fair weather.

Contemporary man prides himself on his elaborately developed consciousness. I hope that this may be developed still further. Human consciousness is still far from satisfactory. The activity of the universe, through thousands of millions of years up to the present, can be regarded as a blind but not unreasonable attempt to produce this elaborate consciousness of man. I say "blind" because existence is not aware of whether or not it has an object until it is equipped with consciousness. Although the universe may seem to be moving without a purpose, from the anthropocentric point of view it has progressed fairly well. It has, of course, made innumerable trials, and produced innumerable failures, but it made a hit in producing consciousness.

And this consciousness is now asking itself, "What is existence?" In the campaign to realize itself, consciousness invented the "I." How ever, this "I" is not yet perfectly developed. We must still look forward to the full elaboration of consciousness and the construction of the true "I." Obviously, what is required is research: physiological, psychological, biological, biochemical, and other kinds of research to explore the still mysteriously shrouded wilderness of Zen. Why do I say "wilderness"? Because, absurd though it may seem, almost no research has so far been done in the field of Zen. What an attractive, virgin territory for exploration!

CHAPTER TWELVE

Laughter and Zen

THE CONNECTION between laughter and Zen may not at first sight be obvious. Before we consider this relationship from a theoretical point of view, let us relate one or two Zen stories.

Once, when Hyakujo and his teacher Baso were taking a walk, a wild duck flew by. Baso asked, "What is that?" Hyakujo answered, "A wild duck." "Where did it go?" asked Baso. Hyakujo replied, "It is gone." At that moment, Baso tweaked Hyakujo's nose violently. Hyakujo yelled with pain. "There," said Baso, "where can it go?" The effect of this shock treatment was that Hyakujo was suddenly enlightened. The next day he went to pay homage to Baso and, returning to his room, started to cry aloud. A monk asked him what was the matter and Hyakujo told him to ask Baso. When the monk did this, Baso replied, "Ask Hyakujo." The monk was perplexed and returned to ask Hyakujo what was happening. This time Hyakujo laughed heartily. The monk could not make head or tail of the matter, complaining that Hyakujo said, "I cried a while ago, and I laugh now." And he went on laughing louder still. The long-pent-up flood of internal pressure was releasing itself. When one attains kensho this discharge of internal pressure may last for as long as three days. It is like an uncontrollable forest fire.

Hyakujo studied Zen with his teacher for another twenty years. When he was mature and was going out to mix with the world as a man of Zen, he approached Baso to pay his farewell tribute to his teacher. Seeing him coming, Baso raised his *hossu* (a kind of baton, the top of which is ornamented with long white hair) straight up. Hyakujo said, "Are you in the use of it, or apart from the use?" Baso hung the *hossu* on a corner of his chair. After a little while he asked Hyakujo, "Henceforward, how do you open those two leaves of your mouth to work for others?" At this Hyakujo took the *hossu* and raised it straight up. Baso said, "Are you in the use of it, or apart from it?" Hyakujo hung the *hossu* on the corner of the chair. Just at that moment, a great roar, like hundreds of thunderbolts falling, rained on Hyakujo's head. The text says Baso gave the cry with all his majesty, and Hyakujo was deafened for three days. Not only for three days, but all through his life the teachings of Baso must have sounded in Hyakujo's ears, shutting out all other sounds.

A Zen saying goes, "If your understanding is the same as that of your teacher, you take away half of the teacher's worth; when your understanding surpasses that of your teacher you are worthy to succeed him." Doing the same thing that one's teacher does will lead only to a decline in the teaching.

Yakusan, a Chinese Zen master, went one moonlit night up the hill behind his monastery and gave a thundering laugh. It is said that the sound of that laugh echoed between heaven and earth, and shook the villages below for ten miles around.

In Western literature Bergson's theory of laughter is well known. In Schopenhauer's writings, too, there is a short but fine passage that deals with laughter. Now let us examine this topic from the point of view of Zen.

INTERNAL PRESSURE AND LAUGHTER   The connection between laughter and Zen arises in this way. Zen is largely a matter of how to deal with one's internal pressure. Laughter, too, is a means of liberating internal pressure. Internal pressure comes from nen. We have already discussed nen at some length in chapter 10, but some additional explanation may be helpful. Nen (or nen-thought) is a term with many meanings. It may mean a fragmentary thought or a flash of thought. We hear a crash behind us and react by looking back. This is a reflex movement in which, it is generally believed, there is no thought. But in fact, at the moment of looking back a certain action of the mind is stirring in us. Something that asks, "What is the matter?" makes us look around. An internal pressure is arising in our mind, and it is in fact this that makes us look back. Or, to take another example, there may be a flash of jealousy at another's success, or secret delight at his failure, in spite of an inward reproach that follows immediately and may cause us to feel remorse. Such a fragment of thought that momentarily appears in our mind is called nen.

Nen has another meaning. Suppose a mother is fighting against a tiger to protect her child. There is only one thought in her mind—protection. This is a kind of willpower and is called nen, or in this case, ichi-nen. Ichi means "one" and here implies a full-scale, wholly concentrated action of the mind. A murderer may be driven by the single thought that he must kill such and such a person. This concentrated, persistent intention is also called nen.

Nen is also used to mean ordinary thought. Nen involves the idea of drive, but it is more than that, since it covers all actions of the human mind. Nen is necessarily accompanied by internal pressure because all actions of the mind have that feature. In any nen-thought—for instance, wanting something, grudging a stupid fellow his fine house and beautiful wife, hating a neighbor, loving or delighting in anything or anybody—a certain degree of internal pressure develops in our minds. This is the case even when we think, "It's fine today." We are tempted to accost someone, saying, "It's fine today, isn't it!" in order to discharge our internal pressure. The slightest nen-thought or idea that appears in our mind is thus accompanied by internal pressure, which has both physiological and psychological aspects.

We say in our routine way, "Good morning." "How do you do?" "Did Dorothea go to school?" "I don't want scrambled eggs this morning, I'll have fried eggs." To examine this sort of conversation may seem silly. But Zen takes up the slightest action of the mind and makes a great matter of it. "Good morning" makes a Zen koan. How to dispose of momentary internal pressure is central to the whole question of Zen practice. Now, laughter is one of the great masterpieces of humanity. We invented it to dispose of internal pressure.

OBJECTIFICATION AND LAUGHTER   All of a sudden, someone hits me on the head. I turn around with clenched fist, and find a calm, serene personage standing there—as composed as a telephone pole. Indeed, that is what I knocked against. If when this happens I can imagine the situation as though I were looking at a cartoon and can objectify myself—that is, if I can look clearly at the figure I am cutting at that moment—I will recollect my wrong guess and false excitement, a sudden collapse will occur in my mind, and laughter will involuntarily follow. The laugh immediately cancels the physical and mental excitement—an internal pressure. I may be made the victim of a practical joke and get angry, but if I can objectively realize the joke of it and laugh with others, my anger will be dissolved before I am aware of it, as if it were secretly replaced. To realize is to objectify. The more advanced the degree of objectification, the more complete is the dissolution of internal pressure. Internal pressure is ego, and laughter is the cancellation of ego. In fact, there are no such entities as what we call ego, consciousness, and so on: all derive from the successive manifestations of internal pressure.

Anger attempts the cancellation of internal pressure on outward objects. When all other ways of dissolving internal pressure are blocked, and the only way of discharging it is upon others, anger appears. When internal pressure finds no outlet and is driven inward, we feel sorrow and distress. Crying, barking ("You fool!"), and laughing are all modes of discharge of internal pressure through the drain called the respiratory organs. In laughing, as in expressing anger or sorrow, physical action plays a very important part. If, when you are angry, someone by chance makes you laugh, you will forget your anger for a while; and when the old anger comes back you will find it much moderated. Part of the internal pressure has been physically discharged. When someone is crying, we feel touched with compassion, but from a physical point of view crying is the ego breaking wind and dissipating itself. However, when the ego does not consent to submit, and stubbornly maintains its position, then anger appears. The farmer who curses, lifting his fist against heaven when a hailstorm ruins his crops, rebels against the macrocosmic being.

Laughter draws us close together in intimacy, because our egos are dissolved. The ego shell falls off in the laugh.

THE DISTANCE OF IDEAS   Laughter appears when the distance between two contradictory ideas is suddenly eliminated. When someone hits you on the head, you look back with clenched fists. You think it is an enemy. But you find a pillar. First you get a false idea, then a right one, and the false idea is suddenly absorbed into—or falls into—the right one and is canceled. If you can objectify the situation, the internal pressure generated by the false idea will suddenly vanish because the false idea is canceled. A vacuum appears in place of the vanished internal pressure, and the figure with the clenched fists, finding no resistance, falls into it. We always experience this falling in when the feeling of amusement occurs. We feel as if we were swept off our feet. It is a mental caving in. However, as we have repeatedly emphasized, there is a conspicuously close connection between the respiratory muscles and the brain, and the mental cave-in is immediately transmitted to the diaphragm, which itself physically caves in. The diaphragm starts to convulse, which induces the convulsion of the abdominal muscles, and thus we laugh. This relationship between the mental and the physical caving in must have been experienced by anyone who has ever laughed.

We said that the internal pressure suddenly vanishes. But this is not quite correct. Nothing can vanish. The internal pressure must have been disposed of somehow. How did this happen? The answer is that it was discharged along with the exhalation, making a definite sound: "Ha, ha, ha!" However, another question now arises. Did the discharge of the internal pressure come first, or the cave-in? The cave-in must have discharged the internal pressure, but the cave-in itself must have been induced by the discharge of the internal pressure. The answer is simple: the cave-in is necessarily accompanied by the discharge. They are two aspects of one event. The various components—false idea, excitement, cancellation, cave-in, and discharge—must have appeared in succession in the brain, and been immediately followed by the sudden contraction, and equally abrupt relaxation, of the respiratory muscles, which induced physical cave-in. The latter led to convulsion of the respiratory muscles, which was necessarily accompanied by the escape of breath that constitutes the discharge of internal physical pressure. These physical events were immediately reported to the brain and a feeling of amusement (relaxation and discharge) was produced there. Without this feedback the emotion is not consummated.

The so-called center of emotion may be located in the middle brain, but it should be clear that the brain cannot produce emotional excitement by itself. Emotion must always be accompanied by some bodily manifestation. Emotion, then, is composed of a series of excitements, mental and physical, that occur in alternating succession—mental, physical, mental, physical—and, finally, consummation. We therefore reach the conclusion that all the events occur more or less simultaneously, in rapidly alternating succession. This explains our feeling when we start to laugh: we feel a painful internal confusion, with many impulses needing to be dispersed at the same time—the last becoming the first, and vice versa. This painful confusion is manifest in the turbulent convulsion of the respiratory muscles, a phenomenon that is seldom observed in even the most intense anger or sorrow.

Let us take another example. An answer may be given to a question that conveys a farfetched idea, which is in one sense contradictory to the idea contained in the question but which is at the same time, in another sense, inescapably connected with it. If the degree of linkage is such as to compel the eventual unification of the two ideas, the distance between them is eliminated and we experience a mental cave-in, just as when a balloon bursts with a bang. For example, a man said to his son, who was sulking and looking down, "Look up, my boy, look at the sun." The boy continued to look down. The father said angrily, "Look, where is the sun?" The boy indifferently answered, "The son is here," and looked down all the more sullenly.

We are told that this is not a very successful pun. However, please imagine that it is successful. Suppose that when you come to "The son is here," you suddenly have a sense of amusement. You will feel as though you were about to lose your footing and fall into a pit. There is a certain feeling of collapse. You are forced to fall from "the sun" to "the son." It is due to this sudden and unanticipated cave-in that laughter occurs abruptly and irresistibly. However, in this story there is another reason for cave-in: the son worsted his father by giving a witty answer. Witty repartee is often followed by surprise, admiration, and surrender—an acknowledgment of defeat by the questioner. The fact that we break into a broad smile when a conjuring trick is performed is also a graceful acknowledgment of defeat. Something impossible has been accomplished. The distance between an image of which you said, "Impossible," and the image standing triumphantly before you is canceled in a moment, and sudden cave-in occurs.

If your ego decides to be awkward, and squares its elbows in its resistance to falling into a snare set by someone else, then no cave-in and no falling into it will occur. If the father does not want to take his son's answer kindly, he will not laugh. The son, of course, did not laugh, because he had shut himself up in his ego shell. The son's indifference and his all the more sullen bearing enhance the outsider's feeling of amusement. When you tell a funny story, you must not laugh yourself. You should remain indifferent. A distance is thereby created between the indifferent and the funny images. If you betray yourself as amused, this distance will be canceled.

When the figure of yourself raising your fist against a pillar is objectified and projected on the screen of your brain, you suddenly have a humorous feeling. You feel as if the image itself causes the feeling of amusement, but there must be a psychological background that makes it funny. You do not feel amused if you look at only the last picture in a comic strip. You must follow the sequence from the beginning.

When we laugh, the humorous feeling springs up suddenly at the moment when the diaphragm begins to convulse. How this feeling of humor is produced cannot be explained. You simply feel amused. It is a vital and actual event, like all other emotional incidents. However, the conditions for the production of the humorous feeling can be enumerated. It is the outcome of a sudden and unexpected unification of contradictory ideas, the convulsion of the respiratory muscles that is caused by this, and the wholesale discharge of internal pressure through the respiratory organs.

153

I cited earlier an experiment to test this hypothesis. Bury one of your friends up to his neck in the sand at the beach, and tell him a funny story. He will not laugh. His feeling will be one of bewilderment, a strange mental condition that he himself cannot describe. The unification of contradictory ideas is intellectually performed, but it does not produce the sense of amusement, for the diaphragm cannot convulse. An amused feeling must necessarily be accompanied by an impulse that pushes up from the bottom of the abdomen. Only when this appears can you burst out laughing. In the case of the man in the sand, the diaphragm does not move, no impulse pushes up from the bottom of the abdomen, there is no laughter and no sense of amusement. Instead of the man laughing, it is you and the other spectators who will start to laugh. Because the man who is expected to laugh does not laugh, and instead looks confused and bewildered, the expected image of a laughing man is rapidly absorbed in the image of a man with this queer look. The distance between the two images is canceled, and a mental cave-in occurs. As we have said, an emotion is consummated only when it is allowed to run its full course.

LAUGHTER THAT IS NOT FUNNY If you are tickled under the arms or on the belly, you start to laugh. This is a purely physical laugh. Even here, some sense of amusement may appear, but this is really a sham kind of funniness and may be merely a response of the nervous system to the stimulus arising from the convulsion of the abdomen. It does not contain the mental component of genuine humor, and without this no real feeling of amusement appears. Hence, it is true to say that the convulsion of the diaphragm produces only the physical energy for the feeling of amusement.

If we point out an enemy's faults in order to laugh at him, the laughter is not the result of a humorous feeling but is simply a way of discharging the internal pressure of hatred or a means of discomfiting him. There is another, similar kind of laughter that arises when one observes someone else's faults or failings and secretly (or openly) enjoys a feeling of superiority. This also is an artificial kind of laugh, in which one is really trying to bolster up one's lowly ego. One thinks, "If I were he, I should not be such a failure." The theory that suggests that laughter in general comes from a sense of superiority to others cannot really be upheld; it applies only to this sort of laughter. The fact that a schoolboy laughs when the teacher falls from the platform, or that we laugh if we see something comical stuck to someone's face, or that general laughter occurs when the gentleman presiding over a public meeting has his hat blown off by a sudden gust of wind, does not necessarily support the theory of superiority. Laughter arises in such cases because something unexpected occurs, something quite contradictory to what is supposed to be the case. Two mutually inconsistent images are ludicrously combined in one and the same person.

Some samurai warriors were once taken into custody for political reasons by the government of the Tokugawa shogunate (1603–1868). In the circumstances, they thought they would soon be liberated. They were treated with due respect, because warriors were regarded as distinguished people. But political affairs shifted quickly in those days. As time went by they began to feel uneasy about their fate. One day a pole topped by a little platform, on which an executed prisoner's head would be exhibited to the public, was laid against the wall that bordered the yard outside the rooms where the warriors were detained. It was on the far side of the wall, and the little platform was in such a position that it seemed to be looking into the yard over the wall. The next day another platform appeared, also looking into the yard. And then every day another platform was added to the row. The warriors at first pretended to be indifferent, but by and by they grew nervous. At last a representative of them protested to the guard, saying that they were warriors of a certain standing and that, even if they had been condemned to death, they should not be executed and exposed to the public like common criminals. The guard was much surprised and apologized profusely, saying that there was to be an execution of felons, for which they were preparing, and his workmen had carelessly placed the platforms where they were. They would be taken away at once. When the representative returned and made his report there was a sudden general outburst of laughter. A strange laugh? But it was the wholesale discharge of steam from a boiler that was on the point of blowing up.

There are two great drainage or discharge mechanisms in the human body: one is the large intestine and anus; the other is the respiratory organs. The latter have spiritual importance. The center for both mechanisms is the diaphragm and abdominal muscles—in a word, the tanden. When there is too strong a mental internal pressure, which must be immediately discharged, the respiratory organs are the only agent that can handle it.

SOCIALITY IN LAUGHTER   Laughter depends on an objectification of the situation. So long as one's ego is squaring its elbows, objectification is obstructed and laughter is inhibited. As long as one's interests, appearance, and prestige are in question, a great deal of internal pressure is likely to remain bottled up, and the onset of laughter is checked. If a man slips and falls, he will not smile if he is anxious to save face. If he could join others and take an objective view of the situation he would laugh or smile freely. When you form part of an intimate group, sociality comes into play, the objectification of circumstances is easily realized, and laughter comes readily. But when you are alone you seldom laugh even if you involuntarily do something funny, such as breaking wind or slipping and falling, or if you do something absent-mindedly that might have induced a laugh had you been with friends. There is only slight objectification due to the lack of sociality. Laughter seldom appears among people who have little intimacy with each other. This is also due to the lack of sociality in the group. To join others and laugh at one's own expense is an abandonment of one's ego in a society. Each time you abandon your ego in this way, another ego is found standing in your shoes. Every time the ego is objectified, it casts itself off and another emerges, equipped with a larger and better developed sociality.

The moment the teacher enters the classroom, a bottle of ink falls on his head from the top of the door. If he could laugh at this it would show that he does not have a stiff, rigid ego, and this in turn would help to make others' egos less rigid. Removing the barrier between "you" and "me," it would bring an atmosphere of reconciliation. It is a renunciation of one's ego, and at the same time a step in the development of a larger one.

A gentle smile gives an impression of a peaceful mind, because it shows that the person's internal pressure is gently and peacefully escaping with the smile. Conversely, it shows that there is only a gentle internal pressure, of the kind that can escape peacefully in this way.

PURELY OBJECTIVE INTERNAL PRESSURE   Internal pressure is continuously present in one's mind as long as one is alive, as long as mood is there. Even when one is thinking objectively, admiring something beautiful, absorbed in philosophical speculation, simply thinking of the weather, or saying, "Good morning," a certain degree of internal pressure is generated. Such internal pressure can be called "purely objective internal pressure." It is the manifestation of a peaceful mind.

VARIOUS MODES OF LAUGHTER   A Japanese employee of the American embassy in Japan once found that he was answerable for the misuse of a certain sum of money belonging to the embassy. It was the inevitable result of a complicated set of circumstances. The ambassador was away on official business. When he returned the employee presented himself before the ambassador, who was in a bad humor because of the loss of the money. The man ventured to make his report orally. He described all the particulars in evnry possible detail, explaining how they had inevitably led to such a result. When the ambassador had heard him to the end, he suddenly burst into—a great rage? No, he burst into loud laughter, and with that the matter was settled. A diplomat is diplomatic to the core, and no one can tell what was really in his mind. But perhaps there was every possibility of his bursting into a rage, if only he wanted to, and at the last moment the needle of the compass swung. Sometimes rage and laughter lie but a hairsbreadth apart, and the mode of discharging one and the same internal pressure depends on whether this switch or that is pressed. In fact, of course, at the last moment some factor will decide which switch is pressed.

When I was a small child something induced in me a strong antagonism toward my brother, who was much older than I. I knew I could not fight him. However, the burning anger led me to go into the yard, pick up a large piece of ice from a basin, bring it into the room, and place it on a silver box my brother had taken a fancy to. Presently my brother came into the room. I watched him with bated breath, expecting he would fly into a rage. Fighting was inevitable and I was ready for it, though not without fear. Suddenly my brother exclaimed excitedly, "Who did such—" I thought, "Now it's coming," but he continued, "—a funny thing as this?" and burst out laughing. As soon as I heard my brother laugh I found, strange to say, that all the resentment I had harbored against him was gone, as if it had evaporated into thin air. I could approach him and speak to him with a smile. I, too, was amused by what had happened. It was a wonderful experience for my childish understanding.

Man is often surfeited with his own ego, with its antagonisms, its troubles, difficulties, and internal strife. Consciously or unconsciously, he is seeking, somewhere in the secret part of his mind, a release from such burdens. When he encounters such relief in a smile or a laugh that cancels the world of opposition, he gives a sigh of relief and feels at rest. Each person's ego is like a stockpiled atomic weapon; when a laugh disposes of it, a peaceful world, comfortable to live in, is realized.

We have a physical empathy—a kind of sociality. When someone yawns, I do too. And laughter will follow, releasing socially induced internal pressure.

Everyone knows that a baby, while asleep, occasionally smiles. This seems to be simply a physical expression. The smile and the laugh are privileges that man alone enjoys, and the baby must be taking out the heirloom to see if it is functioning properly. Man has made the smile and the laugh his bosom friends. He has loved them, caressed them, and developed them into a colorful fairyland of ideas. Pointed stories, games of rhyming, plays upon words, puns, jokes, jests, witty retorts, witty remarks, contrasts, contradictions, Falstaffian absurdities, the fool's tomfoolery, Grimaldi's grimaces, chapfallen Chaplin, ludicrous Lucy, cartoons, caricature, farce, comedy—now we are out of breath. Man intentionally devises internal pressure, then objectifies it and enjoys the cave-in. Besides this, he contrives to discharge, under the disguise of laughter, some of his internal tensions—anger, hatred, enmity, jealousy—that his sociality and spiritual pride do not allow him to bellow out in a fit of rage. Laughter is the safety valve of the world. It is a means of disposing of one's ego and abolishing the world of opposition. Laughter rescues the mind; it is a happy invention of human wisdom in the face of the necessity of social life.

ARTISTIC LEVELS OF LAUGHTER   The view that circus clowns, or comedians on the stage with their comic dialogue and storytelling, attempt to give the audience a feeling of its own superiority certainly does not hold true in the case of highly artistic performances. The essence of such performances lies in pure objectification. The higher the degree of objectification, the greater the element of art in the performance. Conversely, a performance that merely flatters the little egos of the audience is not a source of much enjoyment. Man recognizes the production of purely objectified internal pressure as the highest achievement of art. In other words, to be independent of the subjective ego is the highest ideal of art.

CHAPTER THIRTEEN

Pure Existence

WE HAVE SPOKEN RATHER EASILY in this book of the zero level of consciousness, though it is admittedly no easy matter for the beginner to reach this state. There, exhalation is almost stopped, and after a long silence a faint breath stealthily escapes, and then a slight inhalation occurs. This is the third stage of zazen practice (see pages 78–79). At this time neither first, nor second, nor third nen stirs. What dominates is an inwardly voiced sound, "Mu," or its natural modification, "n . . . ," which characterizes the depths of samadhi. Here we encounter the purest form of existence. Traditionally it is called Original Nature or Buddha Nature; we can also call it "one-eon nen." One-eon nen is the hushed silence of the snow-clad Himalayas. Or it can be likened to the eternal silence of the fathomless depths of the sea. There is a koan that runs: "Pick up the silent rock from the depths of the sea without getting your sleeves wet, and bring it to me." The silent rock is yourself. You are asked to pick yourself up from the depths of the sea. But first you will have to find yourself at the bottom of the sea, where eternal silence reigns, with no time, space, or causation and no difference between yourself and others.

EXISTENCE IN ITS PURE FORM   "Isn't such a state of being all but death?" you may ask. "Like the state of a patient in critical condition, or like that of an idiot who has human form but not human faculties?" No, not at all! The condition of being all but dead that occurs in the depths of samadhi is a great thing. There you can discover your

160

true nature. The activity of consciousness, contrary to expectation, conceals the real nature of existence and represents it in a distorted way. First you have to go through absolute samadhi, where the activity of consciousness is reduced to zero level, and where you can vividly see existence in its nakedness. After experiencing this, you once again come back into the world of the ordinary activity of consciousness, and at that moment, consciousness will be found to be brilliantly illuminating. This is positive samadhi. There is a line in the sutras, "The lotus flower in the midst of the flames." Imagine a living lotus flower, with petals like diamonds, emitting the placid light of Nirvana in the midst of incandescent flames. You can never experience this brilliant state of consciousness until the delusive way of thinking has fa'len off in absolute samadhi.

The existence of an animal may seem to be mere living. The plant may live in the same way, at a more primitive level. Yet look at the flowers, with their individual beauty, color, and form. Or see the graceful feathers of the bird, or the splendid color and design on the back of the insect now perching on the rail of the porch. Such colors and designs cannot be found in the most highly developed human art. The flexible, elegant limbs of an animal, the cells of the organisms we see under the microscope, the crystal structure of minerals, whose exquisite formation makes us stare in wonder: what made them as they are? To say that their beauty is simply the product of man's thought is ludicrous. The flower is beautiful and cannot be otherwise. Man appreciates it and cannot fail to do so. A child produces a masterpiece and the adult cannot help admiring it. This is because existence itself is beautiful, and those who look at its forms are existentially moved by their beauty.

We have identified consciousness as the eye of existence. It is deluded only because it is overcast. In absolute samadhi, existence manifests itself in its purest form; in positive samadhi, it displays itself in full bloom.

> "Spring has come round.
> A thousand flowers are in their lovely bloom.
> For what? For whom?" —Hekigan Roku, Case 5

Among the deep mountains and steep ravines, flowers come out unknown to man, and pass away unnoticed. Existence does not exist for others. It is of itself, for itself, by itself.

> In the lonely retreat,
> Among the alpine rocks,
> Caressed by the whispering breeze,
> The wild pink makes merry by herself.

The beauty of nature is the manifestation of existence itself. It is beautiful simply because it is beautiful. To say that color is waves of light and nothing more is pointless. Existence produces its own beauty for itself, and appreciates it by itself.

EXISTENCE AND CONSCIOUSNESS   The blind pushing on of existence, which wanted to recognize itself without being aware of this desire, proved successful when it created human consciousness and thereby obtained its own eye with which to examine itself. Human existence has succeeded in becoming conscious of its own beauty. To this extent it has raised itself to a higher level than can be found in the animal world or in the plant and mineral worlds. This level is rising continuously, and new beauty is now consciously created. This is intentional evolution.

However, as consciousness develops, its problems also become complicated. Not only beauty, but also diseases that have no parallel in the animal kingdom make their appearance in human life: neuroses, schizophrenia, murder, rage, despair. But existence will never collapse. We cannot imagine that what conquered seemingly insurmountable obstacles in the past will ever be frustrated in the future.

Some deplore the present state of the world, regarding the world as being in decline or disintegration, and truly, the "global village" may be facing disaster. People of earlier villages were totally annihilated, as in the Deluge or the ruin of Sodom—and worlds, and perhaps even solar systems and galaxies, have been pulverized in earlier eons, as the rings of Saturn, the asteroid belt, and cosmic dust in the Milky Way may indicate.

While intellectuals and religious activists earnestly pursue the cause of domestic and international harmony, and while ideologists and industrialists work to achieve national security and wealth, existence simply pushes on and on. It may be deluded, it may become awakened. Crisis and despair are simply phases. "Time and the hour run through the roughest day." That it cannot but exist has made existence pass through all sorts of emergencies, and has led it to what it is. It must surely pursue the same course in the future.

DISEASES OF THE MIND   Those who are afflicted with mental troubles often do not realize that they are suffering from illness. In fact, almost all people are suffering from nervous disorders, and almost all people think of the mind as naturally that way. They never think of a remedy, since they are not aware of the disorder. Literature is the mirror of the human mind. All the sufferings that are described in books are the results of mental disorders, yet there is no sign that the characters in modern novels—or their authors—recognize this. Rushing to destruction, being driven by passion to the point of total ruin: all this is admired. Nevertheless, it is a fever of the mind. People die of mental illness, just as they die of physical diseases. Physical disease is attended by a monitor called the mind. In mental illness the monitor himself is sick. He is deranged and helplessly leads the way to ultimate destruction.

One's true freedom of mind consists in not being dragged on by one's own mind. To be free in this way constitutes true freedom of mind and enables us to exercise genuine free will. The environment is a mere accompaniment.

THROWNNESS   "Thrownness" is a term that appears in Heidegger's *Being and Time*. No one seems to take it as a disease and an object of possible remedy, and Heidegger seems to regard it as the basic mood of *Dasein*.

Many present-day intellectuals feel that they have been given their seats in this troubled world against their will. In that respect, thrownness can certainly be called their basic mood. The following passages from *Being and Time* relating to thrownness exemplify this characteristic:

"This characteristic of Dasein's Being—this "that it is"—is veiled in its 'whence' and 'whither', yet disclosed in itself all the more unveiledly; we call it the *"throwwnness"* of this entity into its 'there'; indeed, it is thrown in such a way that, as Being-in-the-world, it is the 'there'. The expression 'throwwnness' is meant to suggest the *facticity of its being delivered over*."

"Has Dasein as itself ever decided freely whether it wants to come into "Dasein" or not, and will it ever be able to make such a decision?"

"As being, Dasein is something that has been thrown; it has been brought into its 'there', but *not* of its own accord."

"As existent, it never comes back behind its throwwnness in such a way that it might first release this "that-it-is-and-has-to-be" from *its Being*-its-Self and lead it into the 'there'."

"Having been thrown into Being-towards-death, Dasein flees—proximally and for the most part—in the face of this throwwnness, which has been more or less explicitly revealed."[1]

Since Hamlet said, "To be, or not to be—that is the question," or rather, since man first appeared on earth, human beings have questioned the meaning of life. "Whence did I come, and whither am I going? Was I not given this insipid life of the world without being consulted?" These questions have tormented young people and are a primary cause of their disaffection—all because the truth of existence is not recognized.

This being is one's own being. From itself it has sprung. A simple thing! But in order to realize it, one has once to meet pure existence in the depths of absolute samadhi.

The animal lives its life blindly; it entertains no doubts. The child, too, lives its life wholeheartedly, because it accepts the positive nature of existence. Only an adult is uneasy, because he has consciousness, which never feels at ease until it has seen through the secret of its own existence. To ask what is the meaning of life is to inquire about the aim of life. But think, does the sun shine with an aim? Has the baby come into the world with an aim? Existence only exists. It is impossible for it to be otherwise. Life is for life's sake, art for art's sake, love for love's sake. A mother loves her baby because she loves it.

The delusive nature of consciousness comes from the fact that it necessarily belongs to the individual ego and serves the ego's individual needs. It cannot go beyond this individuality; it cannot think apart from the individual ego. This blind attachment of consciousness to the individual ego brings about topsy-turvy delusive thought, from which stem (1) the world of opposition between oneself and others, (2) the craving for a constant imperishable ego, (3) the unsuccessful groping for existence, (4) vain searching for the root of the ego, (5) a sense of life as being uneasy, uncanny, or even dreadful, and (6) the eventual dejection of the feeling of thrownness.

The secret of all this bewilderment lies in the failure to grasp the secret of existence.

Each of us has his own world of individual ego set against the environmental world. The world of A's ego is incorporated into B's environment, and vice versa. C contains A and B in his environmental circle. It is the same with D, E, F, and all the rest. Each has his own world of ego and environment, different from that of all others. Emotional conflict and opposition of views and interests are therefore unavoidable, and alienation necessarily follows. This is inevitable as long as human existence is divided into individual beings. Even Sakyamuni Buddha, the successive patriarchs, and all Zen teachers are not exceptions to this. However, mature Zen students hold existence embodied in themselves, and through the cultivation of Buddhahood come to realize the vacancy of the individual ego. They maintain themselves apart from the world of opposition and bring about its ultimate collapse, while those who remain confined in the world of opposition necessarily discriminate between themselves and others, and between themselves and the world, in every thought and action.

DECENTRALIZATION   A baby understands the outer world only from its own situation, through its sensations. However, as it grows up and its intellect develops, it can, in imagination, place itself in other positions and observe things from different viewpoints. In other words, it can decentralize its imaginative perceptions. As it continues to grow up, it also develops the faculty of coping psychologically with far more complicated matters. That is, it becomes able, in imagination, to change the relationship of its ego to all kinds of different states of affairs. It decentralizes its egocentric views, both emotionally and intellectually.

As he matures, man puts himself in the place of others and feels their sufferings. He delights with others, grieves with them. He can experience others' sufferings as his own. That is, he can fuse his existence with that of others. This ability appears quite early on, in his relationship with his mother and with the rest of his family, and it shows itself in his relationship with his lover and with his wife. In the highly developed mind, this fusion can be extended to relations with friends and even with strangers. Such spiritual understanding can be called a kind of humanism. However, it will have only a weak foundation, as it lacks the perfect realization of existence. Zen takes this foundation to be the beginning of everything. All conduct is based on this foundation.

THE HABITUAL (DELUSIVE) WAY OF CONSCIOUSNESS Let us return once more to Heidegger's *Being and Time*. Unfortunately, we find there no mention of decentralization. Such qualities as concern, circumspection, conscience, and resoluteness are mentioned, but they almost all deal with, so to speak, private affairs—and that is not humanism. Such is the condition of Dasein in *Being and Time*. We are not blaming Heidegger. He is a faithful reporter. He depicts Dasein as it is, a being equipped with what we call the delusive way of consciousness. Perhaps Heidegger intended to save Dasein from this miserable condition in the uncompleted part of *Being and Time;* in section 60 we find the following suggestive passage: "When Dasein is resolute, it can become the "conscience" of Others. Only by authentically Being-their-Selves in resoluteness can people authentically be with one another—not by ambiguous and jealous stipulations and talkative fraternizing in the 'they' and in what 'they' want to undertake."[2]

Heidegger speaks of the "context of equipment." He explains that

Dasein maintains its relation with the world through this context. This reveals Dasein's ego-centralization. Dasein makes use of others in the context of equipment. Dasein's consciousness is the watchdog of an egocentric individual being, while Zen understands a being as it is, and not as equipment: mountains as mountains, rivers as rivers, the rose beautiful as a rose, the flower of the weed beautiful as the flower of the weed, an ugly duckling as an ugly duckling. If only you can realize the existence in an ugly duckling, you will find the ugliness suddenly turns, to your surprise, into illuminating beauty. Zen finds brilliant exemplification of existence in delinquent people. It recognizes existence in the animal, the plant, the stone. Zen declares that matter and mind are one. It accepts things as they are.

We find in the drawings of Zen masters many objects and appliances: the sickle, straw raincoat, bamboo hat, earthenware pots, tea utensils, and flower vases. These are not looked upon simply as implements for utilization. The usefulness of each article has the same quality as the mind of the person using it. When the tea master takes up a tea bowl and touches it to his lips, the bowl is alive. You may remember the Zen story I quoted earlier. A monk asked Ummon, "What is the samadhi in particle after particle?" Ummon answered, "Rice in the bowl, water in the pail!" If you look penetratingly into boiled rice, into water in the pail, what an illuminating world of existence you find!

THE WAY OF NANSEN   A monk traveled a long way to see Nansen and found him cutting grass by the roadside. He asked, "What is the way to Nansen?" Nansen answered, "I bought this sickle for thirty cents." The monk said, "I do not ask about the sickle, I ask the way to Nansen." Nansen answered, "I use it in full enjoyment."

When this dialogue is presented by a teacher as a koan, without any preliminary discussion of equipment, even a Zen student of considerable maturity may be puzzled as to how to answer. He will visit his teacher many times, and find it really hard going. In Zen, "subject" and "use" are important terms: the subjectivity of existence and the use of it. In the above koan, this use will eventually be understood by the student. But what is use, after all? Is it something in the context of equipment? No, never. It is quite a different idea. It is the demonstration of existence. Nansen employed the sickle in the context of such use. However, can you demonstrate use? This is what is required of you in presenting an answer to this koan. The student may pass the case in a general way, but a Zen teacher might say, ruminatingly, "You understand? All right, I admit it. However, you have to study it afresh for another thirty years. What is the way . . . ?" And he will mutter to himself. The muttering weighs on your mind, and that gives rise to a new problem. It will be many days later that the student really masters this case.

A brief comment on this topic would be easy. It would run as follows. The monk asked the way to Nansen. If the original text is rendered word for word it runs, "Nansen way," which permits two meanings: "the way to Nansen" and "the way of Nansen." A Zen question often confronts you with the dilemma of two meanings. Whether this monk was conscious of the dilemma, whether he asked Nansen knowing who he was, whether he was a mature Zen student or a novice, is not known, and there is no need to know. What is important is Nansen's answer. We shall first deal with Nansen's last words, "I use it in full enjoyment." Of course he did not use it merely as equipment; it was also used in the context of the use of Zen. In other words, it was the use of Nansen himself. It was Nansen's way of daily life—namely, Buddha's way. When you use a sickle or a hammer or a broom, or when you light a candle before an image of Buddha, if you do it in positive samadhi, it is the use of Buddha Nature. Nansen said, "Ordinary mind, that is the way."

In the Zen monastery, the monks and lay residents work every day, sweeping, washing, cleaning, raking fallen leaves, weeding, tilling, gathering firewood. They are often exhausted by heavy labor. But if you work in a state of positive samadhi, you experience a purification of both body and mind. If you cannot experience this purification, and you find the work to be forced labor, then thrownness appears.

> Morning, sickle in hand,
> Noonday, roaming the forest,
> Gathering and binding wood,

PURE EXISTENCE
Now the evening moon,
Quietly shedding her light
On the path I tread.

How one enjoys cutting wood, gathering and binding it, and carrying it on the shoulders, treading the quiet evening path, dimly lit by the crescent moon. How one enjoys every movement of one's body, just as children enjoy it as they play at keeping house.

"I bought this sickle for thirty cents." Nansen bought the sickle as a boy buys a toy at a toy shop. An adult buys in the context of equipment. You would not apply the context of equipment to Dasein. As long as Dasein is Being-in-the-world, and "solicitous Being-with,"[3] the context of equipment is not applicable to Dasein. But in actual life, as we have seen, the context of equipment secretly creeps into the relationship between man and man under the influence of the delusive way of consciousness. Even in marriage or friendship, the context of equipment will often be found to appear. You can find an all too abundant supply of examples by taking a glance at modern novels. People are generally connected in their daily routine in the context of equipment. Hence arises the distortion of existence, from which stem all the difficulties and sufferings of man's mind.

But "I use it in full enjoyment" solves the problem. In this samadhi, thrownness finds no root to spring up from. You must not understand Nansen's "use" in the context of the user and the used. It is simply that he is using it in full enjoyment. Babies and children use themselves in samadhi every moment and enjoy every moment of life. They are affirmative in every way. The animal is in an animallike samadhi; the plant, a plantlike samadhi; the rock, a rocklike samadhi. We find splendid samadhi in the physical world. Gravitation is samadhi itself! Confronted with a giant magnet, we are forced to feel it. Man alone has lost sight of samadhi, and of purification as well.

Internal pressure is blind. It often falls into error. However, now that it has acquired an eye to see itself with, it has the ability to correct its faults. It attains the capacity for decentralization to an increasing extent with the development of its intellect. This is the first step toward the correction of the delusive way of consciousness. Man has developed humanism, as well as religious movements, aimed at the fusion of individuals into universal existence. However, as we have said, unless one's life is based firmly on a consciously confirmed recognition of existence, this decentralization is resting on an insecure foundation. The outcome is imperfect. Zen clearly recognizes pure existence and on this basis carries through a perfect decentralization.

THE DIRECT EXPERIENCE OF EXISTENCE   Zen students train themselves earnestly in the first place only for the purpose of experiencing existence. However, when this is achieved—when existence is cognized—the business has only begun. Only the first step has been taken. An infinitely long further path extends before us. Hence it is said:

> "Do you want to see the gold-faced Buddha?
> Through countless eons, he is ever on the way."
> *Hekigan Roku,* Case 94

Let us return once more to Heidegger. He thought that if he investigated Dasein, he could reach the true nature of Being. But when he introduces some of his most fundamental ideas, such as Being-in-the-world, thrownness, the context of equipment, anxiety, dread, care, and conscience, we find that, contrary to our expectations, this most scrupulous philosopher brings them in rather too abruptly and easily, without sufficient explanation and reason. We feel a certain misgiving that he has picked them up as he happened to think of them. In addition to this apparently random selection, there is what seems to us a serious oversight, in that some important ideas, such as decentralization, sympathy, love, self-renunciation, the aesthetic sense, attachment, self-interest, hatred, and avarice are not discussed.

Having gone through *Being and Time,* we find ourselves not a step further with regard to the problem of understanding existence. We learn about resoluteness, which is defined in the following terms: "This distinctive and authentic disclosedness, which is attested in Dasein itself by its conscience—*this reticent self-projection upon one's ownmost Being-guilty, in which one is ready for anxiety*—we call 'resoluteness'."[4] From this we learn that resoluteness is supported by Dasein's

attitude of being "ready for anxiety," rather than by the clear understanding of Being. It is a frail conception, based upon a poor foundation. If the problem of life and death could be reduced to the mere
manipulation of this single concept of resoluteness, we should not
undergo the agonizing torments that we actually do in this life.

As this inescapable problem of death is impossible to solve by mere
speculation or reasoning, much less by a single conception, we undertake the practice of zazen, involving as it does many years of tears and
sweat. No peace of mind can be obtained unless it is fought for and
won with our own body and mind. If once our body and mind have
fallen off in absolute samadhi, we are then simply emancipated from
the spell of the problem of life and death.

Zen literature abounds in poetical or word-transcending expressions, which may appear to be rather remote from the kind of approach to Zen that we have advocated in this book. Such expressions
have come into use because when one wants to demonstrate directly
the true nature of existence, one finds that ordinary conceptual description is inadequate. And then there appears that "language samadhi" (page 99) in which the poetical expression of one's samadhi is
understood by those who can place themselves in the same samadhi.
We are greatly helped by this language samadhi in reaching Zen se-
crets. But in spite of this, we wish to say that it is our intense desire to
give a clear and intellectually acceptable demonstration of what has
been regarded as a word-transcending secret. We think that this can be
done, at least to a certain extent, if we make the fullest use of the
achievements of modern culture. It will require the cooperation
of many scientists and thinkers, and above all, the appearance of Zen
genius. Genius may be a rare natural gift, but if you confine yourself to
a single topic, working with a broad mental perspective, and persist
in it, you will find yourself a genius.

When consciousness has lost its root, it finds itself floating like a
piece of duckweed. Thrownness comes from this rootlessness. Only
when consciousness is awakened and firmly grasps its root can it stand
securely by itself. Examining Dasein, shrouded as it is in thrownness,
and neglecting to investigate the origin of this thrownness, one cannot
hope to understand the true nature of the human being. The author of

Being and Time must have recognized this. In his later works he emerges as a quite different writer and appears to be grappling directly with existence. He speaks like a poet and seeks to penetrate language. When a poet plunges himself deep into his language, he reaches a condition of mental lucidity and serenity. This might be called a sort of positive samadhi. Not only the poet but also the painter penetrates his object, and there appears the silent language samadhi that transcends language. The same phenomenon occurs when a philosopher is engrossed in his speculation. Heidegger came to declare that language is the house of existence, and on another occasion that language is existence. This must be because he experienced language samadhi.

Language samadhi figures a great deal in Zen. We touched on the fringe of it when we spoke of Ummon's "Rice in the bowl, water in the pail." What a splendid world the Zen student finds himself in when he penetrates Zen phrases and verses, for instance those of the *Hekigan Roku* or *Mumonkan*. From there the masterpieces of painting, calligraphy, sculpture, landscape gardening, and poetry of the Zen masters spring forth. True language samadhi will be achieved only by going through and through both absolute and positive samadhi, and through many years of studying Zen literature from all aspects. Then you can attain "mastery of the teachings" and "mastery of its demonstration," and will be able to produce a clear-cut picture of truth using simple expressions and plain words.

CHAPTER FOURTEEN

Pure Cognition and Kensho

NANSEN VIEWS THE FLOWER   Once when speaking with Nansen Osho, Rikko Taifu said, "Jo Hoshi said, 'Heaven and earth and I are of the same root. All things and I are of the same substance.' Isn't that fantastic!" Nansen pointed to a flower in the garden and said, "People of these days see this flower as though they were in a dream."

Setcho, the author of the *Hekigan Roku,* comments on this story (Case 40) in a beautiful verse:

"Hearing, seeing, touching, and knowing are not one and one;
Mountains and rivers should not be viewed in the mirror.
The frosty sky, the setting moon—at midnight;
With whom will the serene waters of the lake reflect the shadows
   in the cold?"

Nansen was an outstanding Zen master to whom we have already referred. Rikko Taifu was a high government official. He studied Zen with Nansen and reached an advanced understanding. They exchanged observations about Zen in their dialogues (*mondō*), of which an example may be quoted here.

Once Rikko said to Nansen, "Your disciple understands Buddhism a little." "How is it during the entire twenty-four hours?" asked Nansen. "He goes about without even a shred of clothing," replied Rikko. Nansen said, "That fellow is still staying outside the hall. He has not realized the Tao. A virtuous ruler does not use clever retainers.''

"He goes about without even a shred of clothing'': this is now a well-known Zen saying, referring to one who has stripped off all worldly attachments and is rid of topsy-turvy delusive thought. He has nothing. Nansen, however, was not satisfied with Rikko's reply, and said, "That fellow is still staying outside the hall,'' by which he meant that the fellow had not yet attained fully the true spirit of Zen. One may wonder why Rikko was criticized unfavorably. Had he not attained what Zen students strive for? A fellow outside the hall, to be more explicit, is one who has not yet been granted the privilege of attending the imperial court. "Clever retainers'' means courtiers who are too clever to be trusted. "Without a shred of clothing'' may have been a fresh and rather original phrase in Rikko's day. It is used to denote nothingness and emptiness. But if a student remains there, thinking that that is the ultimate, he falls far short of true Zen attainment. When taught in this way, Rikko must have nodded his head in assent to Nansen's words. Judging from other descriptions of his behavior, he must have attained that much understanding.

Rikko was quoting from Jo Hoshi (A.D. 382–414) when he said, "Heaven and earth and I are of the same root. All things and I are of the same substance.'' Jo was a disciple of Kumarajiva, who went from Central Asia to China in A.D. 401, translated many Buddhist scriptures, and exercised great influence in the development of Chinese Buddhism. Jo was himself a genius as a Buddhist scholar. He is said to have met an untimely death by execution when, for religious reasons, he refused to obey an order of the ruler of the state, Yo Ko. According to legend, his farewell poem was as follows:

> "The four elements have originally no master;
> The five aggregates are essentially empty.
> Now I confront the sword with my head;
> Let's do it like hewing the spring breeze.''

On another occasion, Jo wrote, "The man who has exhausted truth is vast and void, and leaves no trace. All things are one's own making. He who realizes all things as himself is none other than a sage.''

174

In response to Rikko's quotation, Nansen said, "See this flower: it is said that the Tathagata sees Buddha Nature with his naked eyes. Can you see it?" Rikko was confident of his understanding, but when he looked at the flower he could not see Buddha Nature there, only a peony. Then Nansen passed his judgment: "People of these days see this flower as though they were in a dream." There was no denying the difference in ability; Rikko was obliged to bow to Nansen.

Zen texts are sparing of words and express only the essential point. We are not told whether or not the whole conversation set forth here took place, or whether Nansen skipped the preliminaries and simply gave his judgment. The important point is that Nansen put Zen truth under Rikko's nose.

Nansen introduced here the problem of cognition. Perhaps this was one of the earliest occasions in the history of Zen on which this problem was taken up so specifically. In the four lines of Setcho's verse we find a splendid description of pure cognition:

"Hearing, seeing, touching, and knowing are not one and one;
Mountains and rivers should not be viewed in the mirror.
The frosty sky, the setting moon—at midnight;
With whom will the serene waters of the lake reflect the shadows
   in the cold?"

(1) "Hearing, seeing, touching" represent the auditory, visual, tactile, and other senses; "knowing" means cognition.

(2) "Not one and one" means that sensation and cognition are not to be separated from each other; and cognition and the cognized object are also not strangers to each other but are interrelated, which makes transcendental cognition possible.

(3) "Mountains and rivers" represent the external world.

(4) "The mirror" represents your subjectivity.

(5) "The frosty sky, the setting moon—at midnight" expresses the serene and sublime situation in which external object and sensation meet in pure cognition.

(6) "The serene waters of the lake" are your mind, which exercises pure cognition.

(7) "Reflects the shadows" means pure cognition.

(8) "In the cold" again expresses the serene and sublime state of the mind when it exercises pure cognition. The mind is as serene and silent as the frosty sky, the setting moon, and midnight are purely cold.

"Mountains and rivers should not be viewed in the mirror" means that you should not say, as the idealist does, that the external world is nothing but the projection of the subjective mirror of your mind, and that sensation cannot transcend itself to hit upon the external object. The truth is the opposite of this. In profound silence, deep in the middle of the night, the lake serenely reflects the frosty sky, the setting moon, rivers, trees, and grass. The cognition occurs solemnly and exclusively between you and the objects.

Cognition is accomplished through two processes: first, pure cognition; second, the recognition of pure cognition. In pure cognition there is no subjectivity and no objectivity. Think of the moment your hand touches the cup: there is only the touch. The next moment you recognize that you felt the touch. A touch is first effected just through the interaction between hand and object, and at that moment, pure cognition takes place. The next moment, the pure cognition is recognized by the reflecting action of consciousness, and recognized cognition is completed. Then there arise subjectivity and objectivity, and one says, "There is a cup on the table." But at the moment when pure cognition is still going on, there is no subjectivity and no objectivity, just a touch—with no saying that there is a cup on the table. To put this another way, pure cognition is effected purely through the meeting of the first nen and the object. Transcendental cognition occurs through this meeting, but it is not yet recognized consciously. Husserlian phenomenology does not notice the action of the first nen that transcendentally feels the object, and thus it refuses to acknowledge transcendental cognition.

When Setcho says, "The frosty sky, the setting moon," he is speaking of pure cognition, where there are only the frosty sky and the setting moon; no subjectivity, no objectivity; no one can peep into that moment, not even the person himself who looks at the sky and moon, performing this cognition, because here there is no reflecting action of consciousness. The moment is as solemn and serene as the frosty sky

176

and setting moon are cold and silent. When this is realized, the fourth line becomes very clear: "With whom will the serene waters of the lake reflect the shadows in the cold?" No one can notice the reflection, not even the one who does the reflecting (the doer is the lake, and maybe Setcho, or you yourself), because subjectivity cannot recognize itself.

We now want to try to elucidate further this question of pure cognition and some related matters by reference to the three nen-actions, which we considered in chapter 10.

Although for purposes of description the three nen are distinguished as separate categories of cognition, in fact they simply represent the action of one nen in the stream of consciousness. In the present moment, it acts as the first nen; in the succeeding moment it reflects as the second nen; and in the next moment it effects a synthesis as the third nen. This third nen forms plans and intentions as it synthesizes, and its intentional activity directly gives rise to a new first nen, which receives it and, led by it, starts its activity. The first and third nen therefore perform in succession one and the same intentional activity, one nen appearing now as the action of synthesis, now as the action of acquiring experience from the external world, and it is difficult to say which is the initiator. They go from first to second to third nen, and back to first nen once more, in a circle.

Consciousness endeavors to maintain its integrity by focusing its attention on one thing at a time. Even if one dictates several letters at a time, a single focus of attention will be maintained, shifting from this to that. To perform many nen actions at once is beyond the ability of consciousness, though training, it seems, can enable us to have a subordinate center of attention in addition to the main one.

The first nen can act in two ways: (1) it recognizes objects in the external world, and (2) it can also turn its attention inward. In the first case, it directly receives a stimulus from the external world and gives rise to (a) sensation and (b) thought or intuitive thinking. Sensation sees colors, flowers, mountains, and rivers, while intuitive thinking observes that it is fine weather, or feels love, hatred, and so on toward other people. In the second case, one's attention is turned inward and recollects the past activity of the self. This recollection is reflected upon by the second nen, which in turn is followed by the third nen, and the third nen starts judgment and makes new decisions.

Although the activity of the first nen is independent, it is closely connected with the third nen. In fact, it is always under the influence of the third nen and selectively accepts only a proportion of the stimuli from the external world. The first nen is a baby tied to its mother's apron strings, limited in its sphere of independent activity; or it may be compared to a horse wearing blinkers to prevent its receiving unwanted or dangerous stimuli.

In terms of the second analogy, the psychotic or excessively excitable man would seem to be lacking his blinkers or provided with imperfect ones, and his first nen is overwhelmed with stimuli. This unusual sensitivity may sometimes be conducive to artistic or literary production, but it may also lead to a condition comparable to the panic of a frightened horse. Thronging ideas, the kind of religious devotion in which one feels overcome by the love of God, cases of mental confusion in which the patient experiences so much stimulation that he cannot respond to it all—these are all symptomatic of the uncontrolled release of the first nen. Ordinarily, the third nen controls the intake of stimuli by the first nen, thus maintaining a normal functioning condition of mind. At the same time, however, such a "normal" mind may become stale, or be influenced by a false framework of third nen, or be caught in all sorts of topsy-turvy delusive thought.

To summarize: the nen changes its position, working in different roles as first, second, or third nen. Each nen receives its preceding nen's influence and in turn affects the action of its following nen.

Now, in absolute samadhi, all three nen stop, or almost stop, their activity, and one-eon nen reigns over the whole domain of the mind. After once attaining such a condition of mind and then emerging from it into the world of conscious activity, the Zen student will experience for a certain period of time a condition in which the first nen alone is operative, working intuitively as it always does. The reason for this is as follows. In the history of the evolution of consciousness, it may be assumed that the first nen-action appeared first. It is presumably found even in animals, though perhaps in a less highly developed state

178

than in man. The reflecting action of consciousness (the second nen) presumably arose considerably later in evolution, and the third nen appeared last. As far as we know, this reflecting capacity is not present in animals, who are not self-conscious and might therefore be taken to lack consciousness proper. On this basis, it is understandable that when one enters absolute samadhi it is the most recently developed function that vanishes most quickly. First the third nen disappears, then the second nen dies away, and finally the first nen, the oldest and therefore most tenacious activity of the mind, vanishes. The reverse happens when we emerge from absolute samadhi: the first nen appears first, followed by the second and third.

While the third and second nen are dormant the first nen receives stimuli from the external world without restriction. The screening and modifying action of the third nen is inoperative, so that stimuli rush in, in all their unlimited profusion, and produce powerful impressions as they strike the mind. In the kensho experience it is this strength of impressions that brings before you the objects of the external world with fresh and inspiring originality. Thus, Ummon could exclaim, "Rice in the bowl, water in the pail!" Everything is direct, fresh, impressive, and overwhelmingly abundant at the time of the kensho experience.

PSYCHOTIC AND OTHER EXPERIENCES   The fresh, vivid impressions that may be experienced in psychotic or epileptic seizures, or under the influence of psychedelic drugs, may be considered to arise from the unhampered activity of the first nen, liberated by the collapse of the third nen and its integrative function. Are such experiences, then, the same as that of kensho? I do not think so. In a psychotic patient, each of the three nen malfunctions. In the events that occur under the influence of psychedelic drugs, the first nen appears to regress to a primitive state. LSD users speak of their impression of melting and blending with external objects. In kensho, on the other hand, we find that things keep their individuality very sharply, while at the same time they are all of the same quality.

In both positive and absolute samadhi, pure consciousness dominates.

179

But in the case of the psychotic, his conscious activity either splits in the face of the dilemma facing him, or it is in some way benumbed; the first nen, too, is distorted.

Some psychotic patients find that time sometimes starts to go backward, into the past, while others complain that time and events occur too quickly. Jaspers, for example, quotes the following case: "Klien reports a boy who had attacks during which he would be frightened and run to his mother, saying: 'It's starting again, mother, what is it? Everything starts going so quickly again. Am I talking faster or are you?' He also thought the people on the street were walking faster."[1] Such phenomena can perhaps be explained along the following lines. It is well known that our impression of speed when in a vehicle or airplane derives largely from our seeing other objects, which may be either moving or stationary. Suppose three airplanes are flying in formation. If one of them begins to lose speed, the pilot will quite often have the illusion that his plane has started to fly backward. However, if his attention is focused on the other planes that are passing his, he will have the illusion that they are flying too fast. An analogous effect will perhaps occur when the second and third nen suffer too much from worry and anxiety and become exhausted, or shut their eyes in the face of unpleasant reality. Their reflecting and synthesizing actions will in consequence operate more slowly, and impressions taken in by the first nen will scarcely be reflected upon. That is, in the formation flight of the three nen, the reflecting activity has lost speed. The reflecting activity corresponds to the pilot of the plane that has lost speed; it will have the illusion (depending on the focus of attention) either that time and events seem to go backward or that they pass too quickly.

In some psychotics, and in some normal people too, another phenomenon appears in which overwhelmingly abundant impressions of the first nen supply thickly massed mental contents which, if projected, produce the effect of a slow-motion picture, so that everything seems to occur at a slow tempo. A child's time is thought to pass more slowly than that of an adult because of the abundant, fresh, and impressive first nen, which is allowed to form a larger proportion of the activity of the mind than in an adult. (In this connection see the example of C. Zenji, which will be related later in this chapter.)

When the third nen is possessed by a tormenting idea or demand or by some agony, or when it is in some sort of dilemma and finds it impossible to function normally, it may eventually be driven to self-abandonment or destruction. At such a time, the habitual way of consciousness will also fall away. Such is the case with certain psychotics. The falling off of the habitual way of consciousness is the spontaneous banishment of the egocentric self. One becomes a suffering saint and sometimes entertains messianic ideas. Great spiritual leaders often pass through this stage, and ultimately reach their own way of emancipation. As the saint has himself gone through the experience of suffering, he cannot help preaching to others the way he has found.

With the divided self of the schizophrenic, as the term indicates, the internal agony and self-abandonment have driven the third nen into a split within itself. The third nen is tempted in many directions even under normal circumstances, and such a dilemma will force a potentially weak individual to synthesize for himself an inner reality, consonant with the inner agony, in such a way that the usual range of the third nen is restricted: a part of it is not used, and the remainder is distorted. The first and second nen are affected correspondingly. They themselves split in proportion to the activity of the third nen, and all three nen interact with each other in a most morbid and complicated way, producing symptoms that defy our usual understanding.

Some psychotics are driven to a state of personality collapse. However, at a stage in which the split has not gone so far as to produce mental disintegration, when the first nen works independently in its liberated condition, there often appears an experience that resembles the kensho of Zen. Examples of pseudo-kensho and even genuine kensho can be found in William James's *Varieties of Religious Experience*.

The vivid vision that may be experienced by an epileptic before a seizure may be supposed to come from the desperate action of the first nen, igniting itself, one might say, in response to an extreme mental condition, as in a dying man. The effect is seemingly initiated by a certain physical condition of the brain. In the kensho event we

181

find the same phenomenon of ignition. However, with our zazen practice, we find the first, second, and third nen lucidly illuminated and polished, like stars in the frosty sky—closely interrelated in a formation flight of harmonious mental activity.

IDENTIFICATION OF SELF   Descartes' *"Cogito ergo sum"* seems to be commonly accepted without question. But "I think" is the action of the first nen. If it is not recognized by the reflecting action of the second and third nen, no cognition of it occurs. One must say, "I recognize my thinking, therefore I know I am."

In this case "my thinking" is already a past event and, so to speak, objective, and "I recognize" is, in this present moment, the real and assured "I." This "I" is self-conscious, and is the product of the secondary reflecting and synthesizing activity of the third nen. However, as we have previously explained, this third nen must in turn be recognized by the next-coming reflecting action of consciousness (again the third nen), in order that the stream of consciousness may be maintained. To put it another way, each nen action is not conscious of itself; unless it is noticed and taken up by a succeeding action of reflection, it is not known at all. Thus, we do not directly catch hold of our own nen or mind. In reality, a posterior nen is always pursuing a prior one.

This fact, however, does not make us cast doubt on our own identity. The direct past is retained vividly by the present recognizing action, and we feel confident of the continuation of our own being. But is that all? Where does the warm feeling of this "I" really come from?

The warm feeling comes, in fact, from the *mood* that is latent in each nen—it is the mood that maintains the close, warm, intimate feeling that this is "I." By recognizing this mood or feeling, I sustain my own identity. This mood comes from my own body (including, of course, my brain). After all, this body of mine testifies to the truth of my own identification of myself. I live, I notice and feel my living, and I know that I am. A robot may be given the ability to recognize itself, but it will act only mechanically. If it is not given its own mood, it will not experience this true, warm identification of itself.

182

The warm, identifying feeling or mood can, incidentally, be postulated to have developed into the reflecting action of consciousness concomitantly with the evolution of consciousness, because each nen action was from the beginning accompanied, though latently, by this warm, intimate feeling.

SELF-ALIENATION   In the case of the psychotic person, the sequence of three nen actions—I live, I notice my living, and I know I am—is deranged because of the malfunction or fatigue of the reflecting action, especially that of the third nen. This must necessarily be followed by the third nen's failure to perform normally its identifying function, and by the progressive isolation of the nen from each other. The first nen, especially, becomes isolated in this way. Hence, the psychotic often fails to identify his own sensations, perceptions, and mood as his own and begins to feel alienated from himself.

There must be a great difference in the way of thinking between a man of intuitive disposition and a man who thinks rationally and logically. Recently I traveled for several weeks in the company of a certain Zen master, C. Zenji. I knew him as a man of very quick intuitive judgment. I found in traveling with him that at every odd moment he would lie down on his back and soon be asleep with a snore. A person with a logical turn of mind would find it hard to do this. His brain would be like a bubbling pot, which takes a considerable time to cool down. If such a person practices zazen, he is likely to find stray thoughts persistently rising up in his mind. Such tenacious nervous activity is rather unlikely to occur in an intuitively working mind. Even if a wandering thought should occur in zazen in such a person, it would be like a wisp of white cloud appearing in a blue summer sky, vanishing as quickly as it came.

Letters from C. Zenji are full of abrupt utterances. He is no doubt thinking in a certain orderly, intuitive way, but when he comes to put his thoughts on paper he has to express himself in the conventional, logical manner. The effort to give a rational presentation to impulsive thoughts that throng behind the scenes must necessarily involve selection—choosing and rejecting—and artificial arrangement. C. Zenji speaks fluently, in what might be called a computerlike manner, and his speech is persuasive because he has digested all the facts intuitively, in an instant. Intuition is not a simple action, but goes flashing through all the data almost simultaneously, as a computer does. When he comes to writing, however, C. Zenji must stand aside to observe the ideas to which he wants to give expression. He must resort to the third nen to make an old-fashioned selection and rearrangement, and this is his weak point. It results in a clumsy and abrupt expression of his thoughts. A logical brain, on the other hand, elaborately plots the thread of a discourse and sets out its ideas in an orderly fashion. But this orderliness is often the result of artificial tricks. We may recall Nansen's words: "A virtuous ruler does not use clever retainers." Here "clever" means "plotful," or too clever to be trusted. Such a man may often be successful, but how can he be sure that he did not pass by the door of the direct truth—that is, that he did not distort the truth by the use of apparently reasonable logic?

When C. Zenji was a young monk he once fell from a high place. In the course of falling he felt the process intensely, he says, as if he were watching a slow-motion film of it. The total use of the first nen results in a vivid and greatly enriched picture of its object, and gives the impression that the present moment is extending endlessly, because of its rich fullness. It was with this experience of falling that C. Zenji started to have a clear understanding of Zen truth. When one sees purely as the first nen sees, one can penetrate the object. Zazen is the practice of recovering this intuitive cognition. The overdevelopment of the deluded third nen in the modern civilized mind has resulted in a weakening of the intuitive action of the first nen, which is losing its original function of seeing objects clearly in their every particular. An animal sees, hears, and feels things simply intuitively, and its ability to grasp an object is correspondingly certain. When a dog sniffs his friend he recognizes him accurately. It is useless to say that the dog's scenting another in this way is nothing but electrical or biochemical changes in his nerve cells. The dog actually catches hold of vital material emitted by the other dog, experiencing the other dog's being.

184

It was the long evolutionary development of the sense organs, interdependently with the external world, that gave them their present functions. The dog's olfactory and other senses did not arise suddenly, full-fledged, independently. There was a long, slow evolutionary development, at all stages related to the properties of the external world, and that resulted in the dog's present sensory equipment, which permits it to catch hold of the external world. The animal does not doubt its sensory experience. However, lacking intellectual illumination, its cognition ends by being a purely animal one.

Human beings, too, believe in the information provided by the sense organs. It is the third nen (reason) that throws doubt on this information. But the third nen can, by its very nature, get in touch with the object only indirectly, and it is in no position to cast doubt on the cognitive action of the first nen. The first nen may be able to effect only an intuitive recognition of an object, but the important point lies in this recognition: that there an object is. That is enough to constitute pure cognition. The details can be filled in intellectually.

It was the development of the third nen that made man a superior being to the animal. But the first nen is not the less important. The two together form the two wheels of a cart: if the one is imperfect, the other becomes damaged, too.

How Does "Transcendental Cognition" Come About?
In the evolution of living things, we find that the throb of life appeared from chaos, and specialized itself in two directions: on the one hand, it developed sensation, which experiences the external world, and on the other it came to relate to an increased degree of complexity in the external world. At the beginning, the structure of the agent—the amoeba, for example—is very simple, and likewise its world is relatively simple. By degrees the structure becomes more complex on both sides. The sensation and the world that is sensed are fundamentally of the same nature, and they have interacted in the course of evolution to arrive at their current biological, psychological, and sociological status. They have never been isolated from each other. Sensation is, by nature, "Being-in-the-world." Therefore, when the first nen

185

works independently of the interference of the third nen, it comes into direct contact with the external world, and the latter is recognized purely as it is.

Idealist philosophers, it seems, have unconsciously assumed that sensation and perception must have developed independently of the external world, and that they are therefore isolated from it. Thus, they naturally conclude that sensation cannot exercise transcendental cognition of the external world.

The idea that sensation and perception have from the outset been interwoven with the world, and that by their nature they can cognitively hit right upon external objects, may still be objected to by the meticulous philosopher as inadequate and unjustifiable. However, is it not proved correct by common-sense judgment? Even the confirmed idealist employs such judgments in his daily life, and treats the things he sees and touches as existing in the external world.* When we analyze these problems in terms of the first, second, and third nen, we reach the conclusion that common-sense judgment is right, and we can understand why common sense should turn a deaf ear to what the philosophers say.

When my hand touches the cup on the table, my tactile feeling (the first nen) is provoked by the cup, and it realizes that there is an external object. This cannot be denied. Then the second and third nen recognize both the first nen and the first nen's cognition of the existence of the external object. Isn't that enough? Truth is always simple. The existence of the external object is caught by the tactile feeling, the first nen, and this first nen and its content are recognized by the second and third nen. There the spontaneous cognition of the external object in the transcendental sense is realized. And that is what common sense is doing every moment.

As a matter of fact, all the various qualities of the cup are not known to me at once. But I can deepen my cognition of the cup by adding to

---

*Compare Wittgenstein's remark when he heard Moore's proof of an external world: "Those philosophers who have denied the existence of Matter have not wished to deny that under my trousers I wear pants." (Quoted by John Wisdom in *Philosophy and Psychoanalysis* [Oxford: Blackwell, 1957], p. 129.)—ED.

it many other experiences of the cup from other angles and directions. Faulty understanding of the cup can be corrected; revisions can be made. In other words, my knowledge of the cup is improved. Correct knowledge is correct cognition. Knowledge can be revised by direct experience. We cannot expect perfect cognition, but only have it subject to the possibility of revision. An obvious example of cognition subject to revision is in the relations between man and man. Man is a complex being. Cognition of him is deepened by long observation from various angles. A long acquaintance with a man with whom I could not at first make friends may well produce a friendly feeling: "There is a friend."

THE THIRD NEN In an ordinary man, the third nen generally suffers from its own delusive pattern of thought. It wriggles in thrownness, looks at objects in the context of equipment, always dreading, always caught in anxiety. It is egocentric, and carries with it a wastebasket in which it keeps hatred, foolishness, stupidity, anger, greed, jealousy, and so on.

As I have already mentioned, a child can enjoy the sight of the falling leaves, bees flying in the sunshine, and so forth; but the adult cannot. He does not see beauty in the cup on the table but sees only the utility of the object. Perhaps his wife has brought him the cup, and he may even look at her in the same way. A friend told me a story that illustrates this attitude. "Once," he said, "I heard that an important person was on his way to visit me at home. I hurriedly began sweeping the rooms and putting things in order. My wife reproached me, saying, 'Sweeping is my job; please go to the front hall to receive him.' I handed her the broom as if to attach a stick to her hand. To my astonishment, I suddenly realized that I was handling my wife just as I handled the broom. Since then I have coined a proverb: 'Man thinks of his wife as a broomstick.' "

I do not wish to belittle the importance of the third nen or to blame it. On the contrary, the third nen is the master of the mind. When it is purified of its delusive thought patterns, it can work in perfect harmony with the first nen. But in most people, it is deluded. There are friction and division, with the first nen yielding or becoming damaged and the second nen becoming numbed, with mental illness as a possible result.

Delusion comes from egocentric thought patterns, generated by an ego that binds the true man. No one restricts you but you yourself. Your true freedom is attained in being free from yourself.

In order to recover the genuine cognitive faculty, we must accomplish Zen restoration. This is the process of liberating the first nen (sensation) from the control of the third nen, and the third nen from the control of egocentric individuality. As long as this egocentricity persists, we cannot see existence in its pure form. The Zen student trains himself to eliminate his egocentric, individual ego, returning to a condition of absolute mental nakedness.

Zen restoration can in some respects be compared to what is termed phenomenological reduction, but there are important differences between the two. It may be useful to clarify this point. Let us first quote a passage from Husserl:

"The ego as a person, as a thing in the world, and the mental life as the mental life of this person, are arranged—no matter even if quite indefinitely—on objective time; they are all transcendent and epistemologically null. Only through a reduction, the same one we have already called *phenomenological reduction,* do I attain an absolute datum which no longer presents anything transcendent. Even if I should put in question the ego and the world and the ego's mental life as such, still my simply 'seeing' reflection on what is given in the apperception of the relevant mental process and on my ego, yields the *phenomenon* of this apperception; the phenomenon, so to say, of 'perception construed as my perception'. Of course, I can also make use of the natural mode of reflection here, and relate this phenomenon to my ego, postulating this ego as an empirical reality through saying again: I have this phenomenon, it is mine. Then in order to get back to the pure phenomenon, I would have to put the ego, as well as time and the world once more into question, and thereby display a pure phenomenon, the pure *cogitatio.* But while I am perceiving I can also look, by way of purely 'seeing', at the perception, at it itself as it is there, and ignore its relation to the ego, or at least abstract from it.

Then the perception which is thereby grasped and delimited in 'seeing' is an absolutely given, pure phenomenon in the phenomenological sense, renouncing anything transcendent.''[2]

Husserl is saying here that his "seeing" looks at his perception, which is freed from the ego by the process of reduction, and he thus gets to the pure phenomenon. This "seeing" must, according to our understanding, be the action of the third nen; and Husserl's perception must be the action of the first nen. According to Husserl, this first nen's perception is, before reduction, the action of the ego, and epistemologically null. In order to get to the pure phenomenon, this first nen must be freed from the ego and purified by reduction. Husserl says nothing about the third nen's relationship with the ego. He seems to take it for granted that the third nen's "seeing" is intuitive and pure, and has nothing to do with the ego. But we believe that the activity of the third nen is usually distorted by the deluded ego (which is the activity of the third nen itself) and that it has to be freed from this distortion. In order to achieve this, we believe it is necessary to undertake arduous training in zazen. It is not something that can be effected by a process of mental abstraction. We attach great importance to this point. In short, in our view, we must first effect the liberation of the third nen, then the first nen will naturally resume its function of cognizing the external world as it is there. Husserl, however, does not recognize the first nen's cognition of the external world. These are important respects in which we differ from Husserl.

If we read the above quotation in the light of the theory of the three nen-actions, we find Husserl's complicated sentences not so difficult to understand. It is very simple: the third nen is looking at the first nen, and that is all. And as all nen actions are actions within your mind, they are not to be doubted and are entitled to be called absolute data. But the objects of the external world, sensed by the first nen, are outside your mind, so that such information is regarded by Husserl as transcendent. (Phenomenological theory is, in fact, considerably more complicated than we have indicated. However, the simple outline given here is adequate for our present purposes.)

Husserl stresses the third nen's "seeing," but this "seeing" learns about the external world only through information provided by the first nen and therefore has no authentic right to talk about the external world. Thus, Husserl's discussion is limited to the events occurring within one's own mind, and from the outset precludes cognition of the external world.

Husserl also speaks of "seeing" as if it were a simple thing that could easily be realized in practice. However, if you try, you will find it very difficult, if not impossible, to carry out in the way suggested for phenomenological reduction. Look at the book on your desk, as an experiment, and try to use pure intuition ("seeing") to catch your perception that is looking at the book. You will find yourself bewildered as to how you should do it. When the Zen student looks at the book in this way, if he is as mature as Nansen was, he sees the book Dasein (there is). Nansen did it. When he looked at the peony, to put it in the Buddhist way, he saw Buddha Nature there. This is direct cognition by the first nen, which Rikko was not capable of: he could see only the peony. This is the difference between intuitive penetration of the object and conceptual understanding.

This topic is important, and it is perhaps worth going over it once more to make our ideas clear. The first nen is what Husserl calls perception. He says it must be construed by "seeing" (pure intuition). Then, according to him, you get the phenomenon of the perception construed as your perception (that is, the genuinely given datum, which is not transcendent). To put it another way, Husserl demands that the first nen be perceived by the third nen, which employs pure intuition, and then one has the perception construed as pure perception. This recognition of the first nen by the third nen does not, of course, transcend itself to hit directly upon the external object.

Nansen's cognition, on the other hand, is the work of the first nen, which directly (intuitively) penetrates the object and thereby achieves transcendental cognition. For Husserl, this action of the first nen is a personal, psychological, individual experience—epistemologically of no value. The argument thus boils down to whether or not the first nen can be relied upon epistemologically. In Zen, we insist that the first nen, when acting in a purely intuitive manner, is unquestionably able to achieve transcendental cognition.

Husserl speaks only of the "seeing" (the pure intuition) of the third

190

nen; he does not recognize that of the first nen, which he regards as a personal, psychological experience. However, surely intuition proper, whether personal or impersonal, is always pure and direct. It becomes impure only when it is contaminated by the third nen. The first nen, left to itself, intuitively accepts stimuli from the outside world, spontaneously performing transcendental cognition. The truth is simple because it is a direct fact.

Let us return once more to the experiment and gaze at the book. If you are not mature in Zen you will see the book only with your ordinary understanding. You may think that you have somehow to direct your attention to an "essence" or "idea" or "universal." But where is the essence of the book?

Husserl says that "the ego as a person, as a thing in the world," is to be eliminated by phenomenological reduction. Ego as a thing in the world is really the routine activity of consciousness, which is burdened with topsy-turvy delusive thought. What Husserl is saying can be boiled down to the statement that if you stop the activity of routine consciousness, topsy-turvy delusive thought in personal, psychological, individual experience will fall away, and pure consciousness will appear. If this interpretation is correct, then we can only say that this is exactly what Zen students try to do, sitting on their cushions. However, we know from hard experience how difficult it is to eliminate the activity of routine consciousness. We Zen people do zazen for months and years. We often sit through the whole night without sleeping in order to train ourselves to eliminate the individual ego "as a thing in the world." If you want to experience any form of realization with the book on the desk, whether it be phenomenological reduction, or intuitive cognition, or seeing Dasein, or Zen experience, you must first put the book aside and start to eliminate your own topsy-turvy delusive way of thinking. After you have done this, you may return to the book. And see! What a different world you find there! The book radiates essence, idea, and universal quality. You have accomplished an epistemological revolution. Your cognition transcends itself and hits right upon the book. And kensho is just that.

Husserl started something very important for the Western world by introducing the idea of practice. His suggestion should be carried a stage further to include the fully developed practice that constitutes zazen, for this is the only way in which pure intuition can really be attained. If you truly achieve samadhi, everything is spontaneously resolved.

We may note here that, as far as we are aware, the idea of the first, second, and third nen has never explicitly appeared in the work of Western writers. Husserl recognizes them in a sense, his "seeing" being analogous to the third nen and his "retention" to the second nen. Zen masters of earlier times have said, "Cultivate your first nen," and "Don't use the second nen." However, by second nen they are referring to topsy-turvy mental activity, which we call the "deluded third nen." Our use of the term "second nen" to refer to the reflecting action of consciousness is not paralleled elsewhere in Zen literature, as far as I know.

CHAPTER FIFTEEN

Kensho Experiences

IN THE PREVIOUS CHAPTER we were concerned with discussions of a rather theoretical nature. We want now to describe some actual experiences, which will serve to illustrate some of our ideas. Several of these experiences are of kensho. It has long been held that detailed and exact description of the kensho experience is next to impossible. "In a moment too short to measure the universe changed on its axis and my search was over." This is a typical comment of one who has just experienced kensho. The person runs into it, realizes it, just as he drinks water and knows whether it is hot or cold—but cannot describe it. However, someday a Zen genius will appear and make it possible to penetrate this inviolable moment, to take hold of it and describe it.

In the history of literature we can trace the steps of man's gradual success in penetrating the dark sphere of his own consciousness. Zazen also can be regarded as a practice of descending into the darkness of the human mind. Although the Zen student does not do it intentionally, he often finds himself exploring a region of the mind of which quite probably no psychologist has ever had so much as a glimpse. This does not imply that we despise psychology. On the contrary, we have the greatest respect for this and other sciences, and it is our earnest wish that their methods and concepts be brought to bear on the study of Zen.

THE EXPERIENCE OF A GIRL   Recently a young girl, attending a sesshin of the Zen group in Honolulu, left the roshi's room in the detached cottage after finishing her *dokusan* (private interview with the roshi). She descended the steps of the porch, which was perfumed by the cross-shaped purple flowers of the sandpaper vine, and walked a few steps barefooted on the lawn, where the pale yellow, powder-like blossoms of the royal palm were continuously falling. As she passed the graceful trunk of the tree, she took out her handkerchief, feeling as if she were prompted to do so by an unknown agent, and blew her nose. It was just at that moment that the world suddenly changed.

Thanks to her earnest sitting in zazen, the activity of her first nen had shifted to the dimension of pure existence. At such a moment one is replete with a quietly flooding internal pressure, which requires liberation. Unconsciously responding to this need, she took out her handkerchief and blew her nose, and it was at that moment that her existence was shaken by a sharp shock. Simultaneously, as if caused by the shock, the curtain of her mind fell down, and the scene changed.

At the moment of kensho, intuitively activated sensation takes the initiative. In her case the stimulation received by the mucous membrane of her nostrils gave the impetus required. Although the world in front of her was the same old world, its aspect underwent a complete change. For a while she stood in mute amazement, gazing at the sight newly revealed there, and then she felt an emotional welling up—different from anything she had experienced before—as if an indescribably pure spring were overflowing within her. It was an endless stream of ample volume: the outburst of the great delight of which we hear so much. She felt for the first time that she was experiencing kensho. However, she did not know what providence made her experience it. She was aware only of the stream of great delight that ran through her entire body, producing a sense of purification of her existence. Kensho is initiated by the purification of sensation, which hitherto has been latent and stale or distorted, for reasons that we have discussed elsewhere. The trees, the grass, the gatepost ushering her to the inner court, the irregularly arranged steppingstones of volcanic rock, the bright crimson of ginger flowers, the white sand of the stone garden—all retaining their individual shape, color, and character—were marvelously fresh and new.

Until now, she and the world had been strangers to one another. Consciousness, led by her age-old, customary way of viewing things, had told her that they were they, she was she, and there was no inter-psychic communication. Now, however, everything was enjoying free communion, harmoniously united.

It may be instructive to compare the experience we have just described with one vividly recounted by Proust in a famous passage: "I raised to my lips a spoonful of the tea in which I had soaked a morsel of the cake. No sooner had the warm liquid, and the crumbs with it, touched my palate than a shudder ran through my whole body, and I stopped, intent upon the extraordinary changes that were taking place. An exquisite pleasure had invaded my senses, but individual, detached, with no suggestion of its origin. And at once the vicissitudes of life had become indifferent to me, its disasters innocuous, its brevity illusory—this new sensation having had on me the effect which love has of filling me with a precious essence; or rather this essence was not in me, it was myself. I had ceased now to feel mediocre, acciden-tal, mortal."[1]

One can find many passages comparable to this, both in Proust and elsewhere. There is undoubtedly a similarity between kensho and the feelings of oneness with external sights and sounds which are so often described, and which, indeed, many people experience in appropriate conditions. Yet there are important differences, too. Something is lacking by way of preparatory training or development, so that the ex-perience fails to be fully understood or grasped, and it tends to be transitory and elusive. We can see this in another passage from Proust: "We came down towards Hudimesnil; suddenly I was overwhelmed with that profound happiness which I had not often felt since Com-bray; happiness analogous to that which had been given me by—among other things—the steeples of Martinville. But this time it remained incomplete. I had just seen, standing a little way back from the steep ridge over which we were passing, three trees, probably marking the entrance to a shady avenue, which made a pattern at which I was look-ing now not for the first time; I could not succeed in reconstructing

the place from which they had been, as it were, detached, but I felt
that it had been familiar to me once. . . .

"I looked at the three trees; I could see them plainly, but my mind
felt that they were concealing something which it had not grasped, as
when things are placed out of our reach, so that our fingers, stretched
out at arm's-length, can only touch for a moment their outer surface,
and can take hold of nothing. . . . Or had I indeed never seen them
before; did they conceal beneath their surface, like the trees, like the
tufts of grass that I had seen beside the Guermantes way, a meaning as
obscure, as hard to grasp as is a distant past, so that, whereas they were
pleading with me that I would master a new idea, I imagined that I
had to identify something in my memory? Or again were they concealing no hidden thought, and was it simply my strained vision that
made me see them double in time as one occasionally sees things
double in space? I could not tell. And yet all the time they were coming toward me; perhaps some fabulous apparition, a ring of witches or
of norns who would propound their oracles to me. I chose rather to
believe that they were phantoms of the past, dear companions of my
childhood, vanished friends who recalled our common memories.
Like ghosts they seemed to be appealing to me to take them with me,
to bring them back to life. In their simple, passionate gesticulation I
could discern the helpless anguish of a beloved person who has lost the
power of speech, and feels that he will never be able to say to us what
he wishes to say and we can never guess. Presently, at a cross-roads,
the carriage left them. It was bearing me away from what alone I
believed to be true, what would have made me truly happy; it was
like my life.

"I watched the trees gradually withdraw, waving their despairing
arms, seeming to say to me: 'What you fail to learn from us today,
you will never know. If you allow us to drop back into the hollow of
this road from which we sought to raise ourselves up to you, a whole
part of yourself which we were bringing to you will fall for ever into
the abyss.' "[2]

THE CASE OF MARTIN LUTHER   In the chapter on mysticism in
William James's *Varieties of Religious Experience,* we find the following

passage: "The simplest rudiment of mystical experience would seem to be that deepened sense of the significance of a maxim or formula which occasionally sweeps over one. 'I've heard that said all my life', we exclaim, 'but I never realized its full meaning until now'. 'When a fellow-monk,' said Luther, 'one day repeated the words of the Creed: "I believe in the forgiveness of sins," I saw the Scripture in an entirely new light; and straightway I felt as if I were born anew. It was as if I had found the door of paradise thrown wide open.' This sense of deeper significance is not confined to rational propositions. Single words, and conjunctions of words, effects of light on land and sea, odors and musical sounds, all bring it when the mind is tuned aright. Most of us can remember the strangely moving power of passages in certain poems read when we were young, irrational doorways as they were through which the mystery of fact, the wildness and the pangs of life, stole into our hearts and thrilled them. The words have now perhaps become mere polished surfaces for us; but lyric poetry and music are alive and significant only in proportion as they fetch these vague vistas of a life continuous with our own, beckoning and inviting, yet ever eluding our pursuit. We are alive or dead to the eternal inner message of the arts according as we have kept or lost this mystical susceptibility."[3]

THE CASE OF DOGEN ZENJI   Luther's example is paralleled by the experiences of many Zen students. Dogen Zenji (1200–1253) went to China and trained himself under Nyojo Zenji of Mount Tendo. Once, when Dogen was sitting in the zendo with other monks, Nyojo Zenji entered and scolded an idle monk sitting beside Dogen. On hearing Nyojo Zenji's words, Dogen quite suddenly underwent a deep experience. Before this, Dogen had already undergone kensho over and over again, but this time the experience was quite exhaustive. He immediately went to Nyojo Zenji's room, burned incense, paid homage with nine bows, and presented his view. People today are apt to make light of such ritual, but behavior accompanied by sublime experience itself becomes sublime.

Nyojo Zenji accepted Dogen's presentation with approbation and acknowledged that he had completed "the Great Cause" (that is, *satori,* or enlightenment). One might wonder what relation scolding words can have to the principle of Zen. Scolding, crying, lamenting, laughing, bellowing—all human behavior is simply the manifestation of one's being. Particularly when you sit face to face with a psychotic person, listening to his outpourings, or when you watch at your beloved one's bedside, you will feel and realize this in the core of your mind: truly, there he is. If you can only see that the person is there truly, this very moment, whatever you see and whatever you hear will tell you the profound meaning of existence. That is because of what James calls "mystical susceptibility." The more the person is ailing, or suffering, or deranged, or delinquent, the more vividly his being there and suffering is felt. This susceptibility should surely be the psychotherapist's fundamental attitude and the basis of his therapy.

However, with the Zen student, nothing can be mystical except that one exists. The fact that one exists is the root fact that defies all demonstration. Therefore, when a monk asked Gudo, "Spring has come round, a thousand flowers are in their lovely bloom. For what? For whom?" Gudo's answer was, "Throughout eons, it is unthinkable." Fine! But one might also say, "It is for itself, of itself, by itself, in itself."

FROM MR. P.'s MANUSCRIPT   Following is an excerpt from Mr. P.'s manuscript: ". . . how long a time had passed I did not know. I chanced to come to myself in utter darkness. Dark! I cannot understand anything. I cannot meet myself. Where is this? Where am I? I cannot determine where I am or who it is that seeks such an answer. In an eager struggle to recover my self that is missing, I am rubbing and pressing myself to call it back to me. But I am not moving my hands or making my body stir, but only absorbedly shaking myself as in a dream. It is terrible to have consciousness which wants to awake, but finds the usual self does not come back. One is puzzled, but is not sware of being puzzled. And there is no knowing what to do with oneself.

"I make a strenuous effort, as when one strives to come up to the surface from the deep bottom of a lake. Darkness runs past, it runs rapidly as in a space flight. Oh! at last my eyes open. Indeed! This is

the meditation hall of the monastery. What time is it now? It has become light here around. It seems the sun shines brightly out of doors.
There is nothing, it seems, in this spacious hall. Why? It is quiet and
cool like a long autumnal night whose profound silence gives you a
faint ringing in the ears.

"At length I remember that all the monks went out this morning
on their *takuhatsu* trip. I have been sitting all alone in this hall. I did
not know when I entered samadhi, or whether I was asleep, and how
long a time had passed.

"This occurred a day after my arrival at this monastery. I had had
this sort of experience several times in my life, and it was no surprise
to me."

What is the meaning of "I cannot meet myself" or "the usual self
does not come back"? It signifies that Mr. P. could not identify himself in the context of time, space, and causation. Where? When?
Why? What? How? These are not known. Where am I? What time is
it now? Why and how and what and who am I? These questions are
not answered. In short, I do not know the whereabouts of myself.
Therefore, I cannot find myself.

In absolute samadhi, time, space, and causation drop off. And when
consciousness comes out of a deep samadhi, it takes time to recover its
framework of cognition (time, space, and causation), and the ego is
not immediately identified.

This phenomenon seems more likely to occur in a new environment
(as in this case). If the ego is placed in unfamiliar circumstances, its
reaction to the environment seems slower than when it is in familiar
surroundings. This is because certain subtle interrelationships are usually established between consciousness and a familiar environment
(for example, in the form of sounds and other stimuli), and the ego
reacts to the environment more quickly, and returns to normal faster,
when it is in these conditions than when it is in unfamiliar circumstances.

In the present case it is doubtful whether Mr. p. had been asleep.
Even if he had been, the important feature of the situation is not altered. To catch consciousness when it is deprived of its framework of
cognition (time, space, and causation) gives one some understanding

199

of what might be called the world of superconsciousness, where there is no ego. Many a Zen student experiences this when he deprives himself of sleep, as in a severe sesshin. And such an experience dimensionally widens his zazen and the capacity of his consciousness.

A SCHOOLTEACHER'S EXPERIENCE I was sitting in the lotus position in a chair in the library upstairs in my school. There were no classes, as it was summer vacation. I did not know how long a time had passed but suddenly, and in total darkness, I became aware of myself. Dark! I could not discover where I was. As in a dream, I was trying to locate myself, and suddenly it became light. I saw that it was bright day, though I had thought it was the depth of night.

The light came flooding over my shoulders, as I was seated with my back to the window. I was not yet sure whether it was morning or afternoon. Perhaps I wanted to know the time. My hand stretched to the watch on the desk, and I picked it up. At that moment, I encountered a very strange phenomenon. The watch seemed to be part of me. There was no differentiation between my hand and the watch. Truly, an extraordinary feeling! It was quite a different sensation from my ordinary routine one, and it impressed me strongly. I kept looking at the watch for some moments in amazement. The watch was its usual shape and gold color, and as far as these qualities were concerned, it was a quite different thing from my hand, which was holding it. Yet in another dimensional quality, it was not different from my hand.

When one looks at one's hand, one casually identifies it as one's own. This is done almost unconsciously. A person who is alienated from himself (that is, in a state of depersonalization) may find that his hand does not seem part of himself, just as his watch does not seem to be. In the present case, the situation was just the opposite: the watch was identified as part of myself. It was this that caused the amazement. The experience was not bewildering but was deeply impressive.

Some moments passed while I looked at the watch, and then I perhaps wanted to ascertain the general situation. I turned my eyes in another direction and saw bookshelves standing along the wall. They were several meters from me but were directly coming into me. What does this phrase "coming into me" mean? It implies that there was no spatial resistance between them and me. In a word, they and I were one. If I am you, you also are me. In the field of vision, they and I are distinct structures, each separately standing in its place. However, just as my own existence is intimate and warm to me, so now are they intimate and warm to me. We are not strangers; another me is standing there.

This phenomenon will perhaps be more easily understood if we recollect certain experiences of our childhood, as, for example, when the Christmas tree, with dolls and stars of silver paper and the like, stood there as the counterpart of ourselves, just as the mirror reflects our image. While the structural differentiation of he-being-he and me-being-me may be clear, psychologically no discrimination is felt. In a child's mind, time and space are not yet firmly rooted as in an adult's, and cognition outside the ordinary framework of consciousness often occurs.

In absolute samadhi the activity of consciousness is blocked, and when one comes out of it, it takes some time for adult cognition to resume its normal functioning. During the process of recovery, a psychological state comparable to that of a child frequently appears. It is said that a duelist who had gone through his first duel found his fingers stuck to the hilt of his sword and had to get someone else to separate his fingers from it, one by one. A state of desperation had produced strong mental and physical pressure, and it took some time for it to die away. The same is true of absolute samadhi.

Kensho is generally accompanied by a sudden and intense feeling of delight, but at this moment of my experience I felt nothing of the sort. I just kept watching in simple amazement. The wall, the windows, the floor, and once again the shelves and books—they were changed. They seemed just about to jump from their places to meet me, and at the same time remained motionless, hushed and silent. The film suddenly stopped, and the picture on the screen remained fixed—but alive. It was a breathtaking continuum of the present.

Silence like the depths of a moonlit night! Yet there was an un-voiced cry of jubilation. All the books turned their faces toward me. They had been sleeping there a long time, like the enchanted princess. They were awakening now, though still sleepy. They seemed to wriggle, as though they might suddenly stretch out their hands, rather like a baby in a silent film who starts to throw itself into its mother's arms.

Voices could be heard in the next room. Some students had come in for summer training. Or rather, they had been there a long time, shouting and moving something heavy. Perhaps it was their activity that had made me come to myself. I began to feel the brightness around me. By and by I could ruminate on the situation and say composedly to myself, "Now at last I have arrived where I should be." I was in a clear, quiet mood. Days later, when I reflected on this moment, a delightful feeling began to arise within me for the first time.

I don't know whether or not this was kensho, and I don't care. Subsequently I experienced something similar several times, and I could believe that I was gradually coming to understand Zen.

Some people may say, "He was dreaming." Others may laugh and say, "Kensho and the like are simply autohypnotism." They may be right. Subjective experience is open to doubt in many ways. Certainly, one can imagine that one was asleep, dreaming, or the victim of autosuggestion. However, the important point is not whether this sort of experience is the result of dreaming or autosuggestion but that in it the habitual way of consciousness falls off.

In fact, the experience is not what would be called sleep in the ordinary sense of the word. Zazen controls even sleep. The core of the mind is always kept awake, even when you are in the condition in which you are not aware of yourself. By repeatedly experiencing this, consciousness itself becomes familiar with the world beyond the boundary of its own activity and begins to cultivate a wider vision. This is the development of consciousness. By degrees you will be able to see Buddha Nature with your naked eyes. And again, my experience was not so-called makyō (a "devil's condition": ma, devil; kyō, condition), in which one sees, in the course of one's meditation, bizarre visions (hallucinations) of devils, wild animals, Bodhisattvas, Buddhas, and other strange figures. When one establishes jishu-zammai, makyo does not appear.

As to the suggestion that this state is one of autohypnosis or a product of autosuggestion, it is perhaps worth remarking that these are not something peculiar. Consciousness always carries out a sort of autosuggestion to itself. One's confidence is a kind of autosuggestion. Intention or determination entertained by consciousness can be effectively maintained only when it operates under a strong self-hypnotic influence by consciousness over consciousness itself; or, as we might say, by the action of one nen over the succeeding nen-action.

THE CASE OF MR. M.   When Mr. M. first came to a certain monastery to participate in sesshin there, he was a retired industrialist, about seventy years old. He said he had never previously learned or practiced zazen. However, he was very earnest and attentive to everything. He behaved briskly and applied himself eagerly to the routine work of the monastery that was required of all participants, such as sweeping, cleaning, raking the fallen leaves, and weeding the garden. He seemed to understand that action had something to do with Zen discipline. After that he appeared at every sesshin of the monastery, and three years later he had kensho, as he had expected.

Once, when his study of Zen had made considerable progress, and we expected something from him, he asked me to make a thorough investigation of his posture. He was something of a self-made man, who had gone through the whirlpools of life, and his rather stout constitution seemed to show annual rings of distortion. The balance of the left and right sides of the chest and trunk was a little off, and the middle part of the spinal column described a slight curve. The left shoulder was a little higher than the right and protruded. His body inclined slightly to the right. "Don't you feel a pain in your right buttock when you sit for a long time?" I asked. He seemed a little surprised at my question, and acknowledged that he did. "Bring your navel directly under your nose," I said, and found he was quick to understand. He gave one swing to his body and the correct posture was achieved. And then he said with the delighted expression of someone who has been relieved of a chronic trouble, "I know. It is not the shoulder that is really faulty. I have to bring my waist back into position. Isn't that so?"

I advised him to use a mirror to study his posture. Later I was told by one of his friends, who had also started zazen, that when Mr. M.

returned home he pinned a string to the middle of the top of the frame of his full-length mirror and let it hang down like a plumb line. Then he adjusted the position of his nose and navel to the vertical line of the string. I had never thought of doing that. Mr. M. had the wisdom to use what knowledge he could get from others and add to it his own ideas. This wisdom, I thought, made him successful in zazen practice as well as in his worldly career, for he had begun life as a penniless youth.

He also consulted me about breathing. Shortly before this, however, I had had a rather disappointing experience in connection with my recommendation of the bamboo method to a group of people, and I thought it prudent to tell him only what I thought was most fundamental. It was a general talk about how to strengthen the tanden by making the diaphragm and abdominal muscles work in opposition, and I suggested that everyone must work out the method most suited to his constitution. However, I was anxious about his reaction to my talk, and on the next day, when sesshin started, I was rather attentive to his behavior. But there was no need to be especially attentive, for something very conspicuous happened. At first I thought I heard a faint continuous sound that seemed to be coming from outside the zendo. The head monk gave an admonition, saying, "You should not make a sound with your nose." At this the sound stopped, but a few minutes later it started again and this time seemed to be louder than before. It resounded in the hush of the hall, as if in defiance of the head monk's warning, and it seemed to be aimed at attracting the attention of everyone else. At last I realized that the sound was coming from the nose of Mr. M., who was sitting next to me.

It was really a remarkable way of breathing. For about ten seconds he exhaled continuously, producing a buzzing sound, "Zzzzz," there was a short interval for inhalation, then the sound restarted: "Zzzzz." He was giving considerable strain to the respiratory muscles to push out his breath. There was no waxing and waning, no interval for a brief stop, as in the bamboo method, but a broad and straight stream of exhalation.

The head monk gave his warning several times, and each time it was followed by a brief silence, after which the buzzing resumed, resounding through the hall. It was disturbing to the young monks, and Mr. M. was required to leave and continue his practice in a corner of the main hall of the temple. I followed him and seated myself facing him on the opposite side of the room. He was not aware of making the sound. Toward the end of the sesshin, his face assumed a different expression. There was no movement. His face was like the mask of the old man in a Noh play. The eyes of the mask of the old man are open, but Mr. M.'s eyes were almost covered by his lowered eyelids. His face was placid, peaceful, and expressionless, like that of a dead man.

He moved like a person who was dreaming. He walked as a Noh player walks. He was forgetful of his surroundings. He was in either positive or absolute samadhi throughout the whole day. I invited him to sit through the night on the eve of the last day of the sesshin. I cannot recollect if he was still making the buzzing sound, but probably he was not, as I remember nothing in particular about his breathing. On the morning of the last day, he attained kensho. And all day he was experiencing many things, which he told me about. "I must tell you, quite a miraculous thing happened to me. In the brief period after lunch, while we were still sitting in the dining room, the idea suddenly came to me that this room, these utensils, and those people sitting here— they are myself. It was too strange. When I returned to my place, I looked out into the garden, and found the stones, trees, and everything appeared the same way."

Soon after returning home, he developed an irregular pulse and was told by his doctor that it was the result of contracting his respiratory muscles too strongly while he had chronic hypertension. On the doctor's advice he stopped doing zazen for three months and the symptoms disappeared. He reappeared at the monastery after ten months' vacation and told me what was in his mind. "I have pondered deeply and have reached a conclusion. I do not want to become great and extraordinary in Zen, as one might once have hoped for oneself." Certainly he had imposed a great strain on himself, such as a serious Zen student does when he wants to master every secret of the universe. He continued: "I, such a common man, want only to live quietly and do for others what I can, living my remaining years like a *myōkōjin* [good and pure person] or a *mokujiki-jōnin* [a sage who eats raw food].

I do not want kensho. As for the problem of life and death, I do not find in myself much attachment now, and I do not attempt to do such strenuous zazen as before. If wandering thoughts come, let them come. I rather enjoy them."

He had reached an advanced condition. If I were to try to make some comment on his words it would involve a long discussion. For the present, it would be enough to quote some Zen sayings: "I do not seek holiness or enlightenment." "I do not avoid dirt, nor want to get rid of attachment."

But alas! He died soon after I left Japan, not because of his chronic hypertension but of quite unexpected cancer. But he had already predicted his death when he said the words I have just quoted.

CHAPTER SIXTEEN

A Personal Narrative

WHEN I WAS THIRTEEN YEARS OLD I had an experience that may be said to have established the keynote of my life. At this age we are on the eve of youth. We still retain a fresh memory of the dreamland of childhood, but at the same time the activity of our consciousness is almost fully developed.

The experience occurred during a calligraphy lesson. The teacher was something of an artist, and very gentle in disposition. He did not bother much about discipline and keeping order. He would go around quietly among the boys, teaching them individually. When he was so inclined, he would take the brush of one of the pupils and execute a beautiful piece of calligraphy, and this always pleased the children very much. On such occasions pupils near his desk would gather around him, while mischievous boys sitting farther away would take advantage of the opportunity and get up to all sorts of tricks. That day they were extremely unruly. I wanted to cut myself off from them and tried deliberately to concentrate on my work. Fortunately, my seat was situated in a corner and I could do this rather easily. In retrospect, I realize that my breathing while doing calligraphy naturally resembled that of zazen, especially the bamboo method. Before I was aware of it, the noisy fuss of the classroom was far away, as in a dream. Then the time must have come when I heard nothing and felt nothing. How long this state lasted I do not know, but the period of complete forgetfulness of myself and my surroundings must have continued for some time.

In a profound silence—as though the tower of Babel had long been left deserted, and stars shed light upon the ruins, and then, after many ages had passed, a stranger from a distant land happened to visit the remains one moonlit night, carrying his staff with him on his solitary wanderings, and his heart filled with deep emotion—in such eternal silence or midnight quietness, as if suddenly aroused by chance, I came to myself, and found lying on my desk a piece of calligraphy. It was clear and beautiful, in black and white. Gazing for a moment at it, I suddenly came to notice the far more beautiful peacefulness of my mind and the quiet breathing that occupied the whole of my being, and I was filled with deep emotion.

The Chinese Rip Van Winkle strayed into the legendary Land of Peach Blossoms and found a remote, ancient people belonging to a peaceful, mythological age, surviving to live their secret life there. In the noontide silence of bright spring, all was hushed, while countless flowers in full bloom covered the hills and valleys. He must have been greatly impressed, as was I at the moment of coming back to myself.

I felt I must not move lest I disturb the peaceful state of my body and mind. I knew where this peace and silence came from: it was all from my body, which had lost its usual sensation. Where were my legs? my loins? my trunk? I knew I was sitting on a chair but had no feeling of being seated. The usual sensation of the body—in fact, the sensation of my own existence—did not come back to me. This loss of sensation brought home the silence and peace of my body and mind. The hand that held the brush was moving slowly of itself. The most important thing was that I should not move my head to left or right; this I knew instinctively.

When the bell rang at the end of the hour, I wondered what would become of me. I could stand up without mishap, but I found with great regret that the peace was departing from me.

This experience developed into a passion with me, and at the next calligraphy period I intentionally tried to regain the land of legend. In order to bring about the effect, I knew from instinct that I must not move my body. I also knew the importance of holding my breath and minimizing the sensation of my whole body. I knew the skin must be lullabied to sleep. From the memory of yesterday's childhood, I knew how to manipulate my body, skin, and breath. The child playing hide-and-seek hides himself behind the curtain with bated breath—and instinctively practices zazen.

What has happened by chance is often difficult to repeat when it is sought deliberately. Chance is a genius. Monsters drawn by the leaking of rain or the grain of wood may be wonderful masterpieces, but imitations of them are generally useless. The revival of my dream of the legendary land, which I sought each time I entered the calligraphy classroom, seemed at times successful in a way but generally ended in only partial success. It was rather irritating. I changed my plan and, seeking a secluded place, took a walk every evening to the bank of a stream, and, following wisdom that was also taught by chance, I gazed at the evening star.

I stood motionless and breathless, with my neck and shoulders steadily fixed, as though I were turned into a statue. It was late autumn. The still air of the calm evening wrapped the skin of my face and body, and that was enough to quieten the activity of my mind and body. A musical, tremorlike sensation occurred around my ears, neck, and cheeks and gradually spread itself all over my body. Presently off-sensation started to set in, and my limbs vanished. Quietness, like the night growing old, melted into the solitude of the evening and filled my entire body. In those days, I had no conception of zazen, but this was a fine samadhi as I was standing there.

Dusk silently gathered around, the twilight deepened, and over the lonely grassland a faint sound of footsteps approached. Rustle, rustle. It seemed that a man with a dog passed by. That made me come to myself and think, "Now it is time to go." I started to move my body quietly. Taking great care not to disturb the lingering peace of samadhi, I stepped out, walking slowly and gently. Harmonized with the stillness of the darkening hills and valley, it was a continuum of moment after moment's happiness in serenity.

From about that time, a certain disdainful feeling toward man's world started to creep into my mind and gradually occupied it. The deceitful life of adults seemed disgusting. Standing in sharp contrast to mundane life, the dreamy garden of pastoral poetry came to my mind in sweet recollection. However, to my regret, as I grew older, I began to feel the legendary Land of Peach Blossoms leaving me. Many a time I looked back and tried to catch hold of the passing dream.

At the back gate I was loath to part from my fleeting spring; and coming round to the front door, I was repelled by the adult world of fighting and deceit. I pledged to myself that I would never allow myself to enter and be contaminated by the world of lying and cupidity.

And what actually happened? "When the three parts become hairy, you do not listen your parents." Yes, and not only that, but I did not listen to my own inner voice. As I grew up, I forgot my revulsion and wallowed slavishly in the ordinary affairs of life. I indulged in all sorts of vices: heartlessness, cruelty, hatred, stealing, fraud, and flattery.

I pretended at this time to be stout-hearted and put on a bold front with a haughty manner, but in truth I was a coward. I dreaded dying. The fact was that I was suffering from a neurosis, but I was not aware of this, being so engrossed in it. In waking and sleeping, I was preoccupied with the thought that when I died I would be consumed and there would be nothing left of me. It was a state of complete despair that I did not know how to handle. There was no place to take refuge. We can find a way out of almost anything if we do not mind degrading ourselves in the world, but this problem of death is inescapable.

Even during sleep, it seemed, I went through cruel tortures, and I found myself worn out on awakening in the morning. And at the very moment of my awakening, without a moment's respite, a voice came ringing in my ears: "You must die!" Suddenly I would feel choked, and my heart would beat violently. It was as though I were living in an air raid that went on all day and all night—the psychological warfare of death.

Was I born to undergo this agony? This world was literally a living hell. It puzzled me to see people living nonchalantly. "Don't you feel frightened at the thought of death?" I eagerly asked an old man of good worldly understanding. "I have already lost my teeth," he said, "my eyesight is dim, my hairs can be counted. I have forwarded my petty effects already." What stupidity! Don't be a liar! Acknowledge

210

your real concern! I felt I would like to hold him down and make him confess the truth. I had once been a devout Christian. With trembling hands I opened the Bible. If only I could regain the belief that had once made me secure. But alas! All was gone.

Generations before us, there were men, writers and thinkers, with pure Christian faith. But they lost their faith, one after another, and when they did, they died agonizing deaths. Modern intellectuals are cursed people.

I furtively bent my legs to sit in meditation. I had no teacher, and found my own way of sitting. However, strange to say, I found my mind calmed down. Wandering thoughts came and went, but the uneasiness of mind that had made me bewildered was diminishing, as if a fog had lifted, and my feeling was eased, though I did not know why. I thought that zazen might pacify my nerves. This casual guesswork was, it seems, correct. Much later I had time to think about the theory of Zen, but Zen is not, in my view, philosophy or mysticism. It is simply a practice of readjustment of nervous activity. That is, it restores the distorted nervous system to its normal functioning. And it must be pursued earnestly.

I learned that an outstanding Zen master, chief abbot of a principal Zen temple in Kyoto, was visiting my district in response to an invitation from a laymen's Zen society, and that a sesshin was to be held at a certain temple. I went to take part in this and arrived on the evening before the first day. The next morning I jumped out of bed at the signal bell at four o'clock, put away my bedding, and dressed quickly. Soon the morning service started, and after that I was told by a monk to go to the roshi's room for dokusan.

I walked along a long, dimly lit porch, one side of which seemed to face a garden. On the other side were dark rooms, all closed and silent. I came to a staircase, ascended it, and entered an anteroom. It was dark and I could hardly find my way. At the end of the room one of the sliding doors that separated it from the next room was open, inviting me to pass through. There seemed to be no human being stirring in this part of the huge building, and at the same time everything seemed to be watching me. The next room was raised a step higher.

I entered, and found it dimly lit. I had been told I would see the roshi in this room. Looking carefully, I could see someone sitting with the alcove behind him, as if settled down on the bottom of the darkness. The dimmest light was thrown upon him, making his figure faintly discernible.

I made my formal bows before him and said I was a beginner and asked him to give me instruction. The eyes of the roshi, which up to then had seemed almost closed, opened slightly and looked at me. I shall never forget the movement of his eyes and the light they emitted. They were living beings in themselves. They were not human, but the eyes of samadhi. Then once again they almost closed. Presently he said, "Work on the sound of one hand." He quietly lifted up his hand, and held it for a while, and that was the extent of his demonstration. There was no individual bargaining. His action was meant to make contact with man's suffering. In other words, a hand was held out from samadhi. One was supposed to touch it, accept it, and then all would go well. The encounter was brief, but it contained something convincing. I felt like a driver given directions at a crossroads.

Breakfast was served at break of day. Everything was refreshing, and especially the pure sound of the handbell, rung by the head monk, which penetrated my heart. After breakfast, there was a little free time. I entered a detached shrine called Taishi-do, which was dedicated to the ancient Buddhist teacher Kobo Daishi, the founder of many elements of Japanese culture. This temple was one that pilgrims visited. I sat in a corner of the room for meditation and continued until lunchtime without a break.

One's original intention is highly valued in Zen, because it is eager and intense. In my case, this proved vividly true. From the first moment of the first day of *sanzen* (studying Zen), I seemed to enter into a sort of steady samadhi, which continued until the sound of a gong at lunchtime. Then I came to myself. It was early summer. The time was eleven in the morning. Cool southeast breezes were blowing through the room, and rows of hanging paper lanterns, dedicated by pilgrims, were swinging merrily in the wind. At the sight of them, I was struck by dizzy vibrations, like the shocks of an earthquake. With a tremendous roar, all the hills, valleys, temple buildings, and the shrine with me in it went tumbling down into the abyss. Even flying birds fell to the ground with their wings broken.

Along an embankment that was holding back a flood, a single stone rolled down, and at this shock the bank collapsed, and hundreds of thousands of tons of water surged into the streets of the city. The visual oscillation at the sight of the swinging lanterns brought about a whirling in my brain and an overflowing of internal pressure. The breach went down to rock-bottom level, allowing the flooding internal pressure to rage unchecked. The higher the pressure, the greater the destruction. From the earliest times, the head monks in Zen monasteries have taxed their ingenuity to produce the maximum internal pressure in students. They declare that from the "great doubt" springs great satori, and they encourage the monks to doubt and doubt.

In my case, dread of death had driven me into an unbearable state. A condemned criminal has nowhere to run to, however much he may weep and shout. I could not remember what crime I might have committed in my previous life, but this misery of mine was too much. If God had really made the world like this, I could only curse Him with unfeigned animosity. However, in a corner of my mind a ray of hope had emerged when I first thought that zazen might help to pacify my nerves. I had a presentiment of there being some means of escape there. And in the disciplined framework of sesshin, sitting formally, things adjusted themselves to open a road in my mind, and I entered samadhi.

This entering into samadhi is absolutely necessary. Samadhi is the cleansing of consciousness, and when consciousness is purified, emancipation is, in fact, already accomplished. The moment I saw the lanterns swing, a stone rolled down from the embankment—the first sign of its imminent collapse—and in that moment a great transformation was effected by consciousness itself, which became awakened. Consciousness does not understand at this stage how or why, but it suddenly finds itself relieved of all its earlier agonies. And when consciousness becomes aware of this liberation, rapture comes overwhelmingly.

213

Human energy is simply energy. Depending on the way the pipes are installed and on which taps are open, it can be turned into ecstasy, anger, or laughter. At the moment one attains kensho the tap is fully opened and pure water gushes out in an endless stream. Spiritually, it causes an overflowing of wild joy; physically, it sends the blood rushing through the entire body. It is said traditionally that on the occasion of kensho the discharge of internal pressure will last for three days, and the person undergoing this is encouraged to lie down quietly. Considering the agonies he has gone through, kensho and its aftermath can be compared to a convalescent period after an illness.

To return to my story: the lunch gong kept sounding, as if set in motion by the swinging of the lanterns; I reeled to my feet and, still as if in a dream, began walking slowly. I walked like a man recovering from a long illness, who is learning how to walk again. I came to the roofed passage connecting the shrine to the main building, crossed a bridgelike walk, and entered the main hall. All was silent, with no human shadow stirring. Everyone had gone to the dining room. The inner part of the hall, extending far back, was dark, and I could see there the Buddha's seat, shining faintly black. The golden lotus flowers were peeping out from behind an embroidered curtain. An image of Pindola stood facing south on the porch. As if attracted by it, I approached and stood by its side. I looked toward the temple gate, where I saw two pilgrims lying with their heads pillowed on the stone base of a pillar. Pindola, too, was looking at them. They were perhaps a hundred paces from the porch where I stood. The spacious, dry ground shone in the noonday light, making the figures of the pilgrims stand out vividly in relief, like projections on a screen. They looked like father and son.

"The father and son are lepers," Pindola said clearly in my ear, almost as if to try to persuade me that it was so. This was half a century ago. By then, all lepers had been taken into institutions and they were not allowed to wander about. But a decade before, when I was very young, they were to be seen on pilgrimages, undertaken in the hope of curing their terrible disease; some had their noses and eyes collapsed—a profoundly affecting sight. The memory of seeing them must have popped up in my mind on this occasion. It was a trick played by consciousness upon itself.

"How do you feel about this?" the same voice continued. "They are lepers. If you are really enlightened, you must have developed the heart of the Bodhisattva Kannon. You can go straight to the father and son, be kind to them, console them from the bottom of your heart. Like Empress Komyo, you can suck up the pus from their sores with that mouth of yours. Can you do that?"

It was in order to ask this question that the voice had first told me that they were lepers. On an occasion like this, consciousness speaks to itself, as if it were a stranger to itself. It is nothing extraordinary; everyone experiences it, for instance in their dreams, as Freud made abundantly clear. When the voice asked me if I could do the sort of thing Empress Komyo had done, my mind wavered in spite of myself, and I involuntarily shrank back. Also, I clearly felt this occurring in me. It was a momentary betrayal of myself that I could not deny. "Then you are not enlightened," the voice muttered. I could but bow down my head and say, "No, sir, I am not."

I had naturally believed that if I only got kensho, the secret of the universe, the problem of death, and everything else would be solved instantly, once and for all. Cut off this arm! Carry away these legs! Even if my life is taken at this moment, I shall not be grieved, so long as I have understood the secret! Where I am from, whither I shall go, the true nature of reality, eternal life, and everything else will be understood as clearly as looking at a picture—so I had imagined. However, at this moment, nothing at all was clear to me. At the bottom of my mind, this "nothing was clear" had been vaguely felt. Hence this grilling. It was the cross-examination of a prosecutor making his preliminary inquiries. Both prosecutor and prosecuted were products of my own consciousness.

Some psychotics complain that they find two people in themselves. Consciousness streams along, forming a continuum of a prior nen succeeded by a posterior nen, and there is no mystery in the fact that the former asks and the latter answers. In this connection the psychotic may be said to be more acutely sensitive than the ordinary person. In an ordinary mind, the habitual way of consciousness reigns unshaken. It fits the impressions of each moment into the framework of its cognition to cook up a supposedly constant, individual ego.

In my experience on the porch (with logic suspended for a while), in the deep part of my mind a voice was saying, "Although you were beginning to think you had kensho, in fact you don't know anything."

Be that as it may, how could I explain the impulsive, delightful feeling that bubbled up within me? Let the prosecutor and lawyers say what they liked; inwardly I was filled with a joyous feeling that came bouncing up like a child at play. I was happy to resign myself to it without reasoning about it. Everything I saw gave me a vivid impression. Pilgrims were arriving at the temple and could be seen coming up to the office that issued amulets. They walked silently under the blazing sun. A priest stamped the amulet with the temple's seal. All was quiet. With deep wooded hills at the back of the temple, the remote singing of cicadas made the atmosphere the more hushed. The pilgrims would take up their staffs and go. It was an extraordinary sight, and, like some movie scenes that I had seen as a child, it left an indelible impression upon me.

In the afternoon a young man invited me to go swimming. Withered victim of the fear of death as I was, the thought of swimming in the sea was instantly attractive, and we set out immediately. I was in the sea for perhaps an hour. When the time came to return, I found the crystallike, pure, and delightful feeling that had filled me until an hour previously had all gone, and (as if it had been secretly substituted) a stale, dirty body like a gunnysack was left to contain my whole being. At no time in my life have I so clearly felt the difference between the purity of the body and its mediocrity, side by side. I scolded myself and told myself that I had got what I deserved for mixing play with the serious pursuit of zazen.

For some readers the idea of the purity of the body and its difference from routine mediocrity will seem absurd, but if you experience it you will understand what I mean. What the purity is and what the mediocrity is cannot readily be explained, but they are palpable facts, actually experienced with the body. What I felt now was a mediocre staleness of my body. The unworldly, pure delight of an hour before had departed, leaving no trace. It was useless to repent.

Much later I came to understand that the delightful feeling and the purity of the body were, in fact, the product of the intuitive action of the first nen. How pure it was! You should simply experience it! However, while I was pushed about in the waves, its purity and freshness were dissipated. I returned to the temple full of repentance. There, after the roshi's lecture and supper, the evening meditation began. Waiting impatiently for it to begin, I tried to recall the memory of the morning's delightful feeling and to restore myself to the same condition.

It was eventually nothing more than a matter of dealing with breath, skin, and guts. Once experienced, you can find the route to return to it rather easily. An initial slight inhalation, and then gentle, soft exhalation, full of pure emotion: this sort of breathing appears naturally when you express something inspiring. I have already dealt with these procedures at length, but perhaps I may be forgiven for repeating certain points here. If, sitting in zazen posture, you hold your breath around the horizon of breathing and almost stop all movements of the respiratory muscles, your body will be reduced to motionlessness. And when you thrust your belly forward and your buttocks backward, the shoulders will be lowered and their tension relieved. If the shoulders are relaxed, all the muscles of the upper body will follow suit. They will be in a state of moderate or quiet tension. Just as there is an optimum cruising speed for a car or airplane, so muscles can also take up a preferred condition of equilibrated strain, and it is this that we call a quiet tension.

The feeling of our bodily existence is maintained by various stimuli arising from the skin and muscles. If this stimulation is lacking, the body will no longer be felt to exist. To put it another way: if you try to fix your body, immobile, in zazen, your breath will spontaneously become bated. Then a certain peaceful and pacifying sensation will appear, first around the most sensitive parts of the body—the forehead, cheeks, ears, hands, and arms—and then spread to the chest or back. With a little practice you will soon notice a delicate, musical, thrill-like vibration, accompanied by a pacifying sensation. This lull-abies the skin, and off-sensation will follow naturally. The pacifying sensation and off-sensation are closely interrelated; they are separated by only a hairsbreadth. The skin has its own emotion. It acts as the lips of the soul (if the guts are the site of the spirit), and it reflects emotionally the internal condition of the muscles and viscera. At the time I write of, of course, I knew none of this at all clearly. I could only vaguely guess at it. I concentrated on my experience of that morning and tried to revive the condition once again. And at length I was able to recover that delightful feeling.

Zen literature tells us that the delightful feeling that accompanies kensho lasts as long as three days. To tell the truth, I wished to conform to the traditional pattern. When I felt that the delightful feeling was diminishing a little, I used my breathing trick to reactivate it. For about three days things went well, as I had hoped, but gradually during this time the strong internal pressure began to exhaust itself, and I sensed that I was cooking up the feeling artificially. I felt an extra burden imposed on my heart, as happens when we try to arouse a forced emotion. So much for petty tricks, I thought, and I decided to take a new step and make a frontal attack on absolute samadhi. So my hard training in zazen began anew. Sometimes I found I seemed to be approaching absolute samadhi; sometimes I found myself blocked by wandering thoughts. It was not an easy matter. The world I had inhabited in my childhood proved difficult to recapture now that I was a youth with an intensely active consciousness.

If only in those days I had known how to conduct my body and mind, I should have been spared the hardships I underwent. It took thirty years before I began to feel as if I had attained a tiny understanding of Zen. Why was this? Simply because of the lack of organized method and theory. I know that in the old days Zen people did not talk much about the techniques of zazen. They devoted themselves solely to the simple way of sitting, and in the course of five or ten years they invol-untarily developed their own way of practice. And this way proved effective for them, because it was their own. However, they abhorred the idea of merely being masters of a technique and were reluctant to talk about their methods. Even today the idea that zazen can be mastered only after many years of hard and seemingly wasteful effort dies hard. Some monks are fond of going into the mountains and remote valleys for seclusion, and fast and discipline themselves, enduring all sorts of hardships. It is somewhat romantic and, in a way, attractive. However, surely there is no reason why we should not now learn and make use of some basic elements in the technique of zazen in order to attain more quickly the ability to enter absolute samadhi. Once one habituates oneself to absolute samadhi, one can forget technique. One must, of course, not be a slave to it.

We enter absolute samadhi when off-sensation and the state of body-and-mind-fallen-off are both achieved. Then the peace and silence of the Himalayas fill your whole being. One day, in such an absolute silence, I happened to open my eyes. I had been in the habit of sitting with my eyes half-open, but this time I must have closed them before I was aware of it. It was late in the afternoon, and several trees in the garden threw long shadows on the ground. I was unconsciously forced to keep gazing at the sight. It was something I had been accustomed to from childhood, but now I saw it with an artist's understanding. That is to say, a child looks at a sight instinctively, but now I saw it with an intuitive understanding. The understanding led me to a deep appreciation of what I saw. It was the vivid impression of the first nen's pure cognition.

In my first kensho-like experience, which I have described above, I experienced a mental earthquake, in which temple buildings, hills, everything went tumbling down into the abyss with a tremendous noise. But this time I was quietly looking at the shadows of the trees. A moment later I heard a voice muttering somewhere inside me, "It is something. . . ." But no particular delight was stirred up in me. I did not think about whether it was a great or small kensho, or even whether it was definitely kensho at all.

This experience led to another experiment. I started the practice of gazing at a tree, a rock, a hill, a flower, or something similar. One evening, while waiting for a friend, I stood by a willow tree on the bank of a moat, with the site of an old castle on the opposite side, and gazed at the water. It was early winter, with no wind, and all was silent. The water was dark and seemed muddy; duckweed and other water plants were growing in it, and decayed lotus stems were to be seen here and there. I could vaguely make out the red color of a carp among the weeds. It did not move. I fixed my eyes on the red color and moved neither eyes nor body. Ten seconds, it seemed, had not passed before off-sensation started to appear around my shoulders, neck, and cheeks. Dusk was gathering. The shades of night and the still air seemed to thicken around me and wrap me up. It was like covering a doll's face with sheet after sheet of tissue paper. Off-sensation spread rapidly to my chest, arms, abdomen, and back. When the friend came, I was completely absorbed in my standing samadhi, but he said he had not been away more than five minutes.

It gradually became quite easy for me to get into this sort of samadhi whenever I wanted to. Vision and positive samadhi have a close relationship. Gazing at the stitching of a mat, the pattern of a carpet, the grain of a wooden wall, I could enter samadhi in a very short time. I became more and more accustomed to seeing Buddha Nature with my naked eyes.

I practiced walking Zen, too. Every morning I walked for about forty minutes to reach the place where I worked. I went along a river. One side was bordered by a bank; on the other there was a grassy plain. Ta! Ta! Ta! I stalked vigorously along, looking neither right nor left. I called this my walking samadhi. Even on a cold winter morning, before I had gone halfway, my body was comfortably warm. One day I was walking along a path in the grass. It was midwinter. Far ahead of me, a long bridge could be seen. River fog was rising and made the bridge hazy. When I was about two hundred yards from the bridge, I saw the blurred outlines of people carrying sticks as weapons. The contours of the figures, wearing overcoats, were rounded and dull-looking. They were moving in one direction over the bridge and happened to form a group. Then, quite suddenly, a vision flickered through my head of a procession of bandits. The next moment an idea ran through my mind, with striking vividness, that the time of Emperor Jimmu's eastern expedition was just this moment in which I was taking in my breath.

Emperor Jimmu, founder of the Japanese empire, started from western Japan and led his clan and soldiers eastward 2,600 years ago, just as Moses led his people out of Egypt. Coming to the central part of the Japan of those days, he established his capital there and the history of Japan started.

Historical time had dropped away, and the idea possessed me that Jimmu's time and this present moment were one and the same. Even after the figures on the bridge had passed and the appearance of the traffic had changed, the idea remained. But it did not disturb me. I was simply absorbed in the experience that was going on within me. Perhaps I was feeling in the background of my mind that in one's samadhi, time and space fell off. I left the path through the grassy field and climbed up onto the bridge. When I got on the bridge, and saw its modern structure and the clear images of modern people, I returned, as if the scene of a film had suddenly changed, to the cognition of my living in the present-day world.

This experience of mine closely resembled that of some psychotics. The difference is that the psychotic does not return to the present-day world. In R. D. Laing's *Politics of Experience and The Bird of Paradise* there is a chapter entitled "A Ten-Day Voyage," which recounts the experience of a man who took what he called a voyage, during which his time went backward and he was in a highly disturbed mental condition. At the end of this trip, "one morning," to quote the man, "I decided I was not going to take any more sedatives, and that I had got to stop this business going on," and he suddenly left off his voyage and could "join up" with his "present self." "And as I sat on the bed and held my hands together, and as—I suppose in a clumsy way of linking myself up with my present self, I kept on saying my name over and over again and all of a sudden, just like that—I suddenly realized that it was all over."[1]

The true psychotic never conceives this idea that he must stop the business going on. He gives way to his illness and plays the spoiled child. At first he may do this to relieve himself temporarily, but when he has gone too far, in relation to his innate constitution, he will reach a state from which he cannot return. With a strong spirit that stands firm against the flooding assault of mental suffering, such giving way does not occur in the first place. The experience of William James, for instance, which appears in his *Varieties of Religious*

Experience,[2] and the agonies of Tolstoy, described in the same book,[3] are two cases in which extreme mental suffering did not lead to collapse.

When the habitual way of consciousness falls off in samadhi, the sense of time also drops off, and there is no discrimination in time sequence. A subtle coincidence of various ingredients contributed to my vision that showed there to be no difference between the time of Emperor Jimmu and the present moment. The experience was a unique one. It happened only once in my life, and I believe it to be a rare condition. I neither recommend nor disparage that sort of experience, but I do say that one must go through and through the state of having the habitual way of consciousness fallen off.

CHAPTER SEVENTEEN

Stages in Zen Training

IN THIS CHAPTER I want to discuss two classics of Zen literature: first the traditional series of pictures called "In Search of the Missing Ox," and second the Five Ranks or Situations of Tozan.

IN SEARCH OF THE MISSING OX

1. Starting the Search for the Ox. In Buddhist literature, the ox is likened to one's own True Nature. To search for the ox is to investigate this True Nature. The first stage in the sequence is the starting of the investigation.

Consider a young man on the threshold of life. In imagination he will expect many things of his future, sometimes in a joyful mood, sometimes in a pensive one. But what may be in store for him in life is not known to him until it actually happens. He himself probably does not know what he really wants from life, but in his naiveté he may entertain the idea that he should work for others, denying himself, even at the cost of self-sacrifice. "I must grapple with something serious. I want to know how the world is constituted, what my role in it should be. What am I? What am I to expect of myself?" So he may think. Then, perhaps, this youth will start studying, shall we say, the philosophy of economics, and when he thinks he has understood the power structure of the modern world he may rush off into some sort of revolutionary activity. Others will take up the study of literature, philosophy, psychology, physiology, medicine, and so on. However, whatever direction they may take, they tend to find that an intricate traffic network has been set up there, which quite often leads into some sort of complicated maze. Working in a situation that they did not originally envisage, habituation sets in, and before they know what has happened their path in life has become fixed.

However, a feeling that something is missing will make some of them knock at the door of religion.

Zazen is a matter of training yourself to become a Buddha; rather, to return to being a Buddha, for you are one from the beginning.

Now imagine a youth standing at the door of Zen in search of his true nature: he is at the stage of starting the search for the ox.

2. *Finding the Footprints.* Practicing zazen and reading Zen literature, he has acquired a certain understanding of Zen, though he has not yet

224

experienced kensho. At the first stage, when he started his search, he may have doubted whether he could attain his object by going in this direction, but now he is confident that if he follows this path he will eventually reach his destination.

3. *Catching a Glimpse of the Ox.* At length he has come across the ox. But he has seen only its tail and heels. He has had a kensho-like experience, but if he is asked where he came from and whither he is to go, he cannot give a clear answer.

There are varieties of kensho, and have been from the outset. Sakyamuni Buddha's satori was a matter of creating a new world. Before his time, it was not even known whether there was such an event. The unprecedented experience came to him suddenly, striking him like a thunderbolt, and his every problem was solved in an instant. However, if the Buddha had not already been far advanced in his training, he could not have explored in so creative a fashion this region that had never before been visited by any human being. Before this experience, the Buddha had passed the seventh and eighth stages of our sequence and had reached the ninth, "Returning to the Source." His was the thoroughgoing kensho that is real enlightenment. Since his time, there have been many Zen teachers who had already finished the whole course of their training before they had their kensho experience. For many of them it took fifteen or even twenty years before this happened.

Now in the third stage we have a situation analogous to that in which a beginner in painting finds his work admitted, by a lucky chance, to an exhibition of the highest class. His painting is, of course, excellent, but it does not prove his ability as an artist. Everything depends on his future endeavors.

Modern Zen students are told at the outset that there is an event called kensho awaiting them, and when they cross the path of this third stage they naturally take it for the vista that the Buddha saw, for the first time, when he stood on the peak of Zen practice. They are scrambling up among the rocks and bushes, expecting to see this view, and at the first glimpse of it they cry, "That's it!" Of course, what they see is not false, but there is a great difference between their experience and that of the Buddha in content, beauty, and perfection.

4. *Catching the Ox.* At this stage, his kensho has become confirmed. However, as you see in the picture, the ox is inclined to run away willfully, and the man has to hold it back with all his might. In fact, he is experienced enough now to understand the saying, "Heaven and earth and I are of the same root; all things and I are of the same source," but in his everyday life he cannot control his mind as he wishes. Sometimes he burns with anger; sometimes he is possessed by greed, blinded by jealousy, and so on. Unworthy thoughts and ignoble actions occur as of old. He is exhausted by the struggle against his passions and desires, which seem uncontrollable. This is something he did not bargain for: in spite of having attained kensho he

seems to be as mean-spirited as ever. Indeed, kensho has seemingly been the cause of new afflictions. He wants to behave in a certain way but finds himself doing the opposite. His head is in the air, but his body is lying at the foot of the cliff. However, he cannot let go the bridle and tries to keep the ox under control, even though it seems to be beyond him.

5. *Taming the Ox.* After great struggles the ox has at last begun to be moderately tame. This is the time when the trainer thinks that the wild animal is broken in and can perhaps be taught to perform some tricks.

6. *Riding the Ox Home.* The ox is now tame and obedient. Even if you let go of the bridle, it walks quietly homeward, in the evening calm, with you sitting peacefully on its back.

7. *Ox Lost, Man Remaining.* Now kensho, enlightenment, even Zen itself are forgotten. No matter what holy feeling or marvelous state of mind you may experience, the moment you start to concern yourself with it and become conscious of it, it starts to be a burden.

Let events happen as they may, and simply let them stream by. When things have happened, they have happened; when they have gone, they have gon:. The moment you settle down to some fixed view of things, decay is already setting in. "Abiding nowhere, let your mind work." The verse on the Transmission of the Dharma by Buddha Vipasyin, the first of the Past Seven Buddhas, says:

> "Vice and virtue,
> Sin and blessing,
> All is vanity;
> Abide in nothing."

8. *No Ox, No Man.* At the previous stage, "Ox Lost, Man Remaining," you probably thought everything was finished. But now another

stage appears, in which both man and ox are forgotten. There is a Zen verse:

"Last night, two clay bulls fought each other,
Disappearing in the sea in the fighting,
And nothing is heard of them this morning."

The moment your ego appears, circumstances appear. When your ego vanishes, circumstances vanish. Subjectivity and objectivity accompany each other. We have already quoted the story of the guardian deity who wanted to see Tozan Osho but could not. He took some rice and barley from the kitchen and strewed them in the yard. Tozan, seeing them, said to himself, "Who could be so negligent as to do this?" And at that moment the deity could see Tozan. Internal pressure appeared in Tozan's mind like a wisp of cloud in a bright summer sky. It came and faded away silently in the blazing noontide serenity, and then all was quietness again.

This stage corresponds to Rinzai's "Both man and circumstances are deprived" (pages 93–94).

9. *Returning to the Source.* You have only to emerge from the state of "No Ox, No Man" to find that you have simply returned to the source. Just a flip and you are in the warm spring sunshine, with flowers blooming, birds singing, and people picnicking on the grass. If you look carefully at the scene, you find it is the same old world you saw yesterday. The hillsides are covered with cherry blossoms;

the valleys are full of spring flowers. But each of the flowers has its own face and talks to you. The things you see, the sounds you hear are all Buddhas. The old habitual way of consciousness has fallen off, and you have returned to the Pure Land.

Before reaching this stage, you had to go through the stage of "No Ox, No Man." First you penetrated to the inside of yourself. The skins of the onion were peeled off one by one until it was reduced to nothing. That is absolute samadhi. But now you have come out into positive samadhi, in which consciousness is active.

In this stage of "Returning to the Source," what is experienced is in some ways identical to what was experienced at the third stage of "Finding the Ox," but there is all the difference in the world in the degree of profundity.

There is a Zen saying, "Ever shuttling from beginning to end." Your attainment is deepened by repeatedly coming back to the start, to the state of the beginner, and then retracing the path along which you have progressed. In this way your maturity becomes unshakably firm. Even Hakuin Zenji tells us that when he was over sixty he had his satori over again.

10. In Town with Helping Hands. He mingles with the world. The picture shows a potbellied, carefree man—Osho perhaps—who is now beyond caring about his personal appearance. He goes barefoot. He shows his chest. He cares nothing about how he dresses. All this symbolizes his mental nakedness. He carries a basket in which he has something for the townsfolk. His only thought is to bring joy to others.

And what is that in the gourd he is carrying? Perhaps the wine of life.

In the above commentary we have talked in general terms about how one attains maturity in Zen. Let us now change the viewpoint and treat the sequence as a series of steps in attaining samadhi.

1. Starting the search for the ox is the time when the beginner is first initiated into how to sit, and how to regulate his breath and the activity of his mind. At this stage he is naive, compliant, and intensely impressionable. The sound of the head monk's bell rings absolutely pure and seems to penetrate deep into his heart, purifying it. Everything creates a strong impression on his mind. Even a slight movement of his hand or the taking of a step is done with gravity, and this is very important and precious, although he may not realize it. It is much superior to a poor, commonplace kensho.

This beginner's mindfulness should never be lost, all through your training. Unfortunately, many students do lose it later on, substituting for it various "meritorious" achievements to which they often attach great importance. The Zen student is supposed to leave the meritorious region and enter a meritless one.

2. In the second stage, when his practice of zazen begins to get under way, he finds his mind beginning to become quieter. He now finds to his surprise that all this while his normal state of mind has been noisy and agitated, and he had been unaware of it. He begins to realize that he has been suffering from a vague uneasy feeling, the origin of which he could not pin down. Now that he sits in zazen he is largely freed from it. He realizes that zazen may be a means of quieting a disturbed mind.

When he first started the apparently simple practice of counting the breath, he was puzzled to find it not at all an easy matter. But by dint of earnest effort, he becomes able to keep his diffused mind more sharply focused and gradually starts to bring order to the activity of his consciousness. He realizes that another dimension of mind is at work. But he feels himself far from experiencing genuine kensho.

231

3. At this stage ("Catching a Glimpse of the Ox") he experiences, though only occasionally, a kind of samadhi. But it is unstable and he lacks assurance. Nevertheless, his teacher may take his hand and pull him up into the meditation hall, saying, "That's it, that's it." This is part of the teacher's strategy, and he times it according to the student's capacities and needs. Some teachers are very strict and grudging in allowing credit to the pupil; others are less so. All have their individual ways of teaching, and there is reason in their methods.

Generally speaking, when the student is once promoted to the meditation hall he naturally acquires a certain confidence, and his practice gets under way. However, there are instances of students who have studied under very strict teachers for ten or even fifteen years without receiving any acknowledgment of their progress and who one day exploded with genuine enlightenment. This is called sudden and direct satori or enlightenment, in which one undergoes an exhaustive and profound experience all at once, just as Sakyamuni Buddha did. Compared with this sudden and direct enlightenment, the method of gradual, step-by-step advance (the "installment plan" method, we might call it) is termed "ladder Zen." However, whether we go by the ladder or in one jump, everything depends on one's determination to reach the top. Unfortunately, the human will is so weak that unless it is forced to make desperate efforts it is often too lazy to use all its strength and courage to reach the peak. Do not doubt; desperate effort *is* required to attain exhaustive enlightenment.

4. In the fourth stage, "Catching the Ox," an experience something like the following will occur: "How long a time has passed he does not know. Suddenly he comes back to himself, and feels as if he were at the bottom of the fathomless depths of the sea. All is silent. All is dark. Was he asleep? No, his mind is wide awake. An internal strength seems to be welling up within him. He feels as if clad in heavy armor. Is this what the Patriarchs called 'silver mountains and iron cliffs'? His mind is as still and solemn as the snowy ravines of the Himalayas. No joy. No grief. Whether it is night or day, he does not know."

232

Someday you will have this kind of experience. And one day, when you emerge from it, rising from your seat, stepping across the door-sill, looking at the stones and trees in the garden, hearing some tri-fling sound, raising a cup to your lips or passing your fingers over a bowl, suddenly you will find heaven and earth come tumbling down.

On coming to the last extremity in zazen practice, the reversible-figure effect will necessarily occur, and a new vista will be revealed to you. Just as the ripe bean pod splits open at the lightest touch of your fingertips, so your internal pressure brings about a new dimensional development of the mental world.

A hostile critic might say that this is a matter of autosuggestion. But in fact the habitual way of consciousness has dropped off and a new mode of cognition, independent of space, time, and causation, is now at work. You and the external objects of the world are now unified. It is true that they are located outside you, but you and they interpenetrate each other. That is to say, there is no spatial resistance between you and them.

In your earliest days, your daily life was full of such a way of cognition. But as you grew up, the elaborate activity of consciousness consolidated its habitual mode of operation and separated itself from the external world, constructing the world of differentiation and discrimination. But now that habitual way has dropped off, and you are suddenly awakened to a new world. That is kensho. *Ken* means seeing into something; *sho* means one's true nature. You find your true nature within yourself, and at the same time in the external world.

5. Once the ox was caught, you thought you had it for good. But it was not so. Though sometimes you can get into samadhi, at other times you cannot. Now stillness of body and mind seem to appear; now you cannot control wandering thoughts. "It could not have been samadhi," you say. There is no remedy but to try again and again. Last year's harvest is last year's; this year's must be earned by hard work. And so the struggle is renewed, over and over again.

6. Here let us once more discuss the process of entering samadhi. The skin and muscles are normally constantly changing their tension,

and it is largely through this that the sensation of bodily existence is maintained. But in the immobile posture of zazen, little change in muscular and cutaneous tension occurs, and off-sensation develops. The skin reacts very sensitively to this novel experience. A thrill-like sensation that runs through the entire body is experienced. It is like a sort of musical vibration, delightful and delicate, accompanied by a peaceful state of mind and by a beautiful stream of emotion that seems to flow from the heart.

We mentioned earlier that off-sensation is often heralded by this thrill-like tremor, which appears first in the most sensitive parts of the body, such as ears, cheeks, forehead, neck, and arms, and eventually runs down the entire body, dying away in a few minutes. Then peace and stillness start to fill the whole body. Samadhi develops from this stillness. With long practice, however, the delightful bodily sensation does not often appear. One simply sits down, and one immediately begins to enter samadhi.

What is really going on inside the body when samadhi, preceded by these phenomena, appears? Certain chemical changes must be occurring in us. We know that the body is constantly producing all manner of chemical compounds. Perhaps samadhi results from the production of certain specific chemicals in the body. We are much against the use of drugs, such as marijuana, in zazen practice, but we would not oppose the view that zazen training in some way modifies the student's metabolism so that certain chemical substances are produced that facilitate the advent of samadhi. The fact that such substances are internally generated is a source of strength; externally supplied drugs weaken us by making us dependent upon them.

Whatever the physiological basis of samadhi may be, at this stage of "Riding the Ox Home" the student has achieved maturity and enjoys the freedom of his body and mind.

7. At this stage, shikantaza reigns. You pay no particular attention to breathing, posture, and so on. Even lying in bed you can enter absolute samadhi. On the plane of the normal activity of consciousness, working, talking, even riding in a jolting bus, you do not lose your

positive samadhi. Formerly you and samadhi were two—were separated. You attained samadhi with effort. You were working on a dual system. But now this is not so. "Man" is dominating. The realm of the mind has been brought under man's rule. Hence, "Ox Lost, Man Remaining."

8. We can arbitrarily distinguish a number of levels of consciousness:
(a) The uppermost, where thoughts and ideas come and go.
(b) A level that understands but does not form ideas.
(c) A level that is only aware.
(d) A level that simply reflects interior and exterior objects as a mirror does. Even in this stratum, traces of the reflecting action of consciousness will occasionally appear, flashing momentarily upon the scene of your mind.
(e) The deepest level, where not even the faintest reflecting action of consciousness penetrates. Here certain vestiges of mood remain. They are a kind of memory of one's lifetime, and also of one's predecessors. They want to rise up to the surface of consciousness and give expression to themselves. Even if they are not allowed to, they do not fail, remotely but importantly, to affect the trend of the activity of consciousness. They are ever changing, affected by the nen-thoughts that occur moment by moment.

In absolute samadhi, however, the brain's activity is reduced to a minimum and the muddy layers of ancient memory are thoroughly cleansed. The habitual way of consciousness is swept away. Both the reflecting and the reflected vanish: a pitch-dark world. This condition is called "no-thought" samadhi, which is the same as absolute samadhi. It is the stage at which we can say, "No Ox, No Man."

9. In the previous stage a thorough and decisive purification of consciousness was carried out, and the muddy deposits, accumulated through countless eons, were dredged away. Now, in the present stage ("Returning to the Source"), the activity of consciousness starts up once more, with this cleansed condition of mind. It is like putting a brush to a clean sheet of paper: every stroke comes out shining bright.

If you listen to music, it sounds unimaginably exquisite. It is a state of positive samadhi in which the condition of kensho has become permanent. What is said of the Tathagata will be true of you: you find Buddha's face wherever you turn your eyes.

Until yesterday you took great pains to develop the solemn state of absolute samadhi and fiercely checked all activity of consciousness. Now you let consciousness gaily open into full bloom.

10.   Finally the world of antagonism has dissolved; the habitual way of consciousness has totally dropped away. You no longer wear the old ceremonial dress. You go barefoot, with chest bare. Everything is welcome. Wandering thoughts? All right! This is the Buddha's great *dhyāna* (meditation) in the busiest activity of consciousness. You enjoy perfect freedom of playful, positive samadhi.

THE PATHOS OF THINGS   What a shock we experienced when we were still quite little children, when we realized for the first time that we must pass away, one by one, alone and separately, leaving behind us our loved ones—father, mother, brothers, sisters. Perhaps you can remember this critical moment in your own childhood, when you first experienced this sense of the "pathos of things." It is not improbable that you were thrown by it into a kind of neurosis for a while; you had sad, sorrowful feelings toward others, perhaps even toward plants and animals. What you unconsciously felt at this time was a loss of unity with others, a deprivation of love.

It is from this deprivation of love that the feeling of the pathos of things stems. On a stroll in the moonlight in the country, or even on a busy street corner, we feel a certain yearning for something we cannot quite catch hold of. We do not know what it is, but the feeling infiltrates our whole being. The mysterious, misty veil of the moonlight reminds us of eternity and distant lands, which in turn makes us sensitive to the mutability of our actual life and brings about the melancholy mood. The pathos of things is a kind of homesickness. It is a sorrowful expression of the love we have lost, a yearning for homeland, faces, things, even for living beings and nonliving things in general.

The sense of the pathos of things is often to be found at the bottom of our sense of beauty, particularly when the former is the expression of love obstructed by something fateful in life. Man is sometimes defined as the being who hates others. However, so long as he is a "Being-in-the-world," he lives with other people, and he and they are inseparable from each other. He cannot help feeling that he lacks something when he is deprived of the chance of loving others and of being loved by them. Especially when you once experience absolute samadhi, in which your egocentric, illusory thought falls away, you invariably develop love toward others. Then, however, you find that you must go through the frustrations of actual life. How are we to escape from this dilemma, from this seemingly irreconcilable conflict between separateness, distinction, and hostility on the one hand, and love on the other? Is this dilemma human fate?

Eternal cultivation of Holy Buddhahood after enlightenment helps us to solve this problem. Many Zen stories show how this problem was solved by our predecessors. Constant practice and experience of absolute samadhi give you the vision that enables you to see Buddha Nature with your naked eyes. Compassion and love toward strangers appear spontaneously. You understand Sakyamuni Buddha's exclamation on the occasion of his enlightenment: "All the beings in the universe are endowed with the virtue and wisdom of the Tathagata." You experience yourself the feelings of others—their sorrow, delight, humor, their whole personality—just as if they were your own feelings. The more firmly your samadhi is established, the more steadily does the illusory way of thinking fall away, and the less often does discriminatory thinking occur. A new system of cognition is formed within you.

We want now to illustrate and develop some of these points by discussing another well-known Zen topic, Tozan's Five Ranks.

TOZAN'S FIVE RANKS   In searching for the ox, we were mainly dealing with the process of attaining enlightenment. Tozan's Five Ranks are concerned with matters after enlightenment: that is, with the cultivation of Holy Buddhahood. Certain Buddhist schools assert that there are fifty-two stages through which the enlightened person has

237

to pass before he reaches the true maturity of the Buddha. However, Tozan's Five Ranks are sufficient to enable us to grasp the essential points. Before commenting on them in detail, however, we must introduce and explain certain essential terms used in describing these ranks.

When one attains kensho and the habitual way of consciousness falls off, there appears what is called *daien-kyōchi;* this may be translated as "the great perfect Mirror of Wisdom" (*dai,* great; *en,* round, which here means "rounded maturity" and hence "perfect"; *kyō,* mirror; *chi,* wisdom). Everyone is innately equipped with this Mirror of Wisdom. However, in most people it has long been veiled because of the activity of our topsy-turvy delusive thought. In absolute samadhi the veil is cleared away and the perfect mirror is allowed to appear. This condition constitutes Tozan's First Rank. The Mirror of Wisdom, however, still remains in darkness in the absolute samadhi of the First Rank. This rank corresponds to the eighth stage of searching for the ox, illustrated by the circle, in which body and mind have fallen off.

The great Mirror of Wisdom becomes brilliantly lit in the positive samadhi of one whose cultivation of Holy Buddhahood has reached full maturity. The remaining four ranks refer to this sphere of positive samadhi. We should note here that the fact that, apart from the first, Tozan's ranks all relate to positive samadhi should not be taken as belittling the importance of absolute samadhi. The latter is the foundation of all Zen practice, and that is why Tozan places it first. The brilliance of the mirror in positive samadhi is comparable to that of broad daylight, the silence and oblivion of absolute samadhi to the darkness of midnight.

The great Mirror of Wisdom is also referred to by the Zen terms *shō* (authentic or genuine) and *honbun* (*hon,* original; *bun,* part). Honbun can be described as absolute, genuine, dark, and empty; it is a state of "no-thought." However, if you settle down in this dark, empty, thought-less condition, your development will come to an end. You must return to the world, to the state in which your consciousness operates normally, and live in positive samadhi. Here, however, you are necessarily bound by the restrictions of time, space, and causation, and you live in the world of individuality, confrontation, and differentiation. However, when you have once experienced the absolute equality of the great Mirror of Wisdom, you can go on to attain a freedom of mind that goes beyond such discrimination. This maturity, in which, while yet living in the world of time, space, and causation, you transcend the limits of that world, is called the Wisdom of Equality. It is to this maturity that Tozan's ranks point the way.

Let us put these matters in another way. At an early stage in the cultivation of Holy Buddhahood, you may often find yourself failing to behave well; you do not what you would wish to do but what you hate. You say, "It should not be so," but to no avail. However, as you go on, you begin to lose these discriminating motivations and ultimately come to find equality in distinction. It is this state that constitutes Tozan's Second Rank.

We used the words "Sho" and "honbun" to characterize the First Rank, which we connect with the world of equality. The Second Rank relates to the world of differentiation and distinction, which in Zen terminology is called *hen* (periphery). The two words "Sho" and "Hen" have no exact equivalents in English, and we shall not try to translate them here. However, to suggest their meanings, we will list contrasting terms that can be associated with them; in each pair, the first term represents Sho and the second Hen: absolute, relative; equality, distinction; emptiness, form; absolute samadhi, positive samadhi; darkness, light; yin, yang; no-thought, thought; inward, outward; central, peripheral; reason, matter; reality, appearance.

Here we have a series of concepts that are in opposition to each other. However, in actual life, we find that we simply exist. When we are in absolute samadhi, we are in absolute quietness. When we are in positive samadhi, we are in vigorous activity. There is only one stream of existence, the continuum of the present. However, when we take up philosophical speculation again, we are once more confronted by ideas of reality and appearance, absolute and relative, and so on. Then once again we return to the continuum of one single existence. Sho and Hen alternate, each retaining, so to speak, a vague memory of the other. Thus, two situations can be considered: "Hen

239

in Sho" (Tozan's First Rank) and "Sho in Hen" (Tozan's Second Rank).

To go on from there, we abolish entirely the dualistic idea of Sho and Hen—absolute and relative, and so on—and bring about a synthesis and integration of them. There then remains the Real in its true sense. That is to say, when you are in absolute samadhi, you are in absolute samadhi; when you are in positive samadhi, you are in positive samadhi. There is only one fact—that you exist. This returning to "existing," with the resumption of the activity of consciousness, constitutes Tozan's Third Rank, "Coming from Sho."

These remarks are, perhaps, sufficient introduction to Tozan's verses and our commentary on them. We shall deal with the Fourth and Fifth ranks in their turn below. The reader should understand that the Five Ranks are not to be thought of as so many grades of achievement but simply as different conditions. There is, however, a customary sequence in which the different states that Tozan depicts occur, and the Five Ranks follow this sequence.

In the following paragraphs we give first the relevant verse by Tozan and then our commentary on it.

1. Hen in Sho
At dead of night, with no moon,
Meeting, yet not knowing each other,
You have a vague memory of old days.

"At dead of night, with no moon." When you are in absolute samadhi everything is darkness, emptiness, and silence, like the depths of a moonless night.

"Meeting, yet not knowing each other." In absolute samadhi you are not aware of your state. You regain your Original Nature, but you do not recognize it. This is because you are the samadhi itself and the Original Nature itself. Together, the two lines indicate that you have returned to the darkness of the absolute (Sho). You have regained your babyhood.

"You have a vague memory of old days." In absolute samadhi the Great Death is realized. But this is not the end of the story. Jishu-zammai, which presides in samadhi, is in a sense a nen-action, as it is a manifestation of will (or spiritual) power. Hence, the relative, phenomenal world (Hen) must always be found in the absolute (Sho) as a vague memory of old days.

These ideas of relative and absolute—Hen and Sho—are, of course, the product of conceptual thinking. What is essential in our experience of life is simply the fact that we exist. Our existence must necessarily combine both the relative and the absolute. However, in absolute samadhi, it is the latter that occupies the central position, while the former is subsidiary. In positive samadhi the reverse is the case.

In the experience of kensho we find that all objects maintain their individuality while at the same time existing in a unity. They are not strangers to one another. They intercommunicate among themselves, displaying differentiation in unity and at the same time unity in differentiation. This is because kensho occurs on the dividing line between absolute and positive samadhi. Kensho occurs at the moment when you come out of absolute samadhi and stand on the threshold of positive samadhi. When you thus experience unity in differentiation, the Second Rank, "Sho in Hen," appears.

2. Sho in Hen
At dawn the old woman finds the ancient mirror,
Immediate and intimate, but nothing particular;
There's no need to search for your own face.

"At dawn the old woman finds the ancient mirror." At the dawning of the activity of consciousness, the old woman comes across the mirror that she had used to reflect her face when young. That is to say, she emerges from the darkness of the absolute (Sho) into the light of the ordinary phenomenal world (Hen) and finds the mirror, which she had been provided with from birth but which, as she grew up, she had gradually lost under the influence of the habitual way of consciousness. She suddenly finds this mirror again, sees her reflection in it, and discovers once again her own Original Face.

When reflected, there she is. She is nowhere else, but is here, as she is. And she is nothing but this "herself," who had appeared in the world as an individual among others. There is no herself apart from this present herself. There is no mode of her being other than the fact that she is as she is just now.

Until a moment ago she was searching after the truth, in the deluded belief that there is something Real, that is, some fundamental truth called Reality, or Being, or Buddha, apart from the ordinary sentient beings and things of the world. In fact, this present world and its beings, just as she finds them, are the sought-for Reality and the world of Buddha.

When you attain kensho, on all sides of you, right, left, before, behind, above, and below, you find Buddhas making merry. And you yourself participate in this delightful party, which goes on, strange to say, in a voiceless serenity, with every scene and every individual shining and animated, yet silent, like scattered jewels. The bell tower, the rows of tiles on the roof, the trees in the garden, the stones, the flowers are all overflowing with joy, like happy children in the kindergarten playground. This is the world of children's art, a highly intensified expression of existence. Everything is all right as it is. Is there anything else to be sought? What you had looked upon as the merely contingent phenomena of the surrounding world are real and true.

"Immediate and intimate, but nothing particular." The woman finds the ancient mirror to be "intimate" because it is her own self. "Nothing particular" means that truth is immediate and simple; there is no special truth that can be arrived at only by complicated thought and speculation.

"There's no need to search for your own face." This line refers to a story told by the Buddha that appears in one of the sutras. A girl loved to look at her reflection in a mirror. One day she looked and could not see her face. She thought she must have lost her head and started to make a great fuss searching for it. The Buddha tells us that we have Buddha Nature from the outset; why seek for it far away?

When you are in absolute samadhi, you realize existence in absolute silence. In active life, you do the same in positive samadhi. It is all right to regard absolute samadhi as something absolute, and positive samadhi as belonging to the relative, phenomenal world. But remember that these are two phases of one existence. By experiencing the First and Second ranks we demonstrate for ourselves that these two phases alternate, mutually reverting one into the other. And by experiencing repeated alternations we attain maturity and eventually arrive at the synthesis of the two phases, which is represented by the Third Rank.

In order to reach the state in which we combine the two phases in one existence, we have to go through them again and again. In Japanese, this is called *ego* (*e*, reversion; *go*, mutual), which may be roughly translated as "interconversion."

3. Coming from Sho
In emptiness is the way found, pure and clear;
Don't mention the name of the emperor;
You have the universe under your sway.

The Third Rank stems from this interconversion. In other words, it is the result of synthesis. Interconversion is found only between the First and Second ranks. It does not occur in the remainder because it has already been realized in them. They are thus independent and perfect in themselves.

What does "coming" mean? It means coming from absolute samadhi into the activity of positive samadhi. In the Third Rank we build our behavior on the foundation of Sho (the Real). It is for this reason that, in the Rinzai sect, this rank is regarded as the general base and center wherein we should, as a rule, abide in our ordinary daily life. Coming and acting from the Real (Sho), making it the keynote of our life—that is the meaning of the Third Rank.

"In emptiness is the way found, pure and clear." In absolute samadhi there is no activity of consciousness, no nen-thought in your mind. Everything is empty and pure. Then, when your consciousness once again resumes its activity, there is no obstruction to encumber your mind. The way is open to you in all directions. You have absolute freedom of action. Therefore, "In emptiness is the way found."

"Don't mention the name of the emperor." This line refers to the fact that in the old days it was customary for Oriental people to call the emperor not by his actual name but by his title. The emperor was regarded as a sort of absolute being, and it was thought that to give him a name would be a desecration. That absolute Being evades all description is a tenet of philosophy generally. Our topic here, the Real (Sho), is absolute. Absolute is absolute. It is in itself, by itself, for itself, and of itself. It is not to be described but directly caught hold of. And again, once you get the idea that you have realized it, you are thinking about it as an object and have become separated from it. You yourself must become absolute.

"You have the universe under your sway." You are the master of the Real. Come out of the Real and use your freedom of activity. Everthing is empty, like outer space; you can go anywhere and everywhere; you have perfect freedom.

As a person, you are mature in this rank. But Tozan now sets up two more ranks. There is profound significance is this, which we must now try to explain.

4. Perfection in Hen
Two swords are crossed; the spirits of the warrior—
Like a lotus flower shining in the fire—
Soar high, penetrating through space.

The Fourth Rank is reached when you acquire maturity in both understanding and demonstrating Zen truth. It is in this rank that your consciousness is polished and emits a shining light, like that of jewels. The activity of your consciousness is developed into a living masterpiece.

"Two swords are crossed." The swords crossed in fighting are to be taken as representing the most highly intensified concentration of mind. The point is not fighting but the brilliantly intense condition of the mind.

"Like a lotus flower shining in the fire." This is a special flower referred to in the sutras. Imagine a lotus flower bedecked with jewels, serenely emitting glittering, flashing reflections from the midst of roaring flames. This lotus in the flames forms the central image of this verse.

In a person mature in Zen, in positive samadhi and with his mind perfectly clear and pure, even the simplest, most trivial action, such as lighting a candle before the image of the Buddha, or the movement of his feet in white socks, stepping along the corridor like two white rabbits, takes on an indescribable beauty. It is a masterpiece of movement. We have referred to this previously when discussing Kasan's "Beating the drum." Dancing is one of the most highly developed modes of human movement, the result of highly sophisticated training and practice. For the person mature in Zen, comparably exquisite actions and postures arise spontaneously, without artifice. His consciousness and his every action shine like jewels in the fire. Each action is a highly intensified expression of his existence. The overflowing spiritual power of the artist at the moment of creation is the constant condition of his daily life.

When one attains the maturity of this Fourth Rank, even though one may have been a mediocrity before, one acquires profound insight and begins to look perceptively into other people's minds. This is because the mature person places himself in the position of the person before him, thinks with him, delights with him, deplores with him, understands him.

With regard to Zen, the person at this stage develops maturity in understanding and in demonstrating the truths of Zen. The maturity of understanding manifests itself as a seemingly inspired ability to cut through the Gordian knots of koans with unprecedented quickness and clarity. As for the demonstration, the route to enlightenment is now as clear to him as if he were looking at an aerial photograph; he can point out simply and clearly all the hills, passes, gorges, and streams where his students are now struggling. He can give them the exactly appropriate help and guidance that they need. He displays the all-around ability and activity of the three-faced, six-armed Buddha.

It will be apparent now why this rank is called "Perfection in Hen." It is the stage of a highly developed activity of consciousness and, of course, of positive samadhi.

It is said in a sutra that the Tathagata sees Buddha Nature with his naked eyes, and the whole field of view, as far as the eye can reach, is alive with Bodhisattvas and Buddhas. What is seen, as it is, is Buddha. For the person who has reached the condition of the Fourth

Rank, this becomes the constant and ordinary state of his daily life. The artist's eye, the musician's ear, the philosopher's wisdom, Kannon's thousand hands and eyes—all are given to him. This explains how the great Zen masters of earlier times were able to leave such masterpieces of painting, calligraphy, sculpture, garden design, and poetry.

Individuality—differentiation between you and others and between you and external objects—is clearly marked. But at the same time you and they interpenetrate each other. The trees and rocks in the garden, casting evening shadows; every piece of furniture, the cushions, tea things; every person and every thing around you, and their appearance, manners, and gestures, which reflect themselves in your eyes, are nothing but Buddha and Bodhisattva. The person who is sitting in front of you, though he may turn into your enemy and fall upon you, can never be hated when you have insight into his life.

It is said in the Bodhisattva's Vow, "Then on each moment's flash of thought, there will grow a lotus flower, and on each lotus flower will be revealed a Buddha. These Buddhas will glorify Sukhavati, the Pure Land, every moment and everywhere." And thus, in every moment's flash of thought, the world of Buddha will be revealed.

Having gone through all the human mind's paths and highways, its mazes, blind alleys, and dead ends—being acquainted with and having tasted through and through the inescapable evil thoughts, self-centered thinking, heartwarming good intentions, ideas for others' benefit, and so on—the maturity of the Fourth Rank is attained. In this state, one enjoys "the king of kings' samadhi."

"Soar high, penetrating through space." As the "towering waves beat the heavens," as lightning flashes through the sky, so the spirit of the master in this rank penetrates through space.

5.   Perfection in Integration
Falling into neither *u* nor *mu,* who can join the master?
While others strive to rise above the common level,
He unites everything, sitting quietly by the fire.

The fair is over. As a great river empties itself at last into the ocean, leaving no trace behind, so the mature Zen master forgets all his merits and achievements and seems to return to the old state of blessed ignorance. The potbellied Osho, depicted at the end of the search for the missing ox, comes barefooted into the marketplace, showing his chest. His appearance symbolizes his spiritual nakedness. However, to your surprise, you may find that he is carrying some wine in that basket, and perhaps something more.

Old Tokusan, a great Zen master, one day mistook the time and came down to the refectory with his bowls. Seppo (then the kitchen master, and later himself a great Zen master) said, "The dinner bell has not yet rung. Where are you off to?" Tokusan nodded, as if to say, "Is that so? I see," and returned to his room. This story has become the basis of a famous koan. In his prime Tokusan had been a vigorous man, famous for using his stick as his Zen spirit prompted him. But now he was as quiet as the Pacific Ocean.

The old man sitting by the fireside, with rheumy eyes and running nose, may seem to be approaching his second childhood. But suddenly he calls to a friend to go out into the garden with him, and together they start filling the well with snow. They carry it energetically from the back yard in buckets on a pole. Their perseverance at this hopeless task is ludicrous, but they keep at it.

He gives counsel to a forsaken young man, lending him a helping hand. Some of the senior monks may admonish him, saying, "That fellow stole money from his father's company and squandered it in dissipation. He was disowned by his family and was sent to prison. Even when he visited us, he extracted money and things from various people with his glib tongue. Once he stole into the sick monks' ward and made off with their money and other possessions. To give him more help is like throwing coins into the sea." He nods, but says, "He is not a bad man. I am awaiting his conversion. If he continues as he is, he will end up a lost man. As for a petty sum of money, it is of little importance. What he now needs most of all is to feel the kindness of other people. I don't care for the moralist's theory that if I give him even the little money I do I should be contributing to his decline. It is a cold theory. I do not agree with it. Some years ago a certain tunnel was being built and they came across a deep fault that seemed to swallow all the concrete they were able to pour into it. It was like an abyss. It seemed impossible to fill it. They were almost in despair. However, they persevered, refusing to admit defeat, and eventually they won. If I turned my back on that man now he would be lost forever."

He recites the Zen saying, "Sin and blessing are all empty. The snake swallows the frog. The toad sucks up the worms. The hawk eats the sparrows. The pheasant eats the snake. The cat catches the rat. The big fish devours the smaller one. And everything is all right. The monk who offended against the commandments does not fall into hell."

Encouraged by these words and by his easy manner, some young monks, avid readers of modern fiction, raise the saying, "The passions themselves are Bodhi." They assert that Sakyamuni Buddha hit the nail on the head there, as modern literature does. Now that the passions are to be given free rein, monks can indulge themselves as they like. But the answer is: "You make a great mistake there, and for this reason. Every nen-thought of yours creates its effect. This is karma. A good intention at this moment leaves you with a good state of mind. An evil thought increases your evil impulses. Every action has its effect. Raising your hand, taking a step, govern your mind's great Mirror of Wisdom. The law of causation is exacting and severe. It is so relentless that you should humbly lower your head as if an air raid were in progress. You should walk quietly as if you were in the imperial presence. Don't be fooled by these writers. They may be widely admired, but where is their maturity?"

He seems to be almost in his dotage, but coming to the point, he is suddenly all alert.

"Falling into neither u nor mu, who can join the master?" U here means form (Hen); mu means emptiness (Sho). He is in neither form nor emptiness. However, while active in the ordinary world of phenomena, he does not leave the Real.

"While others strive to rise above the common level." In the early days of his training in Zen he made every effort to excel. He wanted to emerge distinctly from the ruck, and his struggles to do so were prodigious. However, now:

"He unites everything, sitting quietly by the fire." Everything is integrated in maturity. The struggle is over. He is not dispirited but is above it. He sits quietly by the fireside, an old man with a running nose. He has forgotten Zen and everything like that. But if you observe him carefully, looking at his casual and seemingly trivial actions—his carriage, his manner, his words—you will discover how wonderfully harmonious and mellow they are.

You reach this state of mellow maturity by repeating the cycle, from the First Rank to the Second, the Third, the Fourth, the Fifth, and then coming back once more to the First. Each rank gains in profundity and becomes increasingly mellowed with each repetition. The Third Rank, which can be regarded as the base camp for your ordinary life, is enriched by experience of the Fourth and Fifth ranks, as well as of the First and Second. Training is done by repetition. Each rank is independent of the others and has its own individual character.

Let us end this book with a famous episode in Zen history. The Sixth Patriarch, whose name was Hui-neng (Eno), lost his father when he was three years old, and he and his mother were left in poverty. When he grew up he earned his living by selling firewood in the marketplace. Once he was delivering wood to a customer's shop and, as he was leaving, overheard a man reciting a sutra. When the man came to a passage that ran, "Abiding nowhere, let the mind work," Hui-neng experienced a sudden illumination. (In Japanese the text runs "*Ō musho jū, ni shō go shin*": *Ō*, let; *musho*, nowhere; *jū*, abide; *ni*, and; *shō*, generate; *go*, the; *shin*, mind—"Let him nowhere abide, and generate the mind.") He asked the name of the sutra, and being told that it was the Diamond Sutra, which had been given to the man by the Fifth Patriarch, he determined to go and see this great Zen master. People gave him ten taels of gold to support his mother while he was away. It was over a thousand miles from his town in Kwantung Province, which is a southern district of China, to Wongmui, where the Fifth Patriarch was living, in North China.

Hui-neng traveled all the way in less than thirty days, and paid homage to the Fifth Patriarch, who asked where he had come from and what he expected to receive. Hui-neng replied, "I am a commoner from Sunchow in Kwantung. I have traveled far to pay you respect, and I ask for nothing but Buddhahood." "You are a native from south of the mountains, a savage land," said the Fifth Patriarch. "How can you expect to be a Buddha?" Hui-neng said, "Though there is north and south in the location of men, there is no north and south in Buddha Nature." More questions and answers were exchanged, and the Fifth Patriarch realized that Hui-neng was a potentially great Zen personage. "This barbarian is too bright. Say no more. Go to the rice-pounding cottage and work there."

Hui-neng stayed with the Fifth Patriarch for eight months and completed his Zen training in this short time. He was a natural genius in Zen. One night, in the third watch, the Fifth Patriarch called Hui-neng to his room and transmitted the Dharma to him, giving him at the same time the robe and the bowl that had been handed down from Bodhidharma to successive Patriarchs. Hui-neng was told by his teacher to retire to a remote place and cultivate Holy Buddhahood for ten years before entering on active life as the Sixth Patriarch.

Hui-neng left the Fifth Patriarch and went southward with the robe and bowl. A great commotion occurred among the monks under the Fifth Patriarch when they learned that the robe, the symbol of the Buddha's teachings, had been carried off by a layman who had arrived casually a few months before and to whom they had paid scant attention or respect. The robe and the Buddha's teachings were the self-same thing in their unenlightened eyes. They were greatly agitated, and several hundred of them started in pursuit of Hui-neng to take the robe back. A monk named Wei-ming (Emyo), a general of the fourth rank in lay life, was at the head of the pursuers. He was rough in manner, hot-tempered, but earnest in his studies. He overtook the Sixth Patriarch at a pass in the Taiyu mountains. He must have been a stubborn and persistent man, for he covered over a thousand miles in this pursuit. In those days, traveling was a matter of almost indescribable hardship. A Chinese proverb ran, "Blessed are a thousand days at home; cursed is a single day on a journey." Wei-ming's fellow pursuers dropped off one after another, and he was alone when he came to the Taiyu mountains.

Perhaps the Sixth Patriarch, knowing of Wei-ming's approach, chose this out-of-the-way place to meet him. In the remote mountains, far from any sign of human life, all was silent. Even the breeze was hushed. The Sixth Patriarch placed the robe on a rock beside the road and said, "This robe signifies trust. We should not fight over it. If you want to take it, I leave it to you." Then he stepped back behind some shrubs. Wei-ming tried to approach the robe. He stretched out his arms, but his hands trembled. His legs failed him and he could not move a step. The robe was as heavy as a mountain to him. Perspiration broke out over his whole body. Heaven and earth shook and swung. He became dizzy and almost fell. "Help!" he cried. He realized that the robe should not be touched by an unenlightened man like himself. He collapsed to the ground, and exclaimed, "Lay brother! Lay brother! I have come for the Dharma, not for the robe!" He did not know what he was saying. The Sixth Patriarch came out from his hiding place and sat on a rock. Wei-ming made obeisance and said, "Lay brother, teach me, please!"

"If you have come for the Dharma," said the Sixth Patriarch, "stop thinking of anything. Don't let a single thought stir in your mind, and then I will speak to you." Wei-ming kept himself in meditation. After a while, there came the voice of the Sixth Patriarch: "When you think neither of good nor of evil, at that very moment, what is your Original Face?"

The words went penetrating through Wei-ming's mind. In an instant, he realized his own nature. He was illuminated throughout his entire body. There can be such a critical moment, when one's mind is completely converted. It happened to Saul of Tarsus on the road to Damascus. Persecution, internal strife—and then there comes conversion. One's old way of thinking is totally swept away. When Wei-ming cried out, "Lay brother! Lay brother! I have come for the Dharma, not for the robe!" his mind had already been converted, and the Sixth Patriarch's words were able to have their effect.

What is really meant by the words, "When you think neither of good nor of evil, at that very moment, what is your Original Face?" They hold two meanings. On one level they refer to the revelation of

251

pure existence in absolute samadhi. The other is the aspect that appears in the positive activity of life, in the eternal cultivation of Holy Buddhahood after enlightenment. You attach to nothing and let your mind work of itself. In your business transactions you let go of your last hold on the cliff. In your ordinary daily life you climb up beyond the top of the hundred-foot pole. Bodhidharma has no beard, no eyes, no nose, no mouth, no face, no hands, no legs, and no body.

Reference Notes

EDITOR'S INTRODUCTION

1. For example, Alan Watts, *The Way of Zen* (New York: Pantheon, 1957).
2. In *The Three Pillars of Zen* (Tokyo: Weatherhill, 1965; New York: Harper & Row, 1966).
3. See, for example, S. Cohen, *Drugs of Hallucination* (London: Secker & Warburg, 1965). For a valuable discussion of the whole topic see Robert C. Zaehner, *Mysticism: Sacred and Profane* (Oxford: Clarendon Press, 1957).
4. From David Magarshack's introduction to his translation of *The Idiot* (Harmondsworth, England: Penguin, 1953), p. 8.
5. Ibid., pp. 258–59.
6. Charles T. Tart (ed.), *Altered States of Consciousness: A Book of Readings* (New York: Wiley, 1969). See also Robert E. Ornstein, *The Psychology of Consciousness* (San Francisco: Freeman, 1972).
7. Arthur Waley, *Zen Buddhism and Its Relation to Art* (London: Luzac, 1922), p. 26.
8. Iris Murdoch, *The Sovereignty of Good* (London: Routledge & Kegan Paul, 1970), p. 84.
9. Ibid., p. 34.
10. Ibid., p. 91.

CHAPTER 3. THE PHYSIOLOGY OF ATTENTION

1. William James, *Text-book of Psychology* (London: Macmillan, 1892), pp. 12–13.
2. Arthur C. Guyton, *Function of the Human Body* (Philadelphia and London: Saunders, 1959), pp. 370–72.
3. James, *Text-book of Psychology*, p. 376.

CHAPTER 4. BREATHING IN ZAZEN

1. This figure and the account of normal respiration are adapted, with modifications, from Arthur C. Guyton, *Function of the Human Body*, pp. 220–21.

REFERENCE NOTES

CHAPTER 5. COUNTING AND FOLLOWING THE BREATH

1. N. Das and H. Gastaut, "Variations de l'activité électrique du cerveau, de coeur et des muscles squelettiques au cours de la méditation et de 'l'extase' yogique," *Electroencephalography and Clinical Neurophysiology,* supp. 6 (1955): 211–19. For another paper on this topic see B. K. Anand, G. S. Chhina, and B. Singh, "Some Aspects of Electroencephalographic Studies in Yogis," *Electroencephalography and Clinical Neurophysiology* 13 (1961):452–56.
2. A. Kasamatsu and T. Hirai, "An Electroencephalographic Study of the Zen Meditation (Zazen)," *Folia Psychiatrica et Neurologia Japonica* 20 (1966):315–36.

CHAPTER 13. PURE EXISTENCE

1. Martin Heidegger, *Being and Time,* translated by John Macquarrie and E. Robinson (London: SCM Press, 1962), pp. 174, 271, 329, 330, 399.
2. Ibid., pp. 344–45.
3. Ibid., p. 308.
4. Ibid., p. 343.

CHAPTER 14. PURE COGNITION AND KENSHO

1. Karl Jaspers, *General Psychopathology,* translated by J. Hoenig and M. W. Hamilton (Manchester: Manchester University Press, 1962), p. 83.
2. Edmund Husserl, *The Idea of Phenomenology,* in *Readings in Twentieth-Century Philosophy,* edited by William P. Alston and George Nakhnikian (London: Free Press of Glencoe, 1963), pp. 656–57.

CHAPTER 15. KENSHO EXPERIENCES

1. Marcel Proust, *Swann's Way,* translated by C. K. Scott-Moncrieff (London: Chatto & Windus, 1922), p. 58.
2. Marcel Proust, *Within a Budding Grove,* translated by C. K. Scott-Moncrieff (London: Chatto & Windus, 1924), pp. 20–23.
3. William James, *The Varieties of Religious Experience* (London and New York: Longmans, Green, 1902), pp. 382–83.

CHAPTER 16. A PERSONAL NARRATIVE

1. R. D. Laing, *The Politics of Experience and The Bird of Paradise* (Harmondsworth, England: Penguin, 1967), p. 131.
2. This is recounted on pp. 160–61 of *The Varieties of Religious Experience* by William James (London and New York: Longmans, Green, 1902). James represents this experience as being that of a "French correspondent," but in fact it was his own (see *The Letters of William James,* edited by Henry James [London: Longmans, Green, 1920], vol. 1, p. 145).
3. Ibid., pp. 153–55.

Index

255

The "weathermark" identifies this book as a production of John Weatherhill, Inc., publishers of fine books on Asia and the Pacific. Supervising editor: Suzanne Trumbull. Book design and typography: Meredith Weatherby. Production supervisor: Mitsuo Okado. Composition: Samhwa Printing Co., Seoul. Printing: Kenkyusha Printing Co., Tokyo. Binding: Makoto Binderies, Tokyo. The typeface used is Monotype Perpetua (the main text in 12-point size), with hand-set Perpetua for display.